THE M&S GUIDE TO

ONTARIO COLLEGES

OF APPLIED ARTS AND

TECHNOLOGY

Geographic Distribution of Ontario
Colleges of Applied Arts and Technology (Main Campuses)

(Please contact the main campus of each college for location of affiliated campuses.)

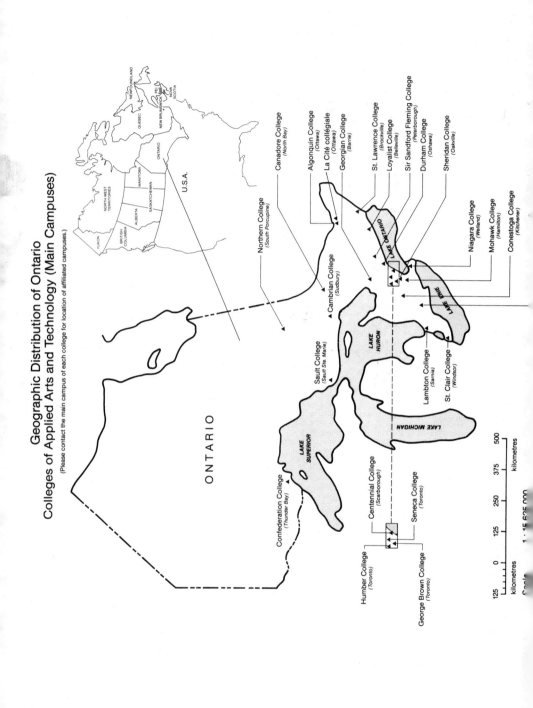

Canadore College
(North Bay)

Algonquin College
(Ottawa)

La Cité collégiale
(Ottawa)

Georgian College
(Barrie)

St. Lawrence College
(Brockville)

Loyalist College
(Belleville)

Sir Sandford Fleming College
(Peterborough)

Durham College
(Oshawa)

Sheridan College
(Oakville)

Niagara College
(Welland)

Mohawk College
(Hamilton)

Conestoga College
(Kitchener)

Northern College
(South Porcupine)

Cambrian College
(Sudbury)

Sault College
(Sault Ste. Marie)

Lambton College
(Sarnia)

St. Clair College
(Windsor)

Confederation College
(Thunder Bay)

Centennial College
(Scarborough)

Seneca College
(Toronto)

Humber College
(Toronto)

George Brown College
(Toronto)

LAKE SUPERIOR

LAKE HURON

LAKE MICHIGAN

LAKE ONTARIO

LAKE ERIE

ONTARIO

U.S.A.

NEWFOUNDLAND

QUEBEC

NEW BRUNSWICK

P.E.I.

NOVA SCOTIA

ONTARIO

MANITOBA

SASKATCHEWAN

ALBERTA

BRITISH COLUMBIA

YUKON

NORTH WEST TERRITORIES

kilometres

125   0   125   250   375   500

kilometres

Scale   1 : 15 625 000

THE M&S GUIDE TO ONTARIO COLLEGES OF APPLIED ARTS AND TECHNOLOGY

Christopher Moore

M&S

McClelland & Stewart acknowledges the support of the Government of Ontario through the Ministry of Culture and Communications.

Canadian Cataloguing in Publication Data

Moore, Christopher
The M&S guide to Ontario colleges of applied arts
and technology

ISBN 0-7710-6092-0

1. Community colleges – Ontario – Guidebooks. I. Title. II. Title:
Guide to Ontario colleges of applied arts
and technology.

LB2328.M66 1993   378′.052′09713   C93-093070-3

The publisher wishes to thank the Association of Colleges of Applied Arts and Technology of Ontario for its help and cooperation in the production of this book. The opinions expressed belong to the author and do not represent the viewpoint of the Association or the Colleges.

The map on page ii is reproduced from *Horizons: Guide to Postsecondary Education in Ontario, 1992-1993*, and appears with the permission of the copyright holders, The Communications Branch of the Ministry of Colleges and Universities, Government of Ontario.

Typesetting by M&S
Printed and bound in Canada

McClelland & Stewart Inc.
The Canadian Publishers
481 University Avenue
Toronto, Ontario
M5G 2E9

CONTENTS

LIST OF BOXES

The Hot News

Colleges make discovery: service matters!

In recent years, money got tight and colleges had to hustle. They began to learn that service to customers really matters – and students are college customers. Today most colleges say they want to be "student-centred." Help them keep their word. Be an active college consumer.

Not just for eighteen-year-olds.

Barely half of new college students were in high school the year before (for universities it's about 80 per cent). Who are the others? Everybody. People from the workforce. Adults changing careers. University graduates, homemakers, international students, ex-dropouts. If you are twenty-four, you won't feel old. Most students say the mix in a college class is terrific. Older students bring life experience, younger ones bring school-savvy.

Hot prospect? Technology careers.

If Canada is going to make it in the world economy, we will need many people doing interesting work for good pay in technology careers. College is where they are going to come from. Many colleges still have room in technology programs.

New central applications process.

If you want to take a full-time, career-oriented program, you don't apply to the college itself, you apply to the Ontario Colleges' Central Applications Service in Guelph. For full details, see "Planning and Applying" in Part Three.

"Oversubscribed" means: Don't count on getting right in!

A lot of people want to go to college, particularly when the economy turns bad. Colleges have not got room for them all. Many programs turn qualified people away. Some have hundreds of qualified applicants for every place available. See "Maximize Your Chances" in Part One.

Things change.

Colleges add and remove programs and services frequently. This book is up to date as of the end of 1992, but check with the colleges for new developments about any program that interests you. And watch for the new edition of this guidebook late in 1994.

PART ONE

Accreditation

If you want to be a nurse, the colleges can train you and give you a diploma. But to practise nursing, you have to become "registered," and an institution called the College of Nurses controls registration. The College of Nurses gives exams to nursing graduates and keeps an eye on the quality of college nursing programs. That's the law.

What about other fields? A technician or technologist earns a college diploma, but his or her prospects for working (outside Ontario, particularly) depend on whether the college's diplomas are recognized. In general they are, but outside accreditation of Ontario's programs would make that more certain. There used to be a system by which Technology programs were given outside accreditation, but the Ministry of Colleges and Universities backed out of that early in the 1980s.

Most program areas are like that. Unless they are forced to by law, colleges duck any kind of independent accreditation. You pretty much have to take their word that they are teaching you what they ought to. Of course, high schools and universities are just the same. And at least the colleges have close ties to the industries that hire (or reject) their grads, and that helps keep them honest. But they could be doing more.

In the early 1990s, the Ontario colleges were discussing a kind of compromise, in which the college system itself would set standards and accredit college programs. Whether this can succeed remains in doubt. Obviously independent accreditation is going to be the most persuasive. Colleges ought to open up their program to fair and unbiased inspection by the appropriate accrediting bodies.

COLLEGES AND CAREERS

Men are a small but growing minority in college Nursing programs.

There are twenty-three colleges of applied arts and technology in Ontario. What do they do? Who do they serve? What can they do for you? In the summer of 1992 I went out and asked a lot of people.

Several times I heard the simple explanation, "We are here to serve business and industry" – by training the people that a big, complicated, changing economy like Ontario's needs. But I liked better an explanation I heard at Durham College in Oshawa. It is still very practical, but it remembers that colleges serve their students too.

"Our mission is economic development. For the community and the province, sure, but also the personal economic development of our students. Our students leave here for good careers. [In recent years, Durham has claimed a placement rate of about 97 per cent.] They have a good standard of living. They are productive in the economy. And because they have money to spend, they support the services of other people. By bettering themselves, they make the country stronger."

Who Goes to College?

Anyone with a high school diploma (or something equivalent) is entitled to apply. Once, high school was all most people needed to enter the workforce. Your grandparents might even remember when Grade 8 was enough. Now the idea is seeping through that "the high school graduate is dead" when it comes to getting a good job. (That's pretty serious when 30 per cent of our students drop out before finishing high school.)

Not only high school graduates go to college. In Ontario, colleges are also the main source of help for adults who don't have high school. The colleges bring many people up to high school diploma level – and then accept them in career-oriented programs. They also do a lot of training in skilled trades and apprenticeships. Increasingly the trades demand a high school diploma, and sometimes more, but some of them can be entered from Grade 10, and the colleges teach them.

So the colleges take people who would otherwise have lousy job prospects – and give them pretty decent ones. Just about everything they do is directly career-related, and they cover many careers. Colleges train people who serve the community, from police to early childhood educators. They train broadcasters and publicists. They prepare advertising people, working musicians, and fashion designers.

They train nurses and other health science specialists. Their business schools turn out accountants, office managers, hotel and restaurant operators. They train technicians and technologists for dozens of careers: maintaining heating systems, running environmental control systems, operating elaborate computer-controlled mills and factories, navigating freighters on the Great Lakes, and flying helicopters over the north woods.

(What the colleges don't do, mostly, is broad liberal arts education, abstract or theoretical research, and career preparation for professionals such as lawyers, engineers, dentists, and teachers. That they leave to the universities.)

More and more, the colleges also train the workforce that is already working. A few colleges have post-diploma programs for people who have already been to college or university. College trainers train the whole workforce of industrial plants and give management seminars for the administrators, too. Most of the hundreds of thousands of people taking part-time and evening courses in the colleges are working people, upgrading their skills and qualifications in order to expand their opportunities.

All this the colleges offer to people who have the standard high school diploma. They make it attractive enough, in fact, to draw in a lot of adults from the workforce and a growing number of university graduates who go to college after collecting a B.A. or B.Sc. But college works on an open access principle. Everyone with a high school diploma or something like it has got pretty much an equal shot at what colleges offer.

Someone at Niagara College told me the colleges offer more people more chances to change their economic circumstances decisively than any other part of the education system. I have been thinking about that for a couple of months as I finished this book. And I find it hard to argue with.

In Hard Times

These are hard times. In the 1990s, people have hard choices and big decisions to make. You know you have to have training to get work, but everyone knows lots of trained people are getting laid off. You have to make a living, but you have to find something that gives you a little satisfaction as well as a pay cheque.

You hear Canadian business complaining about the workforce, but Canadian business has just about the worst record in the developed world for research-and-development and for training its own people. You know Canada needs more skilled tradespeople and fewer lawyers, but university still gets all the prestige. You realize we have to compete in a free-trade world, but our foreign-owned industries are heading south as fast as they can move.

Colleges are close to the heart of all these economic challenges. They are caught up in the problems, but for many people they can also be where some answers lie. You have the possibility of getting in and out of college fast, at a cost you can handle, with a real skill that leads to a real job in the real world. (Of course, you can also end up drifting around college, getting meaningless training for jobs you wouldn't want anyway.) If you get through college and into a career, you may not only be bettering yourself but also contributing to a more prosperous, more innovative, more productive society.

About 125,000 people are taking full-time, diploma-bound programs in the Ontario colleges every year. That is probably not enough, and it is not expanding fast enough. The figure is a lot smaller than the number of university students and we might be better off if the proportions were reversed. But the Ontario college system is still only twenty-five years old. It has achieved enough that Walter Pitman, the distinguished writer, educator, and former member of parliament who knows every level of Ontario's schooling system, calls the college system "the most important innovation in education in Ontario this century."

He's probably right.

WHAT COLLEGE CAN PREPARE YOU FOR

Co-op students in everything from General Arts and Science to Architectural Technology learn and earn on the job as part of their college education.

Colleges ask you to make some big choices right at the start. And often they don't make it easy to choose.

Go to university, and chances are you will start in either a Bachelor of Arts or a Bachelor of Science program. Eventually you will choose a "major," but, as one of the university guidebooks (*Students' Guide to Ontario Universities* by Dyanne Gibson, from University of Toronto Press, 1991, p. 53) says, "an undergraduate degree is basically the same at any university in Ontario." At college, however, you choose from hundreds of different programs aimed at different careers, and they are *not* basically the same. There will be people at your college preparing for careers you have never heard of.

This section is a quick run through the main career areas in which colleges teach. First it covers the PROGRAMS – what the colleges call post-secondary programs (for explanations of the

7

colleges' code words, see "The Jargon" in Part One) – then apprenticeship and training and all the other stuff. PROGRAMS mean, more or less, that you need a high school diploma to get in, you will study for two or three full-time school years, and you will come out with a college diploma and be ready to hold down a job in your field. This book covers the programs offered at all the Ontario Colleges of Applied Arts and Technology, and it also gives summary information about apprenticeship and training courses at the colleges.

Programs

The colleges offer programs that prepare students for careers in four big general areas they call Applied Arts, Business (often including Hospitality and Tourism), Health Sciences, and Technology. That's how the programs are listed in the chapter on each college in this book.

To sort out which colleges offer which programs, use the Index of Programs that follows Part Three, or read the chapters on any colleges that interest you. But – *programs with the same title are not necessarily the same.* Colleges often serve local needs and may tailor their programs accordingly. It is worth checking into each program that interests you, by talking to people at the college itself.

General Programs

Before plunging into the career choices, watch for something called COLLEGE PREPARATORY, GENERAL STUDIES, or GENERAL ARTS AND SCIENCE (GAS). Every college offers something like this, sometimes several versions. If you are not sure what you want to do, or you want to look around, or you need to strengthen your abilities in English or Math or study skills, consider starting in one of these. Some people go into GAS if they can't get straight into the program they want. Others use GAS to prepare for applying to university.

Careers in the Applied Arts

"Applied Arts" is a shaggy heading the colleges use to cover a great many kinds of careers.

Programs in the Community Service area prepare people for a lot of social service jobs. Grads are likely to be employed by a government agency, a non-profit group, or some other public institution. (Note that the basic requirement for many senior positions in social service agencies is a Master's degree in Social Work. In many agencies, you may need further education to move up.)

Most colleges offer a program called SOCIAL SERVICE WORK, leading to careers in community centres, group homes, and social service agencies of many kinds. Some colleges offer a similar program called BEHAVIOURAL SCIENCE. There are many supporting programs aimed at more specific aspects of this field: CHILD AND YOUTH WORK, COMMUNITY WORK, DEVELOPMENTAL SERVICE WORK (for careers with the developmentally handicapped), SIGN LANGUAGE INTERPRETER, INTERVENOR FOR THE DEAF/BLIND, GERONTOLOGY (work with the aged), and others. George Brown has a unique program, WOMEN AND CHILDREN'S ADVOCATE, for workers in women's and children's shelters, and several colleges offer NATIVE SOCIAL SERVICE and BAND MANAGEMENT programs for aboriginal communities. A few colleges offer programs in SOCIAL SCIENCE RESEARCH.

Many colleges offer a program called RECREATION LEADERSHIP for careers in the sports, fitness, and recreation industry, either in community agencies or private clubs. A few have specialized programs in recreation management, arena or ski area operations, fitness, or coaching.

Another standard Applied Arts program is LAW AND SECURITY ADMINISTRATION, which prepares students for police and security careers. College administrators sometimes admit that so many young people want to be police that they could fill every LASA section they opened. LASA grads do proceed to Ontario Police College or the RCMP training depot in Regina. But police force hiring has limits, and in the 1990s it is strongly aimed at achieving equity by hiring more women and minorities. Most LASA grads work in customs and immigration, security work, and various personnel roles. Some colleges have different LASA streams for these careers. CORRECTIONAL WORK is another common program in this area.

In the Education field, all colleges offer EARLY CHILDHOOD EDUCATION, which trains workers for daycare centres and nursery schools. Some programs have a specific focus – older children, children with special needs, native childcare, and so on. Other Education programs at some colleges train Daycare Assistants, Teachers' Aides, Teachers of Adults, and Library Technicians.

Many colleges train media personnel for radio, television, and newspapers, and for technical production roles in several industries. The most common program is JOURNALISM, which may train for either PRINT or BROADCAST or both. Almost as common is RADIO AND TELEVISION BROADCASTING, usually emphasizing either on-air or behind-the-scenes production. Also offered are programs in PHOTOGRAPHY (Loyalist's is Photojournalism, others are more general or cover other photographic careers) and AUDIO-VISUAL PRODUCTION. Algonquin offers TECHNICAL WRITING, which leads to careers writing technical reports, manuals, and specifications. At the creative-arts end of the media, a few colleges have special programs, such as MEDIA ARTS, an all-round film-making program at Sheridan. Sheridan's ANIMATION and COMPUTER ANIMATION programs are well known (Algonquin has ANIMATION FOR TELEVISION), and Fanshawe has MUSIC INDUSTRY ARTS, focused on careers in studio performance and production. Centennial offers BOOK AND MAGAZINE PUBLISHING.

College graduates in GRAPHIC ARTS are likely to work in publishing, design studios, or advertising. Several colleges combine ADVERTISING AND GRAPHIC ARTS, and Sheridan has ILLUSTRATION. George Brown has several PRINTING programs. There are various programs for the advertising industry, some focused on art, some on copywriting, some on marketing, and others combining some or all of these. Several colleges offer PUBLIC RELATIONS. St. Lawrence has a combined ADVERTISING AND PUBLIC RELATIONS program, and Seneca has CORPORATE COMMUNICATIONS.

A few colleges have FASHION DESIGN, FASHION MARKETING, and other programs that prepare students for careers in the design, production, and marketing aspects of the Canadian fashion industry. Humber's FASHION ARTS program includes modelling.

COSMETICS, ESTHETICS, HAIRSTYLING, and other supporting programs are also offered at some colleges.

Several colleges offer programs in INTERIOR DESIGN, which promise to train students not simply as decorators but as planners of all aspects of interior space use. Some include VISUAL MERCHANDISING, which focuses on marketing displays. LANDSCAPE DESIGN, HORTICULTURE, or FLORISTRY are available at some colleges, and a couple of colleges train students to work in COMMUNITY PLANNING (Mohawk) and URBAN DESIGN (Fanshawe). In some of these fields you may work under the supervision of university-trained planners or designers. Others offer more scope for individual initiative and self-employment.

In the Creative Arts, apart from the film and music programs listed above under Media, a few colleges offer FINE ARTS AND CRAFTS, and others specialize in Jewellery, Ceramics, Textiles, or other crafts. Sheridan's CRAFT AND DESIGN covers design and production of fabrics, ceramics, glass, and furniture, and it also offers ART AND ART HISTORY in partnership with the University of Toronto. Fleming has ART CONSERVATION and Algonquin has MUSEUMS TECHNOLOGY, both of which train in the preservation of artworks.

Artistic performance careers that a few colleges prepare students for include MUSIC, usually for the self-employed "gigging" musician, THEATRE ARTS (for stage performers), THEATRE PRODUCTION (for backstage workers), and ARTS ADMINISTRATION.

Careers in Business

All the colleges teach Business programs, and they prepare people for a range of careers in business. Some college business grads are clerk-typists or retail clerks. Others are senior corporate executives or successful entrepreneurs. In Business, unlike most Applied Arts programs, the difference between what colleges and universities do is not so clear. There is overlap between some college and university programs in business. At some schools, transfer from college to university (to add a degree after a diploma) is becoming common.

Particularly when the market is tight, university and college business grads may find themselves competing for the same jobs at the same pay rates. University grads have the edge in prestige and credentials; on the other hand, there are employers who prefer grads of college programs for their practical orientation and their adaptability to local conditions and new technology.

If you are choosing between college or university for a business education, be clear on what each program is and how it suits your ambitions. Note, for instance, that if you want to be a Chartered Accountant or a Certified Management Accountant, you need a university degree. College accounting grads can become Certified General Accountants.

Most college business programs are called BUSINESS or BUSINESS ADMINISTRATION. Business Administration covers more and takes three school years instead of two. At many colleges, most business students take a common first year or semester and then choose among options depending on their future career interests. Many colleges also offer a GENERAL Business program that combines elements from various options.

The main Business/Business Administration options include ACCOUNTING, MARKETING, INFORMATION SYSTEMS (or COMPUTERS or PROGRAMMING), and HUMAN RESOURCES. Some colleges (see Seneca, for example) also offer business training in PUBLIC ADMINISTRATION, PROPERTY MANAGEMENT, DISTRIBUTION, or PURCHASING and MATERIALS MANAGEMENT. INTERNATIONAL BUSINESS is a new field where several colleges have recently developed programs. Most focus on the U.S. market and the North American free-trade environment, but Humber's include Asian and German connections.

Some colleges offer special training in SMALL BUSINESS, others in various aspects of RETAILING or SALES. Confederation has a unique program in INDUSTRIAL RELATIONS. Georgian's Canadian Automotive Institute prepares students for all the business aspects of the AUTOMOTIVE MARKETING industry, and its Canadian Aviation Institute teaches all aspects of AVIATION Ground Operations, from airport and airline management to air traffic control. (Confederation also teaches airport and airline management.)

The other large area covered by college business schools is OFFICE ADMINISTRATION, with programs that range from the fundamental secretarial tasks to RECORDS MANAGEMENT. Specializations offered at many colleges include various kinds of MEDICAL, DENTAL, and LEGAL Office Administration. Some business schools also train LEGAL ASSISTANTS, who assist lawyers in research and administration. George Brown has a unique program in COURT REPORTING, which trains the people who produce the official transcripts of court proceedings for judges and lawyers.

Careers in Hospitality and Tourism

A field of study usually linked to Business schools at the colleges is HOSPITALITY AND TOURISM. Colleges active in this area often run their own restaurant or hospitality centre. Their graduates may be chefs in expensive restaurants, or work for major hotel chains, resorts, tourist attractions, or travel wholesalers and retailers.

The most common program here is HOTEL AND RESTAURANT MANAGEMENT. Several colleges offer courses in TOURISM MANAGEMENT, which deals with the planning and management of tourist-related industries. Many offer TRAVEL AND TOURISM, mostly aimed at careers in travel agencies, and Niagara has TOURS AND ATTRACTIONS. Seneca offers FLIGHT SERVICES for airline flight attendants (attendance at an airline's own training program will still be required after graduation). Colleges offering Hotel and Restaurant programs usually offer CHEF TRAINING or CULINARY MANAGEMENT as well, and some colleges have other specialties in this area, such as Italian cuisine at Canadore and many unique offerings at George Brown's School of Hospitality.

Careers in Health Sciences

NURSING and NURSING ASSISTANT programs are the backbone of Health Sciences in the college system. College nursing departments are proud of their grads. They agree that university-trained nurses with a Bachelor of Science in Nursing may be better trained for managing a ward or handling psycho-social health issues. But they insist that college diploma nurses have the practical hands-on advantage when it comes to putting in an IV or handling an operating-room emergency.

However, with the Canadian health system in a financial bind, the health bureaucrats may eventually prefer to have a few B.Sc.N. nurses supervising a lot of RNAs (Registered Nursing Assistants) and other support staff. The degree nurses from the colleges, caught in the middle, are already being squeezed by hospital cutbacks.

So should you avoid the nursing program at college? No, but you should ask about the future roles – and job prospects – of degree and diploma nurses, particularly in the growing field of community nursing. Meanwhile, the demand for NURSING ASSISTANTS is growing, and the colleges' Health Sciences departments also offer many other programs in health-related fields.

About half the colleges teach DENTAL ASSISTANT and DENTAL HYGIENE. DENTAL HYGIENE, which leads to a career with many job opportunities, good pay, and attractive working conditions, is famous for being the most oversubscribed program in the Ontario college system, with huge numbers of applicants for every place. However, recent reports suggest the job market is becoming less promising, and the high starting salaries for Dental Hygienists are starting to drop. In a related field, George Brown has unique programs in DENTAL TECHNOLOGY and DENTURE THERAPY.

Health Science programs train people for medical support roles in all areas: AMBULANCE AND EMERGENCY CARE, MEDICAL LABORATORY TECHNOLOGY, HEALTH RECORDS MANAGEMENT, RADIOGRAPHY, RESPIRATORY THERAPY, PHARMACY ASSISTANT. George Brown offers ORTHOTIC/PROSTHETIC (construction and fitting of artificial limbs and supports) and CHIROPODY (foot care), Humber has FUNERAL SERVICE EDUCATION (with Cambrian offering the same in French), and Georgian trains OPHTHALMIC DISPENSERS. Several colleges have programs training VETERINARY TECHNICIANS or ANIMAL CARE specialists. Grads may work in support roles in veterinary practices or maintain animals at, for instance, research labs or racetracks.

Careers in Technology

Technology people at the colleges are missionaries. They don't just talk about the programs they offer. They don't just talk about the high pay and job satisfaction awaiting their grads. What they really want to talk about is how desperately Canada *needs* technological skills. Time and again, I found technology professors in the colleges telling me they fear for the economic and social future of Canada, unless we educate ourselves in and about technology.

In 1900 most Canadians were farmers. Now with the help of a lot of technology, 3 per cent of Canadians produce all the food we need and more. Today the same thing is happening in manufacturing. A small number of skilled people, using automated machines and computerized robots, will be doing the work that once employed thousands. Soon it will be the same in many service fields, the place most Canadians work in the 1990s. In more and more areas, the challenging job, the well-paid job, the job with a future, requires a level of comfort with technology that too few of us have.

College is the most likely place to get it. Yet Technology programs have fewer applicants per place than any other kind of program in the college system.

The colleges do not produce Professional Engineers – the universities do that. Colleges produce Engineering Technicians and Engineering Technologists (Technician programs take two years, Technologist programs take three). In theory, professional engineers do theoretical and design work and hold final responsibility for the safety of engineering projects, while technicians and technologists have operating and maintenance roles.

A common rule-of-thumb says that in a well-developed modern economy there should be one technician and one technologist for every engineer. But today Ontario has 70,000 engineers and only 20,000 technicians and technologists. Technology ought to be a growth field, and in recent years programs have been created in several new areas. Indeed, many colleges, concerned about how much their students have to master in Technology programs, are pushing for longer programs, perhaps even a Bachelor of Technology.

A problem in Technology programs: you may feel you have to decide right away that you want to be, for instance, an Electro-Mechanical Precision Instruments Engineering Technician. (Right now you can't even *say* it, let alone know what it means.) Some colleges are grouping their Technology programs together into broad areas with common first-year courses. That way, you choose your specialty *after* you know what it means. But with so much specific content in many programs, the amount they share is limited. Some colleges offer a PRE-TECHNOLOGY year, which can prepare you either for a program or for an apprenticeship (about apprenticeships, see below).

Some colleges combine Civil and Architectural Engineering into one department. ARCHITECTURAL ENGINEERING grads may work in architects' offices, but even more work for municipal authorities and real estate developers. CIVIL ENGINEERING grads work on construction projects and public works of all kinds. Some colleges offer SURVEYING or DRAFTING AND DESIGN programs, and many have CONSTRUCTION ENGINEERING programs.

Aviation programs, offered at a handful of colleges, include FLIGHT, which trains commercial and airline pilots (fixed-wing flying at Confederation, Sault, and Seneca, and helicopters at Canadore), AVIATION MAINTENANCE (including Canadore's and Centennial's AVIONICS, which is the electronics of aviation), and AVIATION ENGINEERING, which concerns aircraft manufacturing. For Georgian's Aviation Ground Operation programs, see Business above.

CHEMICAL ENGINEERING grads frequently do testing and measuring work in a laboratory setting. Other fields linked to Chemical Engineering include PULP AND PAPER ENGINEERING, a Sault College specialty, and METALLURGICAL ENGINEERING, concerned with analyzing metals and minerals.

A new field called ENVIRONMENTAL ENGINEERING combines some of the measuring and testing of Chemical Engineering and some of the public works and construction tasks of Civil Engineering. Various colleges' programs emphasize solid-waste, biochemical, energy-conservation, or other aspects of environmental control.

Many colleges offer ELECTRIC ENGINEERING programs, which

may deal with electric power and electric equipment servicing. Some make HEATING AND REFRIGERATION a special program. ELECTRONIC ENGINEERING may focus on communications or on operating or servicing electronic equipment, or it may be focused on COMPUTER ENGINEERING or on maintaining and operating COMPUTER SYSTEMS. On the software side of computer technology, several colleges offer COMPUTER PROGRAMMER or COMPUTER ANALYST. (Note that Business also offers programs in the management of computer information systems.)

The recent slump in the Ontario manufacturing industry has turned many students away from MECHANICAL ENGINEERING programs, but Technology people argue that in a smaller manufacturing labour force, it will be trained college grads who hold the vital advantage. INDUSTRIAL ENGINEERING programs deal with the operation of large industrial systems, and may have safety or management aspects. STATIONARY ENGINEERING and POWER ENGINEERING train operating engineers to manage large industrial or commercial power plants.

A few colleges have specialized MANUFACTURING ENGINEERING and WELDING programs. As computer control of manufacturing becomes more and more standard, some colleges offer ELECTRO-MECHANICAL ENGINEERING, and others have specialties in INSTRUMENTATION, FLUID POWER/ROBOTICS, or PROCESS CONTROL ENGINEERING, all concerned with the new computer-controlled automation processes.

MOTIVE POWER specialists may work with heavy equipment, automobile engines, marine engines, or small engines. Centennial's School of Transportation has unique strengths in AUTOMOTIVE and other Motive Power careers, including AUTO PARTS MANAGEMENT and AVIONICS. Note, however, that much of automotive training goes on in Apprenticeship and Trades training, covered below.

Several colleges have programs devoted to particular technologies used by specific industries. Cambrian and Northern offer MINING ENGINEERING and, along with some others, GEOLOGICAL ENGINEERING. Conestoga offers programs in WOODWORKING and FURNITURE MAKING. As mentioned, Sault has PULP AND PAPER ENGINEERING. Georgian and St. Lawrence (Cornwall) offer MARINE ENGINEERING, while Georgian also has MARINE NAVIGATION, which trains officers for seagoing and Great Lakes ships.

Several colleges, particularly Fleming's School of Natural Resources, Cambrian (mostly in French), and Sault, offer various courses in RESOURCE MANAGEMENT, which prepare students for careers in forestry, outdoor recreation, and wildlife, and RESOURCE TECHNOLOGY, which includes earth sciences, drilling, and heavy equipment operations. Programs include FORESTRY TECHNOLOGY, which trains students for support positions with professional foresters, FISH AND WILDLIFE TECHNOLOGY (Fleming and Cambrian), Sault's METEOROLOGICAL ENGINEERING, which trains weather forecasters, and AQUACULTURE, TERRAIN AND WATER RESOURCES, and PARKS AND FOREST RECREATION, all unique to Fleming. GEOGRAPHICAL INFORMATION SYSTEMS, at Algonquin and Fleming, applies computers to data-plotting and mapmaking.

Finally, there are unusual Technology fields handled by one or a few colleges, including Seneca's UNDERWATER SKILLS, George Brown's PIANO TECHNICIAN, Humber's PACKAGING and its new PLASTICS programs, and FIRE PROTECTION programs at Algonquin and Seneca.

Apprenticeships, Skilled Trades, and Short Programs

The programs listed so far, from Applied Arts through Technology, tend to be two- or three-year commitments on a full-time basis. You enter with a high school diploma and leave with a college diploma and hopes for a job. But the colleges are also involved in other kinds of training that usually involve a shorter time at college and do not always require high school graduation.

Apprenticeships

APPRENTICESHIPS are much older than the college system. They are the centuries-old way to learn a trade – you apprentice yourself to someone who knows the trade, and slowly work your way up, learning while you earn, until you too are a master of the craft. It can take two years, four years, or more to complete an apprenticeship, and there may be exams at the end.

A few additional wrinkles have been added since the old days. Today apprenticeships are regulated by the provincial government. Your employer during your apprenticeship may be a large company, and being an apprentice may involve being a union member. The colleges are involved too. Colleges do the in-school part of most apprenticeship training. So you learn on the job most of the time and get paid. But for maybe 10 per cent of your apprenticeship, you go to college for what you can't learn on the job. You don't get paid during the college part, but you can collect Unemployment Insurance payments.

Employer, union, Government of Ontario, college, Canada Employment – it is complicated. But apprenticeship is still considered an important part of the job training system. Ways to improve the apprenticeship process are currently being explored. Nearly 20,000 people are taking apprenticeship programs in Ontario, and most of the colleges take part. You can't enroll in an apprenticeship through the colleges, unfortunately, since you need an employer and a registered apprenticeship before the college can start teaching you its part of your learning. But colleges do provide the in-school portion of many of the following apprenticeships – and about 500 more are available.

Some of the fields where apprentices are taken are: Alignment and Brake Mechanic, Automotive Machinist, Auto Body Repairer, Auto Painter, Baker, Boilermaker, Brick and Stone Mason, Butcher, Carpenter, Chemical Plant Operator, Construction Millwright, Cook, Draftsperson, Drywaller, Electrician, Electronics Mechanic, Farm Equipment Mechanic, Fitter, Fuel Systems Mechanic, Furrier, Glazier, Hairstylist, Heavy-duty Equipment Mechanic, Hoisting Engineer, Horticulturalist, Industrial Millwright, Ironworker, Lather, Lineperson, Machinist, Motorcycle Mechanic, Motor Vehicle Mechanic, Mould Maker, Painter, Patternmaker, Plasterer, Plumber, Printer, Radio/TV Repairer, Refrigeration Mechanic, Retail Meat Cutter, Sheetmetal Worker, Sprinkler Installer, Steamfitter, Terrazzo Tiler, Tool and Die Maker, Transmission Mechanic, Truck-trailer Repairer, Welder.

If you might be interested in learning any of these (or other) trades through apprenticeship, talk to an employer or a union, or look up an Apprenticeship Office under the Government of Ontario in your local phone book.

Trades

You can learn a SKILLED TRADE without getting hired into an apprenticeship. Many of the colleges offer skilled trades training in courses that often run for 36 or 52 weeks. At the end you have the basic training and a college certificate to say so.

You can often enter these trades courses with a Grade 10 or equivalent. They cover many of the same career areas as apprenticeships, and some of them are useful background if you want to apply for an apprenticeship.

How to find out what is available? There are two or three doorways. You can contact the college directly, enroll yourself, and pay the fees. Or you may find out about them from the local Canada Employment Centres, which will often pay their clients' tuition and "buy seats" in a college program. And the Government of Ontario Ministry of Skills Development also has programs to support people in trades courses. There are also special programs, such as Women into Trades and Technology, to assist traditionally disadvantaged groups to get into new trades areas. For more about that, see "Special Clients" in Part Three of the book.

Short Programs

The sky is the limit here. More and more, the colleges see themselves training, retraining, upgrading, and "reskilling" every part of the Ontario workforce at all career stages. Whether you are in a job, out of a job, trying to change jobs or move up in your job, the colleges offer training programs of all kinds: short-term, part-time, night-school, on-the-job, or day-release projects that give you time off from work while you study. For people needing skills to get into the workforce, they do basic adult literacy, high-school equivalency, and English as a Second Language. They do customized training programs for employees. They run refreshers and upgrades for working professionals. They have a million career-related night-school courses. They do management training seminars. And they sell consultants' advice to business, industry, and government.

The chapter on each college highlights a few aspects of what each college does in this area. If any of these kinds of training seem to fit your requirements, call your local college and start asking questions.

History of the College System

The Ontario college system has just turned twenty-five. It began in 1967.

In the early 1960s, Ontario schools introduced streaming: Basic, General, Advanced. Only Advanced students (supposed to be about one in three) would have access to university. So Ontario scrambled to create something for the rest. Out of a handful of trade schools and technical institutes, the province began to create the CAATs – Colleges of Applied Arts and Technology.

About the same time, the Canadian government decided to put a lot of money into training the Canadian labour force. Hey, said the provinces, education is a provincial matter. So the federal government turned funds over to the provinces. Ontario grabbed a big share of the money, and brand-new colleges quickly sprouted all over the province. Centennial was the first new college to open its doors, quickly followed by eighteen more. Today there are twenty-three Colleges of Applied Arts and Technology with almost 150 campuses across Ontario.

At the start, the idea seemed to be that bright middle-class kids would go away to university and inherit white-collar professional jobs. Workers' kids would stay home, go to college (they called them commuter colleges for a while), and remain working-class.

Today university is still the place for broad liberal education and for the professions, and the universities still try to maintain the prestige gap. But colleges now train adults in all age groups and at every economic level for careers never dreamed of in 1967. They have become the key place for career-oriented training and retraining of all kinds.

Future of the College System

The big money that created colleges and universities by the dozen in the 1960s and 1970s just isn't available for the 1990s. Ontario will need more colleges, but instead it will probably get more intense use of what already exists. Colleges will be busy all year round and almost around the clock, with more distance learning and independent study. Colleges will get bigger and more crowded. Tuition fees will probably go up sharply. And it will still be hard to get into many programs.

Some experts expect that the colleges will have to "rationalize." The Metro Toronto colleges are starting to trade programs for maximum efficiency. Many colleges have already started to specialize. Programs that need special equipment or expensive technology may eventually be centred at a few colleges (or just one), and most of the others would drop out of that field.

It is hard to imagine the universities taking fewer students, but their share may decline as college becomes the normal post-secondary education for most people preparing themselves for careers. And as the population ages, the mature student is going to be a more and more familiar part of the college scene.

Whatever happens, observers of the Ontario college system seem convinced the colleges will remain the most important job-training institution in the province, not only in preparing young people for careers, but also in continuous learning for everyone from the unskilled to corporate executives.

CHOOSING YOUR PROGRAM

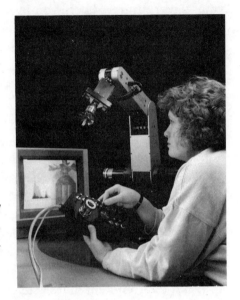

Increasingly industry will need college Technology grads to operate and maintain complex computer-driven machinery.

So – are you going to be an electro-mechanical technologist, or are you going to play bass guitar for a roadhouse bar band? Actually, the colleges can give you some help with either one. But you are going to have to do some choosing. Most college programs are aimed at some *specific* career path.

It is not easy. Some colleges estimate that about 30 per cent of new students enroll in the wrong program and go through a lot of frustration and wasted time before getting straightened out.

There are three parts to choosing a program:

1. figuring out what you want to do,
2. deciding if college can help you,
3. finding out just what a particular program offers.

What You Want To Do

Sorry, this book can't tell you that.

Your whole life experience is going to influence how you see your career future. Where you live, what your parents and your friends' parents do, and what your older siblings choose can have a big influence. Your academic success and your family's ambitions for you play a part. You will be shaped by your experience with part-time jobs, with high-school co-op terms, with volunteering, maybe with the job market itself.

A lot of career counsellors suggest Grade 8 is not too early to start thinking about career directions. Many colleges now offer tours and special events for kids that age, not to sell them on a particular program, but to get them thinking about broad career choices – and how their high school options might fit into them.

Some high school students find teachers and guidance counsellors are a key resource. Many college students I met wanted to emphasize that teachers and guidance counsellors are all university graduates. They may know more about university than college and tend to promote it more actively. (Parents are often like that too.) On the other hand, many college students could point to a particular teacher, counsellor, or acquaintance who had helped them find their way to college.

Adults may find employers and unions prepared to help with career counselling. Canada Employment Centres offer career advice. The colleges offer extensive aptitude and career-preference testing to potential students. (For more information, see "Using the Services" in Part Three of this book.) Usually there is a fee, but some colleges will rebate it if you do enroll in a program. I also met some adult students who had gone back to high school guidance offices five years after they graduated – and got a sympathetic hearing and useful information about colleges.

As your interests focus, you can approach a college directly. Many will put you on their mailing list and send general information and specific program information if you request it.

Can College Help You?

From the section above, "What College Can Train You For," you can get a rough idea of what careers colleges train for. If you want to be a brain surgeon, a sociology professor, an astronomer, or a theologian, there's not much a college can do for you. On the other hand, if you want to be a security officer, a fashion artist, or a dental hygienist, college is almost certainly where you want to be.

In fact, there is a whole group of careers where the colleges have helped create professions. Airport managers used to be mostly retired pilots, and community recreation positions were filled by athletically minded people who drifted into them. As colleges began training in Airport Ground Operations and Recreation Leadership, however, the graduates gradually raised the standards and the general level of expertise in their field.

It gets more complicated where there is either an overlap or a hierarchy in the field that interests you. Do you want to be an Engineering Technologist (from college) or a Professional Engineer (from university)? If you are going into marketing, do you need a college diploma or a university degree in marketing? Will it be nursing or medical school, and if nursing, college or university nursing? Obviously the answer will be shaped by your academic abilities, the state of your finances, and how much time you can commit to your education. Will you consider going on from college to university, or the other way round?

If you have the luxury of choosing between college and university, you will almost certainly encounter the prestige issue. Colleges used to have a second-best reputation, as if they were mostly for those who couldn't make it in university. Many teachers, parents, and university graduates still have that perception, and social attitudes about status and class run very deep.

But now there are too many unemployed B.A.s around, too many teaching assistants in overcrowded university classrooms – and too many college grads making hiring decisions. The prestige gap shrinks a little more each time a university graduate decides to go on to college for post-graduate training that will lead to a career.

For the most part colleges and universities are working different stretches of the post-secondary education beat. You should try to find the one that suits you, not the one with a reputation.

As for choosing between going to college or going straight to work, more and more the world is making that decision for you. There are jobs you can find with a high school diploma (or even without one), but they get harder to find all the time. And often they are not jobs you are going to want to do for the rest of your life. Many people work for a few years while they consider what career they want to pursue and what kind of schooling will suit them best.

What College Programs Offer

Maybe you have some idea what you want to do, and you know that colleges do that kind of training. You are not out of the woods yet.

I met someone who hadn't been happy with his college experience. He knew he was interested in journalism, but he got into a Broadcast Journalism program when he really would have preferred newspapers. He disliked all that radio and TV studio work, and it just didn't work out. *Lesson*: Even similar programs can point in different career directions.

I heard about someone else who started Early Childhood Education at a college. Then she moved to another city and found the ECE program at the college there was not quite the same, and she couldn't simply transfer all her credits to finish her program. *Lesson*: Programs with the same name may not be quite the same.

This book tries to cover the programs offered at the colleges of Ontario. But with so many programs to explore in the Ontario college system, it can't give much detail about any particular one or two that may be right for you. Almost every college promises that if you approach it (usually through the liaison office), it can lay on specific information about particular programs for you. You should be able to tour the areas of the college that interest you, meet with program faculty, even sit in on a class.

So: use this guidebook as a starting point. But if any particular college and program interest you even a little, go to that college and that program. Get the calendar. Get more information. Talk to people about it. Ask what they cover, what they specialize in, how their programs differ from similar programs elsewhere.

A College Day

You arrive in the morning, fight for a (paid) parking space, grab a coffee, and head for your program area. You have the same class schedule as the other people in your full-time program, so over a couple of years you get to know them and the professors. Maybe you rented a locker (often there are not enough to go round), so you aren't hauling books and coats all day. Some programs have a studio or some other room where you can claim your own small space.

Off to class. In a full-time program, you will usually have 20 to 24 hours a week of classes. It used to be more like 28 or 30, but money is tight in the colleges, and hours have been cut back. So you have four or five scheduled class hours a day, a lot of it with the same group of people doing the same program as you. The colleges claim students can learn more by doing independent study or group work than by sitting in class listening to a professor, so those hours should not all be spent at a desk taking down lecture notes.

You should figure on about as much time outside of class working on projects and assignments. Four hours of class and four more doing your own work in the studio, in the computer lab, or at the Resource Centre will keep you busy most of the day. Maybe you did pretty well in the first-year courses, so you have an hour booked for Peer Tutoring – you are getting paid to show the ropes to someone a year behind who is having a hard time. You don't get time to check the Co-op office for job possibilities coming up next term. Tomorrow you better talk to one of the profs or the Co-op staff about that.

After lunch maybe there's a common hour – no classes, and lots of activities scheduled by college clubs and groups, so you take in some of the action. Late afternoon, maybe you have made time for intramural floor hockey.

Back to the house or residence for a couple of hours. In the evening you meet other people from your program for a group assignment. Then you drop by the pub and have a couple to end the day. Part-time job, family time, outside friends, activities . . . it's a pretty busy couple of years.

CHOOSING YOUR COLLEGE

All the colleges have lively men's and women's sports programs. Some colleges offer sports scholarships to top athletes.

Maybe you don't have any choice about your college. Family commitments, or a job, or just a lack of money, may keep you right where you are. Staying home may be the most important aspect of your decision about which college to attend. Fortunately, branch campuses, outreach programs, and Distance Education put a lot of people within reach of at least some college training.

On the other hand, just getting *away* may be a big part of your decision. When the colleges were established twenty-five years ago, they were supposed to be "commuter" campuses and they were not supposed to have residences. Only university students, it seemed, were to have that away-from-home student experience.

All that has changed now. Many colleges draw most of their students from outside their local area, and a lot of students pick their college at least partly by location. Some students want to be in Metro Toronto, others want to be anywhere but. (Colleges in a ring from Belleville to Niagara say they are close, but not too close, to the Big City!) Pick up the calendar from any small-town college, and the cover is sure to be promoting the benefits of that gorgeous outdoor setting and small-college friendliness. Location, lifestyle, sports facilities, cost-of-living – these are all important factors in college choice.

The other reason to go is programs. The colleges go too far when they won't let you transfer your credits from one college's program to another, and they say they are working to get rid of that kind of barrier. But there are real differences too, and real choices to make. Colleges don't take cookie-cutter programs out of a box shipped from Toronto. Mostly they design their own. They try to respond to local needs. They look for special niches no one else is serving. Practically every college has some unique program no other college offers, and even programs with the same title may not be the same.

And they may deliver that program in particular ways. Some colleges let you start in January or February as well as September. Some include co-op work terms in many programs, others do not. You may think it is worth going across the province to take that special program that's right for you.

Still, colleges do overlap. They all have Office Administration programs, they all have Nursing programs. Can you find out if one college's Early Childhood Education or Electrical Engineering Technician diploma is better than another's?

Mostly, no. Without fixed standards, the colleges couldn't compare their programs even if they wanted to. And mostly they haven't wanted to. Several college Nursing Schools hinted to me that their grads do particularly well on the Nursing Registration Exams. But when I asked the College of Nurses about that, it said it doesn't keep that kind of statistic – and wouldn't let the public have the results if it did. If we had the information to rank programs in order of excellence, this book would do so. But mostly it does not exist.

In this book you can find a capsule description of all the colleges of Ontario. The college chapters tell you about the look and feel of each college, where it is and how big or small it is. You can find details about the programs it offers and the way it offers them. There are notes on the services it provides (see also "Using the Services" and "Special Clients" at the back of the book). There is information on student activities, residences, scholarships, sports and recreation facilities at each college.

But you still need to make your own college choice. Some features to look for:

1. Program Clusters.

It's not by accident that George Brown's Hospitality School is world-renowned. Or that Loyalist's Media grads find good jobs in big-city media. Or that Sheridan's Creative Arts programs and Fleming's Resources programs have a high public profile.

When a school has several related programs clustered together, it can assemble good facilities with up-to-date equipment, and give students the opportunity to switch between programs with minimum hassle. It can start to build a reputation, and that helps draw good teachers. A stand-alone program at a college may be first-rate, but I was impressed by the energy levels I sensed at places like Seneca's School of Communication Arts and Georgian's Automotive Institute. Look for colleges that have clusters of programs in any field that interests you.

2. Facilities.

Colleges like their students to do "hands-on" learning (though, as someone told me at Sheridan, "it's really brains-on"). And in almost every field, you can't get "on" without the equipment. Sometimes that means machines or services right in the college, and sometimes it means access to nearby industries. Many colleges have turned their daycare facilities into remarkable Early Childhood Research centres. Durham's pride in its Graphic Design program is connected to its claim to have the best Macintosh computer labs of any college. Algonquin's Museums Technology is strong because of all the big museums in Ottawa-Hull. Ask about the facilities for whatever program you consider.

Nursing schools that train in teaching hospitals boast about that, but ones that are not connected to teaching hospitals say their students get more attention away from all the residents and interns from med school. As the emphasis in nursing moves from hospitals to community activity, you might be more interested in the community learning facilities of your nursing program than in its high-technology operating theatres.

Equipment is particularly important in fast-changing technology fields where the cost of new equipment is staggering. There is increasing talk that many Technology programs will "rationalize" and become concentrated at a few colleges with top-notch facilities and placement opportunities. Humber's Technology Centre, the robotics facilities at Durham and Fleming, and Conestoga's Woodworking Centre are examples of the kind of specialized training centres that may become more common. Check out the facilities for any program you consider.

3. Co-op or Not.

A co-op program is one where you do a couple of four-month, paid work terms between classroom terms in college. It's not available in all programs, and some colleges do a lot more of it than others. Some have no co-op programs. Co-op programs are most common in Business and Technology, scarce in Applied Arts, and almost unknown in Health Sciences. Sometimes it is optional, more often not. Co-op is very popular with students, even though it takes longer to complete a diploma that way.

The biggest co-op colleges are Fanshawe, Georgian, Mohawk, and Seneca. Two that feel they can do fine without it are Durham and (in most fields) Humber. Colleges without co-op often have job internships, practicums, field placements, or other ways to provide job experience. But if that paid co-op term in the middle of the school year appeals to you, it is worth checking to find out which colleges offer co-op learning in the programs that matter to you.

4. Specializations.

Beneath similar titles, programs may be quite different. For instance, one college may have separate Advertising, Graphics, and Public Relations programs, while another college combines Graphics and Advertising, and a third combines Advertising and Public Relations. Even programs called Advertising may be quite different; one emphasizing copywriting, another artwork, and a third sales. Journalism programs may emphasize print or broadcast, or try to combine both.

Colleges can usually tell you how their program specializes and why. Check that their interests and yours are heading in the same direction.

5. Local Connections.

Lambton's Technology programs are closely connected to the industries of Sarnia's Chemical Valley, while Confederation's are linked to the industries of northwest Ontario. George Brown's Community Service programs use the vast network of social agencies of downtown Toronto. Cambrian's Early Childhood Education is linked to French, English, and Native daycares in local communities. The Developmental Services program at St. Clair's Thames campus in Chatham is strong because the Southwest Regional Centre for the developmentally handicapped is right there.

Such connections not only serve local needs, they also ensure that students at those colleges get useful practical experience using local industry facilities. And, being there, you may be making useful contacts for your future. It is getting hard to run Fashion programs if students can't commute to Metro Toronto's garment district. On the other hand, Cambrian is moving into Arts programs because it knows that when students go south to train, they rarely return. So: consider how a college's local connections relate to where you want to work after graduation.

6. Lifestyle.

Close to home or far away? Ten thousand students or two thousand students? Big city or small town? Technology centre or arts school? Athletic facilities and sports scholarships, or big libraries and cultural opportunities? Townhouse residence or highrise? This book tries to give you that kind of information – but which of these ingredients are important to you depends on you.

Would You Consider – Programs Not So Oversubscribed

No college wants to say its programs can't attract students. I asked the colleges to report on programs "which seem to attract fewer applications than their accessibility, job prospects, salary expectations, etc., would seem to warrant."

The most common answer was: "All the Technologies."

Electronic and Mechanical Engineering were the technology areas most often mentioned, and a few schools cited Computer Engineering or Programming. Specialized programs also appeared, including Sault's unique Pulp and Paper program and Centennial's Avionics, a program that promises good pay and good job prospects but still does not have crowds of applicants.

References to low demand for Health Science programs were scarce, although George Brown and Niagara cited Health Records Technician. In Business, Materials Management and Property Management were each mentioned once. Canadore and Durham listed some food service programs. In the Applied Arts, Loyalist mentioned Print Journalism, and La Cité listed its French-language Design Interieur.

MAXIMIZE YOUR CHANCES

College Hospitality grads are becoming the backbone of Ontario's hotel, restaurant, resort, and tourism planning industries.

Many college programs have more applications than places, and they will not take everyone. Not everyone qualified gets in. College staff say these steps can help.

1. Apply on time.

The College system starts to take applications for fall programs on January 1, and the first big deadline is March 1. All qualified applicants up to March 1 have pretty much an equal chance. After March 1, you go on the waiting list. (For details, see Part Three, "Planning and Applying.")

2. Have all the requirements.

Get the calendar, and read the official requirements for the program and college you want. Read them again. If it says you should have Math for Technology, or volunteer experience, or an average over 65 per cent, or a CPR certificate, get it.

3. Get your papers in order.

You will need an official high school transcript or proof of some kind of equivalent standing. You may need proof of some of the things under #2 above. Have them ready.

4. Know what you want – and your second and third choices.

It's tough if you get accepted into a program and then find it isn't what you want. It's tough if someone else gets your spot and then drops out in November. The more everyone's choices are based on good information, the less frustrating it gets all around.

5. Consider the indirect route.

Most applicants are trying to enter career-oriented programs, and they want to start in the fall. Would General Arts and Science or a Pre-Technology year or semester improve your qualifications for the program you want? Could you start in January or February? Look into these routes toward what you want.

6. Keep trying.

Many successful applicants don't take up their acceptance. If you can remain flexible, you might get accepted as late as Labour Day.

7. Talk to the people.

It helps to talk to admissions officers, program faculty, and counsellors before you apply, but if you did not get in, talk to them afterwards too. Maybe it was just the luck of the draw. But find out if there is anything else you could or should be doing.

Changing Male-Female Ratios

Slightly more women than men take diploma courses at the Ontario colleges. But how many men and women you find yourself studying with depends on what program you are in. The male-female ratio ranges from close to 100 per cent women in Office Administration to around 90 per cent men in many Technology programs. Communications and Business programs tend to be more equally divided. Women are the majority in many Community Service and Arts programs and the vast majority in Nursing.

I asked the colleges where the shifts in male/female ratios have been headed lately. Most often, they reported an increasing (but still small) number of men in Nursing and an increasing (but still small) number of women in Technology, with the increase noted particularly in Computers and Electronics.

Other changes? Several colleges noted a strong shift toward equal numbers of men and women in Law and Security Administration, once mostly male. Centennial reported similar trends in Ambulance and Emergency Care ("from all male to half male"), Recreation Leadership (now mostly female), and Accounting (women replacing men as the majority). Loyalist and Fanshawe noted a larger minority of women in Broadcasting, and the Natural Resources school of Fleming has seen more women joining many of its once heavily male Wildlife and Outdoor programs.

One college reported the whole question was passé – "male and female students have long been enrolling in the program of their choice, regardless of tradition." This may be quite a bit too optimistic, but it is probably a good idea to be guided by.

Co-op: Pro and Con

Co-op programs, where you do a couple of four-month paid work terms between semesters in school, are very popular with students, but not all colleges offer co-op. Around the system, I heard a lot of pro and con, but mostly pro.

Pro:

Students love co-op. They like earning some money in the midst of school. They like the hands-on, real-world feeling. They think it will help them land a job. They hear that more than half of co-op graduates get hired where they did a co-op term.

Faculty say the students come back to school very motivated, better equipped to handle the concepts, and much more aware about work habits and job realities. They think co-op helps sell business and industry on the value of colleges and college grads, and they think that it keeps colleges in touch with industry.

Con:

Colleges that don't do co-op say you are in college to learn, not to hold down a job, and it's hard to check if students on co-op are really learning instead of just earning. They say co-op is expensive to organize and causes cuts elsewhere. If you go away for college and then go out of town for two co-ops, you won't be rooted anywhere and you will never really get into college life. They point to students who get hired permanently during their co-op – nice in the short term, but without a diploma, they may end up stuck there.

Mostly, however, non-co-op colleges agree on the value of work experience. They think they can do the same as co-op does by including a lot of short-term, unpaid field placements, practicums, or internships in their non-co-op programs. So maybe the difference is not all that great. Remember that a co-op program will take longer to complete, though you will have that chance to earn money while you are still a student.

THE JARGON

These are some of the code words the colleges use when they talk about themselves. We have tried not to use them too much in this book.

Access. Access Departments mean the people who serve everyone who can't just walk in the door and enroll in a **Program.** Access Departments try to help open college doors to adults, minorities, women, people with disabilities, people lacking qualifications for college, people needing help with language and study skills, working people who need training on an outreach basis, and generally anyone who may not feel like a typical college student, whatever that is.

If you feel you might not be a typical college student, head for Access. (It is also a good place to start looking for aptitude and career-choice testing.) Only eight of the twenty-three colleges have an Access department. If your target college doesn't, start with its Admissions or Counselling Office instead.

Administration. In Business courses, "Administration" is often used to distinguish a three-year program from a two-year program. (Technician and Technologist have roughly the same meaning in Technology programs.)

Advanced, General, and Basic Diplomas. Since the 1960s, Ontario has had three different Ontario Secondary School

Diplomas (OSSD): Advanced, General, and Basic. The General diploma is the key to college. It is the fundamental requirement for entering a college program. An Advanced diploma is mostly intended to provide the requirements for university entrance. Students with Advanced-level OSSDs may be eligible to enter college with credit for some college courses (for more details, see **OAC**). The Basic diploma was originally intended for students heading straight for the workforce. Today, where it is still offered, it is mostly a remedial program for students who have struggled with school. A Basic diploma will not get you into college programs, but most colleges do offer courses to help Basic-level grads to upgrade their skills, either for work or for a college program.

Articulation. In the college code, articulation means links between colleges and high schools at one end and colleges and universities at the other. See "Connections" in the college profiles in this book.

Attrition and **Retention.** Attrition means dropouts. The colleges mostly prefer to talk about retention, which means keeping students from dropping out. But dropping out is a serious problem at all the colleges, and a lot of the services described in "Using the Services" (in Part Three) are supposed to help students to avoid becoming attrition statistics.

Basic – See **Advanced, General, and Basic Diplomas.**

BTSD – Basic Training for Skills Development. Colleges accept students with a high school diploma at the General level. If you dropped out, BTSD is what will bring you up to the level needed for college entry. BTSD has four levels. If you dropped out early, you may have to take all four of them. Most colleges offer BTSD. Talk to Admissions or **Access.**

Catchment Area. When the colleges were established, each was given an official territory or "catchment area," so all of Ontario is divided into twenty-three "catchment areas." (Humber's catchment area is the cities of Etobicoke and York in Metro Toronto, while Confederation's borders those of Northern and Sault to the east and runs all the way west to Manitoba.) Colleges may have special links to the school boards in their catchment area, but for most students, catchment areas don't mean much any more. Students go to any college they want, and some colleges draw 80 per cent of their students from outside their official territory.

Certificate – See **Diploma.**

Challenge Exams – See **Prior Learning Assessment.**

Common Year. You want to go into Business, but you don't know if Accounting is the right path for you, or Marketing, or maybe Materials Management, whatever that is. Many Business Schools (and some in other areas) have a common first year or first semester for many of their programs. It makes sense – you choose your specialty after you learn what it involves, not before. See also **Foundation Year.**

Co-op. In a co-op education program, you will do work placements between the academic semesters at the college. It is a real job in a workplace related to your field of study. Each placement lasts four months, and you get paid. Eighteen of the twenty-three colleges have co-op programs. Most co-ops are in Business and Technology, but they cover other areas as well. Some are optional, but some are not, and in some you need certain marks to qualify. Co-op is very popular.

Diploma and **Certificate.** A diploma is the college's main certification. It is what the college gives to graduates of a **Program** that usually lasts two or three years. Other courses, post-diploma courses, and short programs (of a year or less) usually earn a certificate instead.

Distance Education. Distance Education means any kind of teaching where the student does not come right to the campus for instruction. It can include traditional pen-and-paper correspondence courses, or instruction on audiotape or videotape or television. It can also mean electronic hook-ups through which students in a dozen locations not only hear the professor but ask questions and discuss the material as one group. Distance Education is particularly well developed in Northern Ontario on the Contact

North/Contact Nord network, but it has growing potential throughout the college system.

Fast-track. Some colleges let you start one semester in January and then do the summer semester right after it. You could complete one school year by the end of August and go right into the next one a couple of weeks later. You could do two school years in about fifteen months!

Foundation Year. Foundation year is like **Common Year** – you do it and then you choose from options for later years. But often you can stop after Foundation Year and take a certificate. Some small colleges may offer only the Foundation Year, so you have to go elsewhere to finish the program.

Front-End Services. Front-end services are the ones you need when you are a stranger just trying to find your way into college life: services like the information booth, the admissions department, the counselling service, and the financial aid office. Recently most colleges have figured out that front-end services ought to be near the front entrance and that they should have convenient hours and easy-to-reach telephone service.

General – See **Advanced, General, and Basic Diplomas.**

Learning Outcomes. Learning outcomes means judging any education or training by the results. If you get a Graphic Arts diploma, say, it shouldn't just mean you have jumped through all the college's hoops and collected the piece of paper as your reward. You should actually be able to hold down a job as a Graphic Artist. It seems pretty obvious, but you would be surprised.

Mature Student. Officially, you may become a mature student once the group of people your age has graduated from high school. If you did not complete high school but "your class" has graduated, then the colleges will help you with academic upgrading. But if you are still of high school age, the colleges will refer you back to the school system. Unofficially, people around the colleges may also use the phrase "mature student" (as in Mature Student Societies) to refer to anyone older than the typical college student.

What Is General Education?

Ask line supervisors who actually hire college graduates what they need, and they are pretty clear. They want to hire people who have the knowledge base and the practical skills to become productive employees. But if you ask the president of the corporation, he probably won't know the answer, so he will launch into a speech about society's need for broadly educated generalists.

Some of the top people in the college system must have been spending too much time with the corporate executives, because they decided "General Education" should become a top college priority. They proposed that no matter how focused you might be on a particular program and a particular career, you would have to spend 30 per cent of your brief time at college taking courses in Greek philosophy or Canadian sociology or African history.

Fortunately, this harebrained idea won't catch on. The 30 per cent idea has already vanished, and most of the rest of it will go too. General Education is something you should be accumulating all your life. The colleges are not going to be able to ram it into you in two years.

So don't worry about General Education. What you do need is options. If you are the only woman in an Engineering Technology program, the people in a Women's Studies course could become your vital support network. If you are an Accounting student who only came to this country last year, a Canadian Studies course might be crucial in helping you adjust. If you are working through a tough program in Med Lab Technology, a course in Fine Art might be what keeps you sane.

Your program should leave you some space for outside courses, and you shouldn't let yourself get locked into your special interest. But you can't learn everything in two years, and the college certainly can't do it for you with some arbitrary percentage.

(For the other half of this issue, see the box "About Generic Skills.")

OAC – Ontario Academic Courses / Ontario Academic Credits. OACs are the additional courses that Ontario students can take in high school to earn an Advanced-level high school diploma and make themselves eligible for university. In general, you do not need OACs to apply for college programs – a high school diploma at the General level will do. But if you have some OACs, discuss them with a college Admissions Office or with faculty in the program you are applying for. You may be able to get advanced standing.

Oversubscribed. Oversubscribed means that there are more applicants for a program than there are places in it. Most colleges will tell you which programs are likely to be oversubscribed. For some programs at some colleges, it's just a lottery. Others try to select those most likely to succeed by looking at prior experience, doing assessments, sometimes even comparing marks. If you are looking at an oversubscribed program, make sure you have the qualifications demanded, consider applying at other colleges, and *apply before the deadline* – March 1 for fall programs.

Non-post-secondary Education – See **Post-secondary Education.**

Post-diploma. There are careers where some maturity, some experience of the world, some general education is a real advantage. In these areas, colleges have started creating post-diploma courses open only to students who already have a diploma, a university degree, and/or some experience. Other colleges will let people with those credentials do a shorter version of the standard program. Journalism, Human Resources Management, and some of the Human Services careers are areas where post-diploma programs are becoming more common.

Post-secondary / Non-post-secondary Education. Colleges do both. Post-secondary means you need a high school diploma to get in, and usually it means a **Program** leading to a **Diploma.** Non-post-secondary is everything else: short courses in specific skills, apprenticeship instruction, contract training for business or government, **Upgrading** for dropouts, English as a Second Language for immigrants.

Prior Learning Assessment. Another hot concept in education. If people have learned on the job, or by teaching themselves, or any other way, why make them take courses in what they already know?

If PLA were routine, someone who dropped out of Grade 9 thirty years ago, yet became a topnotch executive secretary through twenty-five years on the job, could walk into college, take some tests (sometimes called Challenge Exams) to prove what she knows, get credit for most of an Office Administration program, and walk out with a two-year diploma after maybe six months of evenings. With the diploma, she could expect better pay, change jobs more easily, maybe go on to more schooling.

It can happen (that story is from Mohawk College), so you should ask. But PLA is a long way from being routine in the colleges.

Program and **Course.** In college talk, a program prepares you for some career. You need a high school diploma to get in, it usually takes two or three school years, you get a **Diploma** at the end, and you are ready for a job in your field. Early Childhood Education is a program; so are Accounting, Dental Hygiene, and Electronic Engineering Technology. When you are in a program, you take a group of courses every semester. (Course also can mean a series of studies that leads to a certificate. A certificate course in Fine Arts taken through Continuing Education might include individual courses in Painting, Sketching, and Sculpting.)

Remediation and **Upgrading.** Roughly, upgrading is what you have to do if you have not got the qualifications you need for some college program. Many colleges offer upgrading that will give you both the training you need and the certificate that goes with it. Remediation usually means you already have the qualifications on paper, but in fact you have not mastered the skills well enough to handle the college workload. You need remediation to master what you are already supposed to know. See **Underpreparedness.**

Retention – See **Attrition.**

Semester – See **Year.**

Technician/Technologist. In the college world, a Technician program (in Mechanical Engineering, say) takes two school years, and a Technologist program takes three school years. In the work world, Technologists can look for a little more responsibility, a little more pay, and some wider prospects for advancement or further education.

Underpreparedness. This is a polite word for a nasty situation. If you have a high school diploma, you are entitled to get into college. But if you can't handle the English or Math requirements of a college program, the college has to deal with the problem of your "underpreparedness." It really means your high school has failed to deliver what it promised you, but colleges have to work with school boards, so they tend not to say that out loud. If the college spots your problem before you flunk out, it will probably steer you to some kind of **Remediation.**

Upgrading – See **Remediation.**

Year and **Semester.** In college and in this book, a year means a school year, and a school year is two semesters. A semester is usually about sixteen weeks, though it can be a little more or a little less. A few college offerings are continuous – 36 or 52 or 64 weeks in a row. But the most common school year is late August or September to May – the fall semester and the winter semester.

If you switch to part-time for a while, or need some extra time to master the material, it might take you three calendar years, or four, or whatever, to complete a "two-year" program. School years and calendar years aren't the same.

Computers

"Need a job? Get into computers!"

People keep telling each other that, and computer courses are still hot properties. After visiting all the colleges, I'm not so sure that computers should be an aim in themselves.

I saw amazing things being done with computers in the colleges. At George Brown, I watched a group of fortyish tool and diemakers. Their craft had been killed by technology. Now they were in front of computer terminals, learning a CAD (Computer-assisted Design) program that let them concoct tool designs right on screen. At Conestoga, I watched the other end of that process, CAM (Computer-assisted Manufacturing). Woodworking students dropped a disk into a huge machine, and it pretty much turned raw wood into the finished office furniture they had designed on-screen.

At Sheridan, I saw fashion design students designing dress patterns. The computer told them instantly how much material they would need, and what the cost would be in any kind of fabric. Then it printed out perfect patterns. At St. Lawrence, they told me how they gave up teaching word-processing to Office Administration students. They just make the computer lab available, and let the computer and some practice show how. At Loyalist, I saw one of the few Surveying programs still offered in the colleges. Society still needs surveyors, but with computerized locating devices, a couple of trained people can do what used to take a dozen. And at Fleming, cartography students were feeding reams of data into a machine that popped some of the most amazing maps I have ever seen.

What's the point? None of these people were computer students. Most of them didn't know much about how computers work. They just use them.

Sure, there are technologists who write programs and maintain computer-driven machinery and business people who manage vast information systems. But in most fields the computer is just a tool you use.

The lesson seems to be – don't worry too much about computers. Get comfortable with them, and know the difference between a keyboard and a mouse. Beyond that, go for what interests you.

Who Drops Out?

Actually, a lot of people drop out. It used to be the dirty little secret of college life. Placing 90 per cent of graduates into jobs didn't mean much if 75 per cent of the students had dropped out before graduating.

There will always be dropouts. People get job offers. They run into a personal crisis or financial problems. Some people "drop up": there's no shame in quitting Nursing to start university Pre-Med. And if you are in the wrong program, it's better to switch.

But with so many people trying to get in, colleges hate to take people who turn into empty seats by November. Dropping out is expensive for you and for the college, and colleges are fighting it. They want to help people make the right choices in the first place. They test applicants, create catch-up courses, and fine-tune the requirements. (If 90 per cent of Technology washouts came in without high school Math for Technology, colleges learn to demand it or put in a Pre-Technology year.) They try to move in fast with counselling and remediation when students start to struggle.

Does all this work? Some colleges think so. But people are less tempted to drop out when jobs are scarce, so it is hard to be sure. Still, students and counsellors say you can cut down your own risk of dropping out. Get your life in some kind of order before you start. Get the information to choose the right program for you. Get yourself prepared (a semester in General Arts and Science, maybe). Get support from the services (faculty, counsellors, financial aid, whatever) before you get in over your head. And sometimes it may still be better to switch than struggle.

PART TWO

Pour les francophones

À ce jour, il n'existe aucun guide des collèges et des cégeps de langue française au Canada. Vous pouvez cependant poursuivre vos études en français dans des collèges ontariens. Bien que publié en anglais, le présent livre couvre les services et programmes offerts en français dans les collèges de l'Ontario.

À la fin de 1992, la Cité collégiale à Ottawa demeurait le seul collège entièrement de langue française du système collégial ontarien. Le gouvernement de l'Ontario s'est engagé, en principe, à créer un collège du Nord et un collège du Sud, mais jusqu'à maintenant aucun des deux n'a été établi.

Cambrian, Canadore et Northern sont des collèges bilingues. Ils offrent des services et quelques programmes en français. Le Collège Cambrian à Sudbury possède la division française la plus importante et la plus autonome. Les deux autres offrent des versions françaises de certains programmes offerts aussi en anglais ou dans les deux langues. (Les programmes bilingues comprennent des cours donnés en français mais exigent également une connaissance de l'anglais.) Parmi les collèges qui ne sont pas officiellement bilingues, certains offrent un ou deux programmes bilingues. Niagara offre plusieurs programmes en français; d'autres institutions en offrent un ou deux, y compris le Collège Georgian (Marketing automobile) et le Collège Seneca (Administration de bureau). Pour plus de détails, veuillez consulter les chapitres sur les différents collèges.

Les francophones possédant une bonne maîtrise de l'anglais s'inscrivent souvent à des programmes offerts par des collèges de langue anglaise. (Après 1989, le Collège Algonquin a transféré à la Cité collégiale ses programmes offerts en français; aujourd'hui 15 % de ses étudiants sont des francophones.) Il arrive que des collèges où l'enseignement se fait essentiellement en anglais offrent quand même des services en français aux étudiants. Vous devriez avoir accès à des services en français à Algonquin, à St-Lawrence (campus de Cornwall), aux collèges Canadore, Cambrian, Northern, Sault et, dans une certaine mesure, au Collège Niagara, parmi d'autres.

ABOUT THIS SECTION

The next twenty-three chapters give you a taste of each of the twenty-three colleges of applied arts and technology in Ontario – not just what they teach, but what they look like, what is important to them, what they do that no one else does, and what services they offer to students.

Each chapter begins with a profile, based not only on college publications and a questionnaire I sent to every college, but also on my own impressions from visiting each college and interviewing everyone from students to college presidents. This book is not published by the college system, by the way, and I do not (and never have) worked for any college. Opinions and judgements in it are my own. If you think I am mistaken or that I missed something worth reporting, I hope you will let me know by completing the comments page at the back of this book.

After the title at the top of each chapter, I have given the location (of the main campus or campuses only) and described each college as large, medium, or small. That description is based on full-time enrollment in career-oriented programs. "Large" refers to the five biggest colleges, Seneca, Humber, Sheridan, Algonquin, and Mohawk, each with 7,500 to 12,000 students. "Small" means the six smallest colleges, Loyalist, Sault, Canadore, La Cité collégiale, Lambton, and Northern, each with less than 3,000. And "medium" refers to the dozen others in the middle, with 3,000 to 7,500 students each. It's worth noting that all the colleges have many times more people enrolled in part-time courses, full-time trades training, and upgrading courses than they have enrolled in full-time diploma programs.

Every college has some special programs or services, and often it has something that is unique in Ontario or in Canada. The section entitled "Worth Going For" highlights one or two stand-out items about each college.

Many colleges have several campuses, sometimes in several cities. The "Campuses" section of each chapter describes all the campuses and what each one offers.

The "Programs" section, the meat of each chapter, lists and describes all the programs offered at the college, including a summary description of trades and apprenticeship training and part-time and outreach offerings. Across Ontario about a third of full-time college students enroll in Applied Arts programs, a third in Business, about 20 per cent in Technology, and about 13 per cent in Health Sciences. In the "Programs" section, you can check how close the college comes to that average, as another indication of its relative strengths. If a college has an unusually large proportion of its students in a particular area, it may have unique strengths or special facilities in that subject.

Several students mentioned to me how intimidated they felt the first time they approached a large, busy college where no one knew they existed. "Getting in the Door" is mostly about finding the college, finding the entrance, and finding the people who can help to orient you. If the college has a toll-free "800" number you can call for information, it's mentioned here.

When it comes to "Support Services," there is a lot of overlap among the colleges. They all have Counselling Offices, Health Services, Daycare. They all offer Peer Tutoring, where experienced students help students who are having trouble with course work. They all guarantee access to people living with disabilities and they all have Special Needs Offices to support those people. They all have policies on safety and equity, and against harassment, sexism, and racism. So services you can expect to find at all colleges are described in detail at the back of the book, under "Using the Services." In the chapter on each college, "Support

Services" looks at a few special features or particular achievements of the college.

The section entitled "Connections" explores links between the college and its local school boards, which often permit students to tailor their high school courses to college programs, even to start acquiring college credits while still in high school. "Connections" also surveys agreements the college has made for advanced standing if you choose to do post-diploma work at university or to combine a diploma and a degree. In general, the universities offer one year's credit for three years of college, but some colleges have worked out better terms with specific universities here or in the United States.

"Scholarships" looks at the efforts the college has made to raise money for its own scholarships and bursaries, including sports scholarships. The financial support that is available to all college students from the Ontario Student Assistance Program (OSAP) is covered in Part Three, "Getting the Money Together." This "Scholarships"section also notes what attention the college pays to its alumni, partly because alumni can be an important source of financial support to a college.

"Where to Live" covers residence and housing possibilities at the college, and notes what proportion of its students comes from outside the local "catchment area," which is the college's official territory.

"Sports and Recreation" surveys the sports facilities at the college and the variety of varsity teams, intramural sports, recreational programs, and other activities run by the college and its students. Some colleges have student-built and student-run Student Centres. Many have pubs, clubs, and other facilities.

Finally, "The City" offers a few words about the community where you will be living if you attend this college, and "Contact" gives you a mailing address for the college and useful phone numbers to call for information.

Following the twenty-three chapters on the colleges, you will find a brief survey of other post-secondary institutions in Ontario. At the very back of the book, there is an index of programs, which shows where specific programs are offered.

ALGONQUIN COLLEGE: *All Things to All People*

Ottawa

Size: Large

Algonquin, like all the Ontario colleges, has integrated computer use into its programs. The colleges claim to have led the way in bringing the microcomputer into the education system.

I heard it over and over at Algonquin College. "We're big in every-thing. We're the only English-language college here and this is a big city, so we have to deliver everything to everyone."

At Algonquin, they seem to be philosophic about that. They take pride in what they do, but instead of proclaiming the wonders of Algonquin, they see themselves as a representative part of a good system. Algonquin's President Philip Killeen declares that Ontario has the best college system in North America, but he thinks that, inside the system, comparing Algonquin to, say, Seneca – another big college in a big city – is like comparing Lob-laws and the A&P. "There's not much to choose between them."

Unlike the smaller colleges, which all like to say they are unique, there is a sameness about the big colleges like Algonquin. Yet Kil-leen's view contrasts strikingly with that of President Robert Gor-don of Humber (another big school in a big city) who thinks

Humber may be the best college in North America and barely considers it as part of any Ontario system.

Algonquin, maybe, has chosen to be "generic college." Instead of seeking high-profile niches in which to build a national reputation, it has been content to offer most things a college can offer and try to do well at all of them. That's not flashy – and since Algonquin is the only college many Ottawa bureaucrats ever see, it probably means the federal government knows less about colleges than it ought to. But opinion seems to be that in its unspectacular way, Algonquin is doing most things reasonably well.

Recently, Algonquin lost one of its distinguishing features. It used to be a bilingual college, with many French-language programs and more francophone students than any other college in Ontario. In 1989, the francophone component of Algonquin was hived off to create a new French-language college in Ottawa, La Cité collégiale. Algonquin is now officially English-language – although 15 per cent of its students are francophones who choose to study in English, and Algonquin still operates in a bilingual (and multicultural) milieu.

Worth Going For

• Museum, Archives, Heritage Programs

Campuses

The Woodroffe campus, the main one, is a sprawling, ordinary-looking complex in Nepean, a suburb on the western edge of Ottawa where a lot of commercial and residential expansion is going on. Algonquin has been consolidating its Ottawa operations at Woodroffe, and expansions are underway there. Transit connections from Woodroffe to the whole of Ottawa are good, but Woodroffe is a long way from downtown. Other Ottawa campuses have been closed – the main one remaining is the Rideau campus, south of the University of Ottawa in Sandy Hill, where many of the Technology programs are offered.

Algonquin's main satellite campus is the School of Renfrew County in Pembroke in the Ottawa Valley. It has about 500 full-time students, a Forestry Technician program, and some standard programs duplicating those offered at Woodroffe. A smaller campus in Perth offers mainly short-term and specialized training, plus the two-year Heritage Carpentry and Millwork diploma, which builds on Lanark County's commitment to architectural preservation.

Programs

Perhaps not surprisingly, Algonquin matches the system "mix" – about a third of students in Applied Arts, roughly another third in Business, 20 per cent in Technology, and 15 per cent in Health Sciences. For most programs, all high school grads and mature students will be considered, but Algonquin assesses applicants through its own pre-admission testing, questionnaires, or (in some cases) portfolios of artwork. It also attracts "adult returners" and university graduates with fast-track, post-diploma programs.

The General Arts and Sciences Program has several options and can serve as a preparatory year for most programs for students needing upgrading or uncertain of their career aims. Algonquin has large programs in English and French as Second Languages.

Applied Arts

Algonquin's Applied Arts programs are clustered into four career-directed sections. There are no co-op programs in Applied Arts, but field placements are abundant.

Programs in Media Studies are large and comprehensive. Radio and Television Broadcasting programs have recently been divided. Print Journalism is also offered – Journalism students run the college paper as part of their coursework. There is an Animation for Television program, linked to a growing local industry. Advertising, Graphic Design, and Public Relations are all offered.

Community Service programs include not only the standard Law and Security Administration, but also a Correctional Worker program and a one-year certificate course in Protective Security for private security workers. There are courses for Library, Museum, and Archives Technicians – the last two, unique in Ontario, cooperate closely with the national capital's museums and archives. The post-diploma one-year certificate in Festival and Event Management is also unique.

Family Studies programs include Child and Youth Work, Developmental Services Work, and Social Service Work. Early Childhood Education is offered both as a standard two-year diploma and as a one-year fast-track option for applicants with degrees or diplomas and work experience. A fine new daycare centre by the main entrance to the Woodroffe campus opened in 1991.

Three Recreation programs are included in the Horticulture/Design/Recreation grouping: a standard Recreation Leadership diploma, a diploma course in Recreation Facilities Management, and a post-diploma certificate in Recreation Work with Older Adults. Horticulture includes both a two-year diploma and an apprenticeship version for registered apprentices. The Horticulture program recently moved to Woodroffe and will be using parts of the campus as a "living laboratory." Interior Design is a three-year program, and faculty stress it is "not decorating," but covers all aspects of interior-space planning.

Business

Algonquin has one of the largest business enrollments in the college system and claims a better than 90 per cent placement rate. A few of the Business Administration programs offer a co-op option.

The heavyweight division of Algonquin's Business school is the three-year Business Administration, where the offerings cover all the options. The first year is a common program for all students. In second year, students specialize in one of Accounting, Finance, Information Systems (which has a co-op option), Human Resource Management, Material and Inventory Management (co-op option), or General Administration.

The two-year Business programs also have a common first year, branching into Accounting, Information, Marketing, and Retail Management options for the second year. The Accounting

Algonquin's new Daycare Centre at the Woodroffe campus doubles as a research laboratory for Early Childhood Education students and staff.

program is available in an intensive fifty-two-week version aimed particularly at older students with work experience. Certificate training is offered in Retail Sales and Small Business Management.

The Computing area includes diplomas in Programming (which has a co-op option) and Desktop Publishing, and certificates in Computer and Microcomputer Operations.

The main Office Administration programs are a one-year certificate in General Office Admin and two-year diplomas in Executive, Medical, or Legal Office Admin. Also offered are a Records certificate and a Records Management diploma, a certificate in Medical Transcription, a Legal Assistant diploma, and Word Processing certificates.

Algonquin opened a new Hospitality Centre with a 100-seat restaurant in 1990 and has been expanding its programs in Hotel and Restaurant Management and Culinary Management. It also offers a variety of certificate and apprenticeship courses in cooking, baking, bartending, retail meatcutting, hairstyling, and front-desk operations.

Health Sciences

Algonquin offers the whole range of standard Health Science courses: Nursing and Nursing Assistant programs (and a nursing program for RNA graduates); Dental Assistant and Dental Hygiene, a one-year Ambulance and Emergency certificate; certificate and diploma course in Health Records; three-year diplomas in Med Lab Technology and Respiratory Therapy; and Pharmacy Assistant.

Technology

Here, too, Algonquin covers the spectrum. The School of Technology and Trades includes apprenticeship and short-term certificate courses as well as two-year technician diplomas and three-year technologist diplomas. For the technologist/technician programs, precise requirements vary, but solid high school math credentials are essential. If you do not have a background in Math for Technology (or something equivalent), you may need to take some preparatory courses.

The three-year programs are Architectural Technology, Construction Technology, Chemical Engineering Technology, Bioengineering Technology, Computer Engineering (hardware) and Computer Programming (software) Technology, Electronics Engineering Technology, Geographic Information Systems (scientific mapping and data-plotting), Survey Technology, and a cluster of Manufacturing, Mechanical, and Industrial Technology programs, which have a common first year. Technical Writer is also a three-year program, starting with technical courses and branching into writing and information skills.

There are two-year Technician versions of many of the Technologist programs, plus programs in Electro-mechanical Engineering Technology, Stationary Engineering, Building Operations, Drafting, Fire Protection and Safety, Printing,

Heating/Refrigeration/Air Conditioning, Instrumentation Control, and Photographic Science.

Part-Time and Continuing Education

"Con Ed" is important at Algonquin; it is big, well-organized, and successful. (One sign of success: the college is pulling in adult learners who start part-time and go on to complete their programs full-time. The average age of Algonquin students is relatively high, and it is climbing.) Bill Conrod, who runs Con Ed at Algonquin, notes that more and more it is the colleges that are filling the need for all kinds of short-term retraining at every level of the workforce – from providing basic credentials to doing high-level management seminars. "If you can't afford to come full-time, don't rule out college," is Conrod's message.

Algonquin offers night and weekend courses, short-term programs, on-the-job upgrading, distance education for students far from any campus, and many other options. It offers the "meat" of most of its post-secondary programs in part-time versions, so working people who want to change their career or add to their qualifications can get started at night-school before committing themselves to full-time study.

Trades Training

As broadly based here as elsewhere, Algonquin has a comprehensive list of offerings in a wide range of trades and apprenticeships. Its automotive apprenticeship courses are extensive, and it is active in many other fields as well.

Getting in the Door

Algonquin does not have a separate telephone number for information, so you may be bounced from department to department (and there are a lot of them) to find out what you need. Approaching the Woodroffe campus by car or bus, you should be able to find the main entrance easily. It may seem large, echoing, institutional, but you will find an information booth just inside the door.

If you are in the Ottawa area, read the newspaper. Once a week, nearly all year round, Algonquin promotes its get-acquainted evenings. Faculty, staff, students, and alumni present general and specific information about most college programs and services. Anyone interested in college is welcome.

Students I talked to gave good reports of Algonquin's Orientation, which they described as very useful, very practical, and not just rah-rah-rah. With a lot of older students enrolling, Algonquin has developed "Smart Start" for older students who find classrooms and studying and the student life strange after years away.

Support Services

Generally, Algonquin is well equipped with all the standard academic and personal support services discussed in Part Three, "Using the Services."

All incoming Algonquin students are tested for communication skills and many are tested for math skills. Depending on the results, they may be directed to remediation classes or tutoring services.

Algonquin claims to have a particularly strong Academic Advisory program. Every student is assigned a faculty advisor who monitors student progress and is available for advice. Faculty advisors are particularly active in the first couple of months, trying to prevent students dropping out if program changes, remediation, counselling, or tutoring can help. You should be able to call on these advisors anytime.

All faculty are trained in this advisory work, and Algonquin has taken the lead in "professional development" courses for faculty at all the eastern Ontario colleges.

Unlike some student governments, the Algonquin Students' Association has been active in student advocacy and helps fund a

College Ombudsman – first in the college system – to investigate student complaints and grievances. The last several years, Public Relations students have dominated the student government.

Connections

Algonquin has had some success forging links with Carleton University, but less with the University of Ottawa. Social Service grads can now move on to Carleton's Bachelor of Social Work program with 1.5 years' credit, and similar accreditations are being negotiated or discussed in other human service fields and business.

Scholarships

Algonquin has never had a major fund-raising drive to raise money for scholarships and bursaries. It has no alumni association. Over the years, however, a number of scholarships and bursaries have been donated.

Where to Live

Eighty per cent of Algonquin's students come from the Ottawa/Ottawa Valley area around the college. With a relatively small proportion of out-of-town students and the housing resources of a big city to call upon, Algonquin has no residences and no plans to build them. There is a housing-search service at Woodroffe and at Pembroke, jointly run by the college and the Student Association, which offers free telephones for students seeking housing.

Sports and Recreation

Sports and recreation are not particularly well developed at Algonquin. The Student Association runs a wide-ranging athletics program, but Athletic facilities are relatively limited, partly because the superbly equipped Nepean Sportsplex is nearby.

There is no student centre. Recreation depends heavily on the Ottawa-Nepean community.

The City

"Ottawa-Hull" is two cities. There's the government town, full of well-paid, middle-class urbanites and suburbanites, often originally from anywhere but Ottawa. Buried underneath that layer there's the rowdier, rougher, working-class tradition of Ottawa Valley farmers, loggers, and river-workers. Nepean, where the Woodroffe campus is located, is the heartland of the suburban, civil-service middle-class community. The Ottawa-Carleton region offers the full range of entertainment, recreation, culture, and shopping. The new home of the NHL's Ottawa Senators is not far from the Woodroffe campus. The federal government helps to support arts and cultural centres and events – don't miss Winterlude on the frozen Rideau Canal. In the long run, a friendly rivalry between La Cité collégiale and Algonquin ought to keep things lively on the college scene in Ottawa.

Contact:

Algonquin College
1385 Woodroffe Ave.
Nepean, Ont. K2G 1V8
(613) 727-9400
Toll free: 1-800-267-7061

About Continuing Education

Continuing Education (some colleges call it Continuous Learning or another name) generally covers all the part-time teaching the colleges do. Con Ed is big. Many colleges have six or eight times as many part-timers as full-time diploma students. Colleges tend to be busy every night and weekends too.

You can take interest courses in Photography or Cooking, but most people who take college Con Ed courses want credits, and they want job-related skills. In some fields, at some colleges, it is possible to do an entire diploma in part-time studies. Indeed, Con Ed may eventually abolish itself, as the distinction between part-time and full-time learning vanishes.

Con Ed is also the main post-diploma arm of the college system. The colleges offer working people all kinds of short-term or part-time courses linked to their careers. Some Con Ed professionals feel they have only begun to tap the potential growth in this area.

Con Ed also reaches out to groups with almost no schooling. Mohawk developed a night-school Health Care Food Service certificate to train the low-wage, low-skill kitchen helpers in nursing homes. One result: the grads discovered schooling was not beyond them, and they began enrolling in other programs with better prospects. Most Con Ed departments will custom-design training for particular institutions or industries.

Something to watch for: inexperienced teachers. Full-time college faculty have an ironclad hours-of-work contract – they turn up their noses at night work. People who teach Con Ed are mostly part-time teachers. They could be excellent teachers. But they come and go, and the college has little control over quality. Some students working toward a diploma by picking up credits in the evenings have encountered instructors who know nothing about how their particular course should fit in the general program.

Something to demand: services. Some colleges already offer counselling and placement services in the evenings to Con Ed students. Some have Part-Time Student Associations to give Con Ed students more input. When are the others going to catch on?

Who Are the Profs?

A pretty well-off bunch, most of them. They have a strong union that has shut down the colleges a couple of times. Labour-management relations are still terrible at some colleges, but the professors won fat settlements and ironclad contracts (including, a few years ago, the right to be called professors). Observers say that, considering their qualifications and responsibilities, college teachers are better paid than either school or university teachers – and that's saying something. Hours of work are pretty good too. Many full-time college professors find time to run part-time businesses or consultancies as well.

But most students I talked to had high praise for their college professors. Because classes are small and there is a lot of contact between students and professors, good teaching is possible. College students who have been to university seem unanimous: college teaching is far better.

In a college program, you spend a couple of years with the same group of students – and the same group of teachers. The professors are available, they spend a lot of time with students, they get on a first-name basis right away, and the best of them become career mentors as well as teachers. You might even play intramural sports with them.

Above all, students like the fact that college professors mostly have practical work experience and can talk about real jobs and real problems. Most college faculty are hired from industry – and those part-time businesses some of them run keep them up-to-date. Ontario colleges have teacher-training programs for the people they hire, but they hire more for work experience than for teaching qualifications.

CAMBRIAN COLLEGE: *Serving the Communities*

Sudbury

Size: Medium

Geological Engineering Technology at Cambrian includes field-camp training every fall. The instruments shown are used in the Geophysics option of the program.

"You come to work here, you better fasten your seatbelt," someone on the Cambrian staff told me. "A lot of the time we set the pace." Cambrian's far from being the largest college around, and you might not think of looking to Sudbury for innovations in education. But at Cambrian they are cocky. They think they do a lot of things ahead of other places, and they don't take a back seat to anybody. There are not many colleges that do a better job of figuring out what communities they ought to serve – and how to do it effectively.

Sudbury and its area is about 40 per cent francophone, but "We're not a bilingual college," Cambrian president Glenn Crombie says firmly. Instead Cambrian is two, soon to be three, colleges in one. Inside Cambrian, there is an English-language college and a French-language college, each setting its own direction with its own set of programs. And with five hundred native students attending, Cambrian has the beginnings of a native college, the Wabnode Institute.

Already there are independent English, French, and native student governments at Cambrian, pursuing their own projects and activities. The bilingual, multicultural part of Cambrian, in fact, is the administrative and service sector, which provides service to all three parts of the college.

At Cambrian they call this "college federalism" and they think it works beautifully. But Cambrian's French-language operation will almost certainly be hived off to become Ontario's second francophone college, the Collège du Nord (for the details, see La Cité collégiale). Eventually there is likely to be at least one native college, too. No matter how well college federalism works, the trend is for separation. Crombie is philosophic about that. "Right now we hold the franchise for French-language and native college education in this area. But if they move the franchise . . ." Meanwhile, for as long as Cambrian does have the franchise, he thinks it has done the right things to serve each of the three communities.

French, English, and native students are not the only communities Cambrian sees itself serving. Across northern Ontario, there are a lot of people in small, isolated communities who will never go away for several years to a big college in a town or city. To reach them, Cambrian has been a pillar of the Contact North distance education network. Well before the provincial government required it to, the college recognized the obligation to serve people with disabilities. Today all the colleges have extensive Special Needs services, but Cambrian was there before most of them and still emphasizes service in that area. The college system award for achievement in that field is named for Glenn Crombie.

Another community Cambrian serves is Sudbury. Ever since the recession of the early 1980s, Sudbury has been learning (the hard way) that it cannot rely on the Big Nickel alone. Attempts to subsidize manufacturers into setting up branch plants have been a waste of time and money. Instead Sudbury is looking to become the capital of northeast Ontario, the place where government services, hospitals, the arts, and educational services – French, English, and native – are concentrated. All those sectors will need educated workers, so Cambrian is a player in all of them.

As the largest post-secondary institution anywhere in Northern Ontario, Cambrian is an important player in Sudbury, and not much goes on there without Cambrian being involved. If a VIP comes to town and meets with five key people, one of them is probably from Cambrian. Colleges in all the northern communities enjoy a local profile that ones in the big southern city cannot match.

Finally, "student-centred" is the hottest buzzword throughout the college system. It's what every college claims to be. But Cambrian seems to have taken student service and student success seriously for quite a while.

Worth Going For

- The Mining-Metallurgy-Geology cluster in Technology
- The Culture and Communications cluster in Applied Arts
- The best college opportunities for French Immersion grads

Campuses

The big Cambrian campus is the Barrydowne campus on a hill at the northeast corner of Sudbury. It seems well designed and laid out, on the whole a comfortable environment to study in. Health Sciences is currently on Regent Street in Sudbury, but long-term planning foresees it moving to Barrydowne. Espanola, Little Current, and Noëlville have satellite campuses with some post-secondary programs, and outreach programs link Cambrian to many other communities in its region.

Programs

Cambrian, with strong English and French component parts, sees itself as an ideal place for Franco-Ontarian students to maintain French in their college studies. (It also wants to attract anglophone immersion graduates – more than half of English-language high school students around Sudbury are in French immersion units.) Cambrian's French-language programs are not a mirror image of the English ones. They do not match the full range of the English-language Culture programs or the Mining-Metallurgy-Geology programs, but they include many programs not offered in English.

Compared to most colleges, Cambrian has a lot of students in Applied Arts and Health Sciences. Technology is small but tightly focused, and Business is unusually small. Cambrian has a few co-op programs, mostly in Business and Technology.

Cambrian offers the General Arts and Sciences Program (in French, Sciences et arts généraux) and College Exploration. GASP is a full program where students accumulate credits withoutp committing themselves to a specific career option, and it accommodates students who did not find space in oversubscribed programs. GASP has a Science option (essentially Pre-Health Sciences) and a Human Services option. College Exploration, tailored to individual needs, is a good way to pick up prerequisites, improve study skills, and consider program options (or reconsider them if you are in danger of failing). Programs where enrollment is limited reserve 10 per cent of their places for College Exploration grads.

Applied Arts

The stand-out cluster in Applied Arts at Cambrian is Communication and Creative Arts. Cambrian thinks Sudbury ought to be Northern Ontario's arts centre, perhaps one day a destination the way Stratford is in the south. But if northern kids go south for artistic training, they don't come back. So Cambrian intends to be the north's centre for artistic training. It offers Music, Community Music (a combination of music and business training for the "gigging" musician), and Visual Arts (ceramics, weaving and textile, painting, printmaking, sculpture, graphic art), and it may soon add Theatre Arts. The Communication side of the cluster consists of Print Journalism, Advertising, Graphic Design, and Public Relations.

The Human Services programs include Child and Youth Work,

Social Services, Developmental Services Work, and Early Child-hood Education (ECE). Cambrian runs anglophone and franco-phone daycare centres on the Barrydowne campus, and offers French, English, and native versions of ECE. The Law and Secu-rity Administration course has Police and Native Justice options, and is complemented by a Correctional Work program.

"Isolated" programs in Applied Arts are Horticulture (building on skills developed for the greening of Sudbury's former "moon-scape" environment), Hotel and Restaurant Management, and a three-year co-op Physical Fitness and Leisure Management pro-gram.

Applied Arts programs unique to the French division of Cam-brian are Techniques d'éducation spécialisées, Techniques juri-diques, Services de réadaptation, Services sociaux (option en gérontologie), and Communication/Interprétation en Langage gestuel. Programs that are roughly comparable to ones offered by the English division are Education des petits, Services sociaux, Administration de la loi et de la sécurité, Techniques des services correctionnels, and Gestion alimentaire et hotelière.

Business

Cambrian offers Business Administration with options in Market-ing, Human Resources Management, and Business Management; Office Administration programs, plus Accounting, Legal Assis-tant, and Information Services. The full-time programs, some of which are co-op, are supplemented by large part-time offerings in business, including the courses of The Enterprise Centre in Sud-bury.

Administration publique is offered only in French. Also avail-able in French are Administration des affaires, Marketing, Comp-tabilité, a one-year program in Gestion de la petite entreprise, and the standard programs in Administration de bureau.

Health Sciences

In French and English, Cambrian has the most comprehensive Health Sciences programs in the north, offering a wide variety of programs. Most of the Health programs are based at the Regent Street campus in Sudbury. The English-language programs are Nursing and Nursing Assistant, Radiography and Medical Lab Technology, Dental Hygiene and Dental Assistant, Pharmacy Assistant, and Ambulance and Emergency Care.

In French, Cambrian offers essentially the same programs: Sciences infirmières, Soins infirmiers auxiliaires, Techniques de radiodiagnostic, Hygiène dentaire, Soins dentaires, Aide pharmaceutique, and Secours ambulancier. There is no French-language Medical Lab Technology, but Cambrian is opening Ontario's only French-language program in Formation en services funéraires.

Technology

Today Sudbury is more than Inco and Falconbridge, the nickel producers that once dominated the local economy (and landscape), and Cambrian has played a notable part in the region's diversification. But mining and refining ore remain important to the region, and Cambrian claims to have the college system's largest programs in the relevant areas. Cambrian has access to the mines of Inco and Science North for training, and it maintains close ties with the big employers in the region.

Cambrian's key Technology programs are in its Mining-Metallurgical-Geological Engineering cluster, six inter-related programs (Technician and Technologist programs in each category) that cover the full range of extracting and processing minerals. It also offers a Mining and Mineral Processing certificate (thirty-two weeks' study and sixteen weeks' paid employment), which is now the minimum standard for Inco employees.

The other English-language Technology programs are Chemical Engineering, Civil Engineering, and Electronics Engineering, each offered in two-year Technician and three-year Technologist programs, and a Technician program in Stationary Engineering. A one-year Instrumentation Engineering program can be entered after two years of Electronics Engineering.

The French division has Techniques et Technologie en Construction (minières et urbaine). Cambrian has created an Institut

canadien de gestion des richesses naturelles, and it already offers
Techniques et Technologie de gestion de la pêche et de la faune
and Techniques et Technologie forestières. Programs similar to
ones offered in English are Technologie du génie électronique and
Techniques et Technologie du génie chimique.

Native Programs

Cambrian's Native programs and its Wabnode Institute are
strongly oriented to community and youth work. There is a Native
option in General Arts and Science and a General Arts Skills
Training course. There is a Native Community Care program
focused on Counselling and Development, a Native Child and
Family Work program, and Binoonjiiyag Kinoomaadwin (Early
Childhood Education). Also offered: First Nations Land Management. Many of the native-oriented programs are now offered
in native communities as well as at the Barrydowne campus.

Part-Time and Continuing Education

The strongest part of Con Ed at Cambrian may be Distance Education (see "The Jargon" in Part One). In both French and
English, Cambrian is an active participant in the Contact North /
Contact Nord network. Courses from many of the main full-time
programs are also offered on a part-time basis at Cambrian in
English and French, so students can pick up specific skills or start
toward a diploma on a part-time basis. There is a good,
easy-to-use calendar, and phone registration is available.

Trades Training

Apprenticeships and skills training are closely integrated into the
Cambrian calendar, with short-term certificate courses corre-
sponding to many of the diploma areas in community work, business, health sciences, and technology. In addition, Cambrian
trains workers in a wide range of industrial, service, and retail

trades. As with the post-secondary area, trades training offerings are not identical in English and French.

Getting in the Door

Cambrian's information service is run by the Liaison department, which has its own 800-number service. Staff are bilingual, but because of the "federal" system at Cambrian, you may be directed to specific areas depending on your interests.

The main campus and its main entrance are easy to find. There is an Information booth at the front door. The Barrydowne campus was built in four stages, and has just recently been reorganized so that all of its "front-end" services are close to the front doors.

Support Services

Like other colleges, Cambrian has developed a Student Success package based upon "Master Student" classes. If you are a new or struggling student, you will be encouraged to take these workshops on study skills, note-taking, time management, and stress management.

There is a strong advisory program, by which faculty in each program monitor the progress of individual students. Six weeks into a semester, program faculty examine the progress of each student, hoping to head off serious problems before it is too late. Students heading toward failure may be encouraged to shift directions and pick up the foundation skills they need. To illustrate: In September, about 200 students enroll in College Explorations to upgrade their qualifications. By January, there are 500.

Student and alumni reps are included in program advisory committees, along with representatives of business, industry, and the professions, and all incoming students are surveyed (on the quality of service, among other things) during the first semester.

Cambrian offers all the usual services: Career Planning and Placement, Financial Aid, Counselling, Daycare, Health Services, Special Needs, Athletics, Learning Resources Centre – but

Cambrian pioneered many Special Needs services for college students. Debbie Giroux, now a Cambrian alumna, demonstrated the Kurzweil synthetic speech reader to the Prince of Wales in 1991. Cambrian President Glenn Crombie looks on.

is unique in the degree to which it offers them separately to French, English, and native clients.

Connections

Like many of the other colleges, Cambrian has not had much success building affiliations with Ontario universities. Late in 1992, however, Cambrian and the local university, Laurentian, signed a wide-ranging collaborative agreement that should lead to improved college-university transfer and to joint programs. Cambrian remains ambitious to expand its own offerings – I heard talk of the college eventually seeking to offer its own degrees, particularly a Bachelor of Technology. (However, the three-year diploma programs that might lead to degrees are only about 10 per cent of Cambrian's course offerings.)

Cambrian has energetic programs to make the college system

better known to high school students. In particular, it does extensive staff-development work with high school teachers, many of
whom know little of the college system and tend to be predisposed
toward the university system they graduated from.

Scholarships

Cambrian has the best fund-raising operation in the Ontario college system. For years, the Cambrian Foundation, operating from
its own downtown offices, has supported itself and brought in
funds for the college. It's a sign that Cambrian has been working to
reduce its dependency on government funds, but it also means
that Cambrian has money for scholarships and bursaries.

Surprisingly, Cambrian's alumni association is in its infancy.
The college publishes a magazine for alumni, offers them placement services, and includes them in advisory committees. An
alumni association executive has recently been established.

Where to Live

In the fall of 1992 Cambrian opened new, townhouse-style residences on the edge of the Barrydowne campus, which can accommodate 300 students, including some with special needs. The
Health Sciences facility on Regent Street can accommodate
another 200 students.

Sports and Recreation

At Cambrian, academic programs and student societies are
divided by language group, but athletic programs are mostly bilingual or multilingual. The athletic complex on the Barrydowne
campus includes a double gym, racquet courts, a weight training
centre, and outdoor sports fields. Cambrian also runs a community fitness centre, linked to its Physical Fitness and Leisure Management program, in Sudbury.

Social and cultural events organized by campus groups tend to be initiated along linguistic and cultural grounds, but there is a fair amount of overlap. When the francophone student government books in Tom Cochrane or Blue Rodeo, everyone attends!

Student activities are still adjusting to the growing number of adult students. For those who need more than pub nights from the college, single-parent support groups, a food bank, a clothing depot, and other services have been developed.

The City

Sudbury gets no respect. It still gets thought of as "Sudbury Saturday Night" (Stompin' Tom Connors's song) – a hard-drinking, hardrock mining town. And it is still a heavy industry, working-class, union town. So, yes, there are lots of taverns, pubs, clubs. Like half the colleges in Northern Ontario, it seems, Cambrian has a Don Cherry's franchise just down the road. But today there's more to Sudbury than that.

Sudbury is adding on services and amenities as it becomes a key centre for northeastern Ontario and for Ontario francophones. Science North, medical centres, the Northern Lights Festival and the festival called "La nuit sur l'étang" – and Cambrian College – are all part of that. Opportunities for recreation, sports, entertainment, shopping, and culture are extensive. And these days it's "greener" than you may think. In 1991 Sudbury was chosen by a magazine poll as one of Canada's ten best cities to live in.

Contact:

Collège Cambrian College
1400 Barrydowne Road
Sudbury, Ont. P3A 3V8
(705) 566-8101
Toll-free: 1-800-461-7145 – Liaison Office, for information.

CANADORE COLLEGE: *Extending Its Boundaries*

North Bay

Size: Small

Canadore's spacious campus includes a lake at the college's back door. In winter it becomes the focus of outdoor activities at Canadore's Winter Carnival.

Canadore is one of the colleges that is larger than it "ought" to be. It began as a satellite campus of Cambrian College, and when it became independent in 1972, it inherited one of the smallest catchment areas in the college system (a population of barely 80,000 people and just six high schools). As a result, Canadore has had to hustle to find a niche.

In that way, Canadore is a good match for the city of North Bay. North Bay used to be the unchallenged "Gateway to the North." Airline routes and new highways have diminished that role, and Sudbury, with a larger population and major industries, has

77

become the region's key service centre. Like its college, North Bay has to scramble to avoid being left in a backwater. Canadore is closely integrated into the city's economic development work, and it now has top-notch facilities for skilled trades training. Canadore College faculty and staff do extensive outreach across Northern Ontario, and they work hard to pull in students from far beyond its local area.

Canadore has focused its efforts in building a few strong program areas – notably Business, Media, Hospitality, and Helicopter Flying. It emphasizes that as a small college, it offers personal attention and small classes – the students to faculty ratio is just seventeen to one. It has also marketed itself effectively as a destination for college students, not only across the north but into southern Ontario too. As a result, two-thirds of Canadore's 2,900 post-secondary students come from elsewhere – including 12 per cent from Metro Toronto.

A unique feature is Canadore's link to Ontario's newest university, Nipissing University, with which it shares a campus. As a result of the association, Canadore is farther advanced on joint degree/diploma relations than most colleges – and could be a good college for students interested in that option.

Canadore is officially bilingual – but mostly in the sense of catering to bilingual francophones. It's mostly an anglophone milieu. Canadore has a much smaller francophone presence than Cambrian, and does not have Cambrian's "federal" system of English and French units. A few programs are available in French, others offer only the possibility of taking some courses in French. As noted below, it also reaches out to aboriginal communities across Northern Ontario.

Worth Going For

- Helicopter Flying and Aircraft Maintenance

Campuses

In recent years, Canadore has consolidated thirteen campuses, mostly scattered in rented premises around North Bay, into just three.

The main campus is the College Drive complex, which it shares with Nipissing University. The campus, designed by renowned architect Ron Thom, sits in a 700-acre woodland environment on a hill northeast of the city, with lakes, streams, and hiking trails radiating out from the college. Canadore people are confident they have the most beautiful college in Ontario.

Canadore's other substantial campus is the brand-new Commerce Court facility in an industrial park close to the city. Once a jeans factory and then the largest empty building in North Bay, Commerce Court has been transformed by extensive renovation into a superb centre for Technology programs and Trades courses. Aviation programs use the heliport north of the city, and Canadore runs training and preparatory courses at outreach campuses, including Sturgeon Falls and Mattawa.

Programs

Canadore has no unusually large or small academic divisions, though it has recently been expanding its programs in Community Service areas.

Canadore offers a two-year College Vocational for high school graduates at the Basic level. It offers several variations of General Arts and Sciences for those uncertain about career choices or unable to gain entry to an oversubscribed program.

Applied Arts

The stand-out cluster in Canadore's Applied Arts programs is Broadcast and Journalism, which includes both Radio and Television Broadcasting and both Radio Journalism and Print Journalism. The media programs are supplemented by a two-year

Graphics Communications program. Canadore supports these programs with well-equipped community radio and television stations on campus and a student-run newspaper. The program has a strong Northern Ontario focus and graduates are placed all over the region. Canadore does Media Studies outreach through its sponsorship of the Northern Ontario Journalism Awards, which bring working journalists from all over the north to Canadore for recognition and professional development.

Another Canadore focus is Hospitality and Tourism. Its programs are Culinary Management, Chef Training (one-year certificate), Italian Culinary Arts (North Bay has a long-established Italian community), and Hotel-Resort-Restaurant with a two-year Management or three-year Administration option – the three-year option is co-op and includes placement opportunities all across Canada. Canadore supports these programs with Hospitality Plus, an outreach program that does short-term training for employees of resorts and hotels.

Community Service courses, some of them quite new to Canadore, are the standard Early Childhood Education, Law and Security Administration, Social Service Work, and Recreation Leadership.

Business

Business programs at Canadore seem focused and well organized. Almost all programs share a common first semester, and related clusters share the second semesters. The accounting area is particularly well developed. Diplomas include: Business, Business Administration, Business Administration Marketing, Business Accounting, and Business Administration Accounting (which also has a co-op option). Canadore also offers two- and three-year programs in Small Business. The business school does outreach through the Centre for Entrepreneurship, run jointly with Nipissing University, and through a Self-Employment Centre.

There are two- and three-year programs in Computer Management, Programmer Analyst, and Business Office Systems, again with common early semesters.

A first year in Office Administration provides a certificate and permits entry into two more years in Executive, Medical, Word Processing, or Legal Office Admin. There is also a two-year Legal Assistant course for law clerks.

Health Sciences

Canadore's Health Sciences division is small (Nursing, the largest program, has fifty places) but its programs include Nursing and Nursing Assistant (with a common first semester), Dental Assistant and Dental Hygiene, Medical Lab Technology, Respiratory Therapy, Technician/Technologist options in Environmental Biology, and Institutional Food Supervision, which focuses on food preparation for health-care institutions.

Technology

Canadore has a small Technology program, built around Civil Engineering (which also has a drafting option), Electronics Engineering (with a robotics option), and Mechanical Engineering. These are all two-year Technician programs except Electronics, which has a Process Control Technologist option. None of them is co-op.

The stand-out Technology programs at Canadore, however, are those in the school of Aviation, where helicopter flying is the focus and students learn their trade under northern aviation conditions. Canadore is the only Ontario college teaching helicopter flying and its Heliport campus is unique. The school has a one-year Helicopter Pilot program, supplemented by two-year Technician programs in Aviation Mechanics and Avionics (Aviation Electronics).

Problem: aviation programs are expensive for the colleges that run them, and recent placement of avionics grads has been disappointing. Canadore has been reducing the number of students it takes – recently, from 18 to 13 in the flying program.

Trades Training

With its recently opened Commerce Court facility, Canadore is expanding its trades and training programs, with apprentice programs in motor vehicle mechanics, fluid power, and training in bricklaying, meatcutting, carpentry, and so on, and a full range of upgrading and skills programs.

French and Native Programs

Canadore is officially a bilingual college, and some of its courses are offered in a bilingual format, particularly in Business, Office Admin, Hospitality, and Nursing.

With 350 native students, Canadore claims to have the largest proportion (not the largest number) of native students of any Ontario college. Its Native Student Services began by offering counselling, mentoring, and student support to native students at Canadore. A native student residence is under development. Canadore is now expanding its academic programming, starting with a Native Social Service Worker program. The Aboriginal Council on Education consults on all native services. The First Nations Resource Centre offers career counselling, seminars, and an outreach role model project. Canadore has also pioneered community outreach programs in race relations, including teacher-training and high school seminars and camps on race relations.

Part-Time and Continuing Education

With the small population in its area, Canadore has a relatively small part-time enrollment, but its schools do a lot of outreach across northeastern Ontario. Business and Computer programs are heavily in demand, and most Business programs can be taken on a part-time basis. The college is doing an increasing amount of consulting and contract training, and in summer it hosts

Artsperience, a month of residential arts courses ranging from Computing for Children to Native Culture.

Getting in the Door

Canadore puts postage-paid information forms in its brochures. Since it is a small campus that depends heavily on successful recruitment, Canadore has to be client-focused, so help should be available. Beside the usual high school liaison programs, Canadore runs Student Ambassador visits and Parent Information Nights wherever there is sufficient interest.

The main campus is not close to downtown and bus service may be slow outside peak hours, but the campus is well signposted and access is easy. The main entrance to the College Drive campus is shared with Nipissing University, but Canadore's Information Booth is close to the main door, and the "front-end" services are grouped nearby and easy to find.

Support Services

Canadore has all the usual student support services. Its Adopt-A-Student program links new students to faculty or staff members for guidance. There is a strong Orientation program (including a parents' day), and many classes include a six-hour Student Success module developed by the Guidance Department that teaches study skills, time management, and how to get help when you need it. Canadore claims that its client-service orientation and small size enable it to give more personal attention to students, resulting in a relatively low dropout rate.

Connections

Canadore is the only college in Ontario that shares its campus with a university. Since Nipissing University is smaller than Canadore and has just achieved degree-granting status, there has been little danger of university snobbery, and as a result Canadore-Nipissing links are strong and growing. There is now direct entry for Canadore graduates into Nipissing, and vice versa. Across the province, about 4 per cent of university students come from colleges. At Nipissing, it's 17 per cent, and they are mostly from Canadore. One additional benefit: by sharing library facilities with Nipissing, Canadore has access to the largest library in the college system.

Scholarships

A few years ago Canadore undertook an Access to Opportunity fund-raising campaign specifically to endow scholarships and bursaries. As a result, funding support is more widely available than at many other colleges. Canadore currently gives $80,000 a year, including 160 entry-level grants and 125 mid-level performance awards. Ask about getting some.

Where to Live

With a catchment area too small to support the college, Canadore draws students from a wide area. Two-thirds of the student body come from other parts of Ontario or beyond.

The college can accommodate 512 students in its townhouse-style residences. Each townhouse has six private study/bedrooms plus a shared kitchen, lounge, and dining area. Residence cost in 1992-93: $2,200-2,400/year. Space is in demand, so apply early.

Canadore also maintains a student housing registry for off-campus apartments and rooms.

Sports and Recreation

Athletic facilities, shared with Nipissing University, include a double-sized gym, weight room, and a network of hiking and skiing trails for varsity and intramural programs and individual use. The college runs a large number of instructional programs and

Townhouse-style residences at Canadore house six students per unit, with private bedroom-studies and shared living space.

fitness courses. Canadore has also developed a voucher system, called "Canadore Bucks," which permits Canadore students to use the YMCA, ski clubs, and other recreational facilities in the North Bay area.

The City

North Bay is a city of 52,000 people on the shore of Lake Nipissing, with good transportation links, a daily paper, radio and television stations, and abundant shopping and recreational facilities. It has always called itself the Gateway to the North, and continues to be a service centre for northern business, transportation, and tourism. It has a new arts centre and Major Junior A hockey.

Contact:

Canadore College
100 College Drive
P.O. Box 5001
North Bay, Ont. P1B 8K9
(705) 474-7600
(705) 495-2862 (TDD)

About Generic Skills

I could be a brilliant Electronics Engineering Technologist and you could be a star in Graphic Arts, but we will need more than that to make our way in our careers. No matter what we do, we need to be able to read clearly, and to write a readable report, and to interpret a column of numbers. We ought to be able to learn new skills and accept new challenges. We should be able to get along productively with other people and talk appropriately to clients.

The colleges call skills like these "generic skills." They are essential, and not just to make us useful and productive employees. They also give the freedom to learn and change when we want to – or need to.

The Conference Board in Canada, a business lobby group, came up with its Employability Skills Profile – "the critical skills required of the Canadian workforce." Under Academic Skills, they listed the ability to communicate, think, and learn. Personal Management Skills include positive attitudes and behaviours, responsibility, and adaptability. And Teamwork Skills mainly means the ability to work with others. Niagara College liked this Employability Skills Profile enough to write it into its own academic goals. Other colleges have similar objectives in their own words.

You won't find a course in "Generic Skills" in your program. Those things can't be taught that way. Generic skills have to be integrated into every program. They have to be everyone's responsibility. So look at your own program. If you don't think it is serious about the generic skills you will need, ask: "Why not?"

CENTENNIAL COLLEGE: *An All-Purpose College*

Scarborough

Size: Medium

Students in the Architectural Engineering Technician program at Centennial can specialize in architectural drafting – on the drawing board and on computer.

Like some other colleges in big cities, Centennial is hard to characterize. It has four campuses, programs in nearly every subject area, and a history of conflict between the college and its unions (not so rare in the college system). Compared to the other Metro Toronto colleges, Scarborough's college is hard to pin down. Humber is innovative and fast-track. George Brown is definitely downtown. Seneca's big in business and innovative in independent learning. And Centennial is . . . ? The answer may be: all-purpose – and committed to co-op.

Centennial moved into co-op education in the mid-1980s, and it has been catching up to some of the long-established co-op colleges. (Seneca is the other co-op college in Toronto.) Centennial now offers co-op in all its three-year Business and Technology programs, and it may extend co-op into more areas in the future.

More than one Centennial student in three identified co-op as the feature that brought him or her to Centennial.

Centennial has programs across the spectrum, including most of the standards offered at many colleges. On the other hand, Centennial has several undoubted strong points. Its School of Transportation, the biggest in Canada, is unparalleled. It has a lively School of Communications and perhaps the most elaborate range of General Arts and Science programs in Ontario. It also has a vigorous student government not afraid to assert student interests. And, of course, Centennial and its students have access to the business and industry of Metro Toronto.

Late in 1992, Centennial got a new president. Cathy Henderson is notable not only for being one of the handful of women college presidents, but also for being a college graduate. She has an Early Childhood Education diploma from Sheridan (and she also has a Ph.D. to go with it). In her previous job as Sheridan's vice-president, Henderson initiated that college's wide-ranging (and much admired) re-examination of the programs it was offering and how it was teaching them. It is a good bet that something similar will soon be under way at Centennial.

Another recent Centennial initiative has been a series of surveys of the college's clients. Centennial polled Scarborough businesses, high school students, and parents on their attitudes to college in general and Centennial in particular. A few of the findings were surprising, some familiar. Some business leaders had found in hiring that a grad with a university bachelor's degree was really little different from one with a college's three-year diploma. For computer skills, their preference for college grads seems to confirm a widespread college belief that colleges have led the way in integrating computers into education. Parents, however, often reflected the prestige gap: they knew colleges did a good job and that college grads got useful skills and good job prospects, but . . . "my kid's going to university!" Students (and teachers) in the schools often had trouble with the variety of college programs and career paths. Everyone seemed to want the colleges to make themselves better known.

Centennial has the smallest post-secondary enrollment of the

Metro colleges (just slightly smaller than George Brown), and all of its four campuses are compact in comparison to those of some of the big colleges. Still, any institution can be intimidating. One student told me that when he first came to Centennial, he was so nervous he had to bring a friend with him just for support. But it didn't last long – barely a year later he was president of the student association. "If someone who was such a dweeb can get to be president, college can't be that bad!"

Worth Going For

- The School of Transportation – Aviation and Automobile
- Co-op opportunities

Campuses

Centennial has four campuses, all substantial. Progress, the main campus and the one that looks most like a college campus, has a spacious, attractive cluster of buildings on Progress Court at the eastern edge of Scarborough ("They can spit into our territory!" someone told me at Oshawa's Durham College). Progress houses Centennial's Business, Engineering, and Technology programs.

Warden Woods, on Warden Avenue between Danforth and St. Clair (south of Warden Subway station), is a former radar factory that looks like an enormous high school. Most Applied Arts and Health Sciences courses are taught there. Ashtonbee Campus, in an industrial zone just north of Warden Woods, is home to the School of Transportation. It has labs, classrooms, a Learning Resource Centre, and student services, but it is dominated by its enormous automotive and aviation workshops. It also houses Centennial's General Arts and Sciences programs.

The East York campus, a former school building on Carlaw Avenue just north of the Pape subway stop, is a TV star – it was featured week after week as Degrassi High. It has just been renovated to become home to Centennial's Communication Arts Centre.

Programs

An all-purpose school, Centennial has its programs distributed among the major areas in proportions roughly typical of the college system as a whole. Only the Business school is slightly larger than average.

Centennial began developing co-op programs in the late 1980s, and co-op work terms are now part of all its three-year programs in Business and Technology.

Centennial has a strong General Arts and Science sector, for those uncertain of their career direction, needing to upgrade their credentials or hone their study skills, or seeking entry to an over-subscribed program. GAS programs include General Studies (aimed toward Applied Arts programs or university entrance), Science Studies (a pre-Technology program), pre-Health Sciences, Visual Arts (preparation for art schools and commercial art programs), Developmental Studies (oriented to study skills and foundations of math, science, language, writing, etc.), and Academic English as a Second Language, which combines language-improvement and academic skills.

Applied Arts

The Applied Arts are divided into several schools at Centennial. A stand-out is the School of Communication, which is building its own studios, newsrooms, and other media facilities at the East York campus. Among the three-year programs are Print Journalism, Broadcasting, which covers both radio and television and is aimed more at production than on-air, and Creative Advertising. In addition there are Corporate Communications and a unique Book and Magazine Publishing program, which attracts many university graduates. Some of these have formalized fast-track options for applicants with academic credentials or job experience. Students do field placements in Metro's media industries.

The Child Studies cluster is built around the standard Early Childhood Education, which is offered at both Warden Woods and Progress. Centennial has three daycare facilities, including a superb new one at Progress, which serve as ECE labs. Other Child Studies programs are a one-year certificate for Early Childhood Assistants (one of the few college programs that accepts Basic-level high school grads), and a one-year Early Childhood Administration program for ECE grads.

The Community Service cluster includes three-year Child and Youth Work, and two-year programs in Social Service Work, Recreation Leadership, and Development Service Work. Rare among the colleges in not having a Law and Security Administration program, Centennial does offer Correctional Work.

The Consumer Services cluster includes a pair of two-year Fashion Marketing programs, in Apparel and in Home Furnishings, a Food Service Supervision program, a one-year Cosmetic Sales program, and a unique post-diploma certificate in Wellness and Lifestyle Management, for the new field of wellness, general fitness, and illness prevention.

Business

All the Business courses at Centennial share a common first year. After one year, you make informed choices about areas of specialization. Most areas offer either two- or three-year options, and all three-year programs are co-op.

As well as standard Business and Business Administration programs, Centennial offers a variety of specialized programs. Accounting has two- and three-year options, a three-year Accountant/Programmer Analyst program, and a thirty-two-week Microcomputer Accounting Clerk program. Marketing also has two- and three-year options, and a three-year program in Automobile Marketing Management. Computer-related programs are Computer Programmer, Computer Programmer/Analyst, Microcomputer Analyst, and Information Systems. Other programs are Financial Services (aimed at banking careers), Operations Management (covering production control and quality assurance), and International Business.

Office Administration programs include one-year General and two-year Executive, Medical, and Legal options. Also offered are short courses in Office Receptionist, Word Processing Operator,

Office Information Administration, and Legal Assistant, a two-year program.

Centennial's Hospitality and Tourism sector has a three-year program in Hospitality and Tourism Administration and two-year programs in Travel Counsellor and Food Service Supervisor (the latter mostly for health care institutions). Centennial runs its own restaurant, Centennial Place, on the Warden Woods campus.

Supporting the Business school is Centennial's national-award-winning Centre for Entrepreneurship, which provides outreach seminars and workshops, networking, and information services.

Health Sciences

Centennial's Health Sciences School has rigorous admission standards (satisfactory high school grades and completion of Centennial's own tests), and it reports a relatively low dropout rate. The School innovated with the preceptor system of teaching, in which every student is assigned a working professional as mentor and advisor. Centennial's programs are very much focused on nursing and are particularly strong on post-diploma upgrades and refreshers. Increasingly, Health Sciences programming is taking into account the shift from hospital-based to community-based care.

As well as the standard Nursing and Nursing Assistant programs, Centennial offers post-diploma certificates for graduate nurses in Operating Room, Community Nursing, Oncology, Orthopaedics, and Gerontology. All Centennial nursing courses make extensive use of the "live lab" of Metro Toronto's hospitals, and the school offers a program for working RNAs to upgrade to RN standing.

For non-nurses with health science credentials, there are certificate programs in Gerontology. Also offered are one-year certificate programs in Ambulance and Emergency Care, Working with the Aged, Home Health Support, Infection Control Practice, and Sterile Supply Processing.

Many new Health Sciences programs have just started or are in development at Centennial. These include Pharmacy Assistant, Correctional Health, Women's Health, Rehabilitation Worker, and Palliative Care. Some but not all will be post-diploma training for nurses.

Technology

Centennial's Technology highlight, unique in Canada, is its School of Transportation, which trains half the aircraft maintenance personnel in Ontario and more than a quarter of the automotive technicians. The school provides training on nearly every kind of transportation machinery: cars, trucks, motorcycles, outboard marine engines, heavy equipment, helicopters, and aircraft. Its huge hangars and shops at the Ashtonbee campus are equipped with up-to-date equipment, including its own aircraft and jet engines. Close connections to the automotive manufacturers keep the school's shops particularly well stocked with late-model vehicles for students to work on.

Wally Manery, head of the school, likes to stress that people who maintain automobiles today are much more than "grease monkeys" – all recently built cars have five or more computers on board, and servicing them is a challenging, ever-changing task involving sophisticated tools. Canada foresees a serious shortage of personnel in this already well-paid field.

Two-year programs at the school are Aviation Technician, Avionics Technician, and Automotive Technician (which has technical and administrative options, one focusing on auto service, the other on service management).

Equally important are the non-diploma courses. The Transportation School is one college sector that has successfully broken out of the lockstep of the September-to-May two-year and three-year programs. There are short certificate courses in Auto Parts Management and Marine and Small Motor Mechanics, as well as in Heavy Equipment Maintenance, and a vital part of the School's offerings is a group of "Modified Apprenticeship Programs," or MAPS.

MAPS provide apprenticeship-type training for servicing various makes of cars, and they are offered in cooperation with major manufacturers and other auto-service corporations. MAPS ensure that service trainees are always working with the most up-to-date

Women are a small but growing part of Centennial's School of Transportation, the largest and best-equipped in Canada.

models and service procedures developed by the manufacturers. MAP apprentices generally work alternating sessions in school and in industry, totalling thirty-two or sixty-four weeks, and they need employer support as well as acceptance by the college. Also offered at the School are a full range of automotive apprenticeship programs (autobody, painter, transmission, brake and alignment, and so on). About 5,000 students study at the School of Transportation every year.

The School of Engineering Technology, at Progress campus, offers a wide range of Technology programs, and all its Technologist programs are co-op. Centennial covers all the standard fields, Architectural, Civil, Electronic, and Mechanical; it is moving strongly into new computerized technology fields; and it has a couple of uncommon specialties.

Architectural offerings are a Technologist program and a Technician program in Drafting. The Technician and Technologist programs in Civil Engineering both specialize in Public Works. The Mechanical Engineering programs have Technician and

Technologist programs in Design, a Technologist program in Industrial Engineering, and a Metal Machining program. There is also a CAD-CAM (Computer-Assisted Design/Manufacturing) Technician program, and Centennial is the only college with Technician and Technologist programs in Fluid Power/Robotics.

There are Technician and Technologist programs in Electronic Engineering and a post-diploma program in Data Communication and Networks. Computer Engineering programs are Technologist programs in Computer Systems and Control Engineering.

Centennial has Technician and Technologist programs in Biological Engineering, both specializing in Industrial Microbiology. It has a Technician program in Environmental Protection, and a one-year Lab Assistant program is available either full-time or part-time.

Part-Time and Continuing Education

Fifty thousand people take part-time courses at Centennial every year, and two-thirds of them are women. As at all the colleges, Centennial's part-timers are rarely there just for interest or amusement. They want specific, usable, job-related skills. Mostly they want credit for their work; some are working toward completing a diploma or certificate.

The college seems well equipped to serve them. You can register by phone or fax. (When will the colleges get organized to let full-time students do that?) You can take part-time courses for credit. Part-timers can enroll in daytime classes along with full-time students. Many programs offer tutorial assistance for students in difficulty. There are even study skills, time management, and introduction-to-college courses for part-timers – and they are *free*.

Getting in the Door

Centennial has an extensive program of orientation sessions,

"Tours du Jour," and student-led information sessions. For anyone interested in Centennial information, the liaison office has an 800 number.

The main Progress Campus is big but well signposted. The bright, open main entrance is easy to find, and most of the key "front-end services" are close by. The other campuses struck me as a little less easy to navigate – ask questions. All the campuses are on the Toronto subway, rapid transit, or bus routes.

Support Services

Centennial, like all the Metro Toronto Colleges, has a multicultural student population (two students in five were born outside Canada). The college runs an annual Multicultural Festival and is committed to equity and non-discrimination.

Centennial has the usual range of support services – see details in Part Three, "Using the Services." Students I talked to thought the support services were good, and they particularly praised the openness of faculty and the Peer Tutoring system (recommended both for students who need tutoring and for those who can provide it). They stressed the importance of seeking out support right from the start.

More than some student governments in the college system, Centennial's takes an advocacy role on behalf of students in academic as well as student life issues. Recent student campaigns helped stop the cancellation of funding for the Peer Tutoring programs.

Connections

Centennial has been building strong connections with high schools in Metro Toronto. Many area high schools now have formal agreements with Centennial. Schools get information about college programs; students can audit college courses and activities, and they are helped to tailor their school courses to fulfil college requirements and earn advanced standing.

The Scarborough Board of Education is going to build its Centre for Alternative Studies on the Progress Campus. At the Centre, 1,200 adults a year will work on their high school diplomas – and get access to College programs and activities. The Centre will also include a Career Planning Centre, open to the whole community.

Centennial has built a joint program in Communication Arts with York University, making it possible to work on both a degree and a diploma. Several programs in that field have fast-track options, by which students with university credentials receive advanced standing.

Scholarships

Centennial reports that almost one hundred academic prizes and bursaries, worth about $60,000, are distributed annually. Centennial does not have a fund-raising campaign for scholarships.

Centennial's alumni now total about 30,000. The college runs an alumni activity program and publishes an alumni magazine, *Ascent*.

Where to Live

Centennial is mostly a commuter campus, with 50 per cent of its students coming direct from local high schools and 55 per cent from Scarborough. Only 15 per cent of students move in order to attend Centennial, and the college has no plans to build student residences. The Housing Office does maintain a housing registry for each of its campuses.

Sports and Recreation

Centennial is right in Metro Toronto, and many students rely more on the city's abundance of entertainment opportunities than on the college itself. But Centennial has well-equipped gyms, weight rooms, and sports fields, and offers a wide-ranging varsity and intramural program. Sports scholarships are available to athletes who maintain satisfactory academic records and hold a place on the Centennial Colts varsity teams.

The City

Scarborough is the huge, multi-ethnic, and economically diverse eastern side of Metropolitan Toronto. It includes industrial districts, leafy suburbs, supermalls, highrise corridors, the waterfront parks along the Scarborough Bluffs, and the mostly undeveloped Rouge River Valley, home to the Metro Toronto Zoo. Both in Scarborough itself and in the metropolitan area, opportunities for entertainment, culture, recreation, and shopping are almost unlimited, and transit networks cover the city. Housing facilities cover the full range, and there are good prospects for both part-time work during college (60 per cent of Metro area college students have evening or weekend jobs) and for full-time careers after college.

Contact:

Centennial College
P.O. Box 631, Station A
Scarborough, Ont. M1K 5E9
(416) 698-4172 – Liaison
Toll-free: 1-800-268-4419 – Admissions

LA CITÉ COLLÉGIALE: *Collège en Français*

Ottawa

Size: Small

Programs in Communications et Medias, a La Cité specialty, cover a wide range, including TV *production, graphic design, and printing techniques.*

Something new emerged in the Ontario college system when La Cité collégiale opened for business in Ottawa in 1989. La Cité is the first college run by and for French-speaking Ontarians, where French is the first language in the classrooms and the corridors, in the president's office and the parking lots.

Not that French was entirely new in Ontario colleges in 1989. From the start, several of the Ontario colleges were bilingual, giving courses or programs and services in French as well as English. Some of these were token efforts by overwhelmingly English-language institutions; others were much more substantial.

As the Franco-Ontarian community became more organized and assertive, it began to campaign for an entirely French-speaking college. Ontario francophones argued that many of their students would have a better college experience if they were not surrounded by English-speakers. They argued that a French college would more effectively reach and serve francophone communities than one where French was a minority language.

The campaign for a college *en français* was strongest around Ottawa – because the Ottawa region has a large, articulate francophone population, and also because the francophone students and faculty of Algonquin College, though they were a small minority there, were a large enough group to be the basis for an entire college. When Ontario's 1986 law to provide Franco-Ontarians with expanded services in French made a francophone college a certainty, it was in the Ottawa region that the first steps were taken.

In 1989, La Cité collégiale took over the responsibilities of both Algonquin College and St. Lawrence College (which had both been bilingual colleges) for providing French-language college services in eastern Ontario. It is a move that is still debated. At Algonquin, they tend to suggest it was not really necessary. At Cambrian in Sudbury, they suggest it would not have been necessary if Algonquin had been run as Cambrian is, with an autonomous French-language division where francophones felt fully at home and in control.

At La Cité collégiale, they see the change as both inevitable and useful. La Cité has already attracted more francophone students than Algonquin ever did, they point out. It draws francophone students from far beyond the Ottawa area. It can "sell" college education to Franco-Ontarians more successfully than any bilingual, English-majority college ever could. Above all, it offers its students an all-French environment no bilingual college can match.

Certainly there is a lively spirit about La Cité collégiale. For its Ottawa campus, La Cité took over a couple of nondescript buildings in an industrial zone in the east of the city, and it has been remarkably successful in making them look and feel like a college campus – though they look forward to the new permanent campus that is being planned. At the same time, the college is also expanding the campuses that provide programs and services to the francophone communities of Hawkesbury and Cornwall.

Students and staff at La Cité – and even Franco-Ontarians with no direct stake in it – take a lot of pride in the college's unique status as *the* college for French-speaking Ontario. The college does a lot of outreach to francophones throughout the province, and it has rapidly established a distinctive presence among the twenty-three Ontario colleges. As well as continuing to run programs that had been offered in French at Algonquin and St. Lawrence, it has established new programs tailored to the needs of the eastern Ontario francophone community.

As the first and only French college, La Cité collégiale sees its mandate extending right across Ontario. La Cité has been the lead institution behind La Caravan technologique, a well-equipped RV that travels the province to promote French-language education services and new technology. The college is working to develop Distance Education to provide its courses more widely. And it gives high priority to upgrading programs, particularly for the francophones of rural communities and the north who never had opportunities or encouragement to stay in school. As French Ontario's own college, it hopes to reach those people – and provide role models for educational success – in a way that a mostly-English bilingual college never could.

La Cité is unlikely to be Ontario's only French college for long. Planning is already advanced for a Collège du Nord to serve Northern Ontario and a Collège du Sud that will serve the 300,000 francophones in communities from Windsor to Welland to Penetanguishene, and also in Metro Toronto. The Collège du Nord will take over the French-language services of Cambrian, Northern, and the other Northern Ontario colleges, and might be based in Sudbury. The Collège du Sud may be a "college without walls," using existing facilities to provide services to many communities. But until they come into being, La Cité will remain unique.

La Cité works in French – but no one will find it hostile to English. Most of La Cité's students (and staff) are bilingual and have lived all their lives hearing English all around them. The college has many contacts with anglophone-run businesses and industries that need a French-language component. Many of the students at La Cité expect to do placements and to find jobs in an

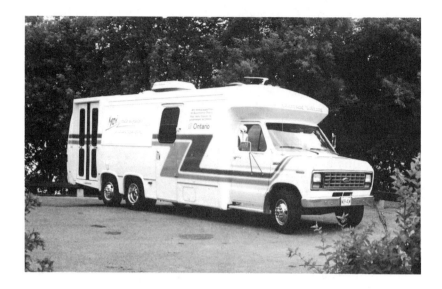

La Caravan technologique, an initiative of La Cité collégiale and other partners, tours Ontario to promote technological innovation – and college education.

English-language milieu. In fact, there might even be an opportunity open at La Cité for some anglophone immersion graduate to become the first anglophone to complete a diploma at Ontario's French-language college. When I asked them about that at La Cité, they couldn't remember any who ever had.

But the real task of La Cité collégiale is to be the best possible French-language college for the francophone community of eastern Ontario. It may be only a few years old, but it already seems to be a resounding success at that.

Worth Going For

- The French-language college experience

Campuses

The main campus in Ottawa is temporarily housed in an industrial zone in the east end of Ottawa. At Hawkesbury, La Cité has taken over the former outreach campus of Algonquin, and it is expanding the academic programs here. At Cornwall it operates from part of the St. Lawrence College campus on Windmill Point.

La Cité plans new buildings in Cornwall and Ottawa. At Cornwall, La Cité will be part of a post-secondary education centre shared with St. Lawrence and the bilingual University of Ottawa. In Ottawa, La Cité has acquired property closer to downtown, where it intends to build an entirely new college campus. The new campus should start replacing the present temporary facilities late in 1994.

Programs

As well as the standard upgrading programs, La Cité offers a two-year Programme collégial préparatoire à l'emploi, and a one-year or two-year Programme général d'arts et sciences. La Cité does not have co-op programs, but most programs include job placements called "stages de formation."

Applied Arts

La Cité's largest Applied Arts cluster is Communications et Médias, with two-year programs in Journalisme, Production télévisuelle, Radiodiffusion, Relations publiques, Publicité, Conception graphique, Techniques de documentation (Bibliotechnique), Techniques d'Imprimerie, and Techniques de Photographie, all at the Ottawa campus.

In Human Services, La Cité offers Éducation des petits, Travail social, Techniques en services de réadaptation, Techniques d'éducation specialisée, and a cluster of security programs consisting of Administration de la loi et de la sécurité, Techniques des services correctionnels, and Protection et sécurité. The Cornwall campus offers Travail social-gérontologie.

Business

In Etudes Administratives et Commerciales, La Cité offers the two-year Commerce programs (options in comptabilité, informatique, and marketing) and the three-year programs in Administration des Affaires (options in comptabilité, gestion, informatique, marketing, and services financiers). Also offered is a two-year Programmeur en informatique and one-year Direction de commerce au détail. Programs in Administration de bureau are one-year programs in Secrétariat général and Opérations d'ordinateurs, and two-year Secrétariat juridique and Soutien administratif. Some of the Business programs are available at Cornwall, which also offers Gestion des petits entreprises.

Health Sciences

In Sciences de la Santé, La Cité has a three-year Sciences infirmières (at Ottawa and Cornwall) and a 1.5-year Soins infirmiers auxiliaires (also at Hawkesbury in a one-year version), Soins dentaires, and Hygiène dentaire, a one-year certificate in Secours ambulancier, Technologie du laboratoire médical (three years), and Thérapie respiratoire (three years).

Technology

La Cité's most innovative Technology cluster is Habitation et Aménagement, which brings together design, construction, and even horticulture. Programs are three-year Design d'intérieur-avancé, two-year Horticulture et aménagement paysager, Technician and Technologist programs in Architecture and in Génie de la construction, plus a one-year Fleuriste certificate.

Also offered are Technician and Technologist programs in Génie mécanique and Génie électronique, Techniques des systèmes informatiques and Technologie des ordonnateurs. The

Cornwall campus offers Techniques des sciences de l'environne-
ment. Hawkesbury has Techniques forestières.

Trades Training

No French-language apprenticeship programs existed until La
Cité began developing fifteen of them. La Cité also offers a limited
number of skilled trades certificates at all three campuses. Given
the need for basic upgrading, literacy skills, and retraining in the
francophone communities of rural and Northern Ontario, La Cité
is developing a strong commitment to all these fields.

Part-Time and Continuing Education

In 1990, when La Cité welcomed its first students, it had more
than twice as many in full-time programs as in part-time. However, Éducation permanente is part of the college mandate, and La
Cité will be expanding its part-time courses. It also has a strong
commitment to Distance Education, in order to make its programs available to francophones unable to come to its campuses.

Getting in the Door

La Cité promotes information-line numbers for all its campuses
and it has a Canada-wide 800 number. The present Ottawa campus is in a mostly industrial and commercial area, but it is not far
from the centre of Gloucester, and it is linked to the rest of the city
by public transit. There is an information counter inside the front
door of the main Ottawa building, and all three campuses are
small enough to be easy to use.

Support Services

Along with the usual support services, all provided in French, of course, La Cité points to its orientation, la Programme d'Acceuil, and to its efforts to reduce drop-out rates by building faculty-student cooperation. There is a lively and active student organization. The enthusiasm that comes from being small, new, and unique is evident throughout the college.

Connections

The University of Ottawa accepts La Cité's nursing grads to advanced standing in its degree nursing program, and discussions are under way for similar linkage in the Administration des affaires program. But as with the English-language institutions, the colleges are considerably more interested – and flexible – than the universities when it comes to creating connections between colleges and universities.

Scholarships

La Cité feels that it is still establishing its reputation and how it is seen by business, industry, and the community. La Cité is not yet ready to start any substantial fund-raising drives, but it does have a small number of scholarships and bursaries.

Where to Live

Already about 30 per cent of La Cite's students come from outside its eastern Ontario territory, and the number may grow, at least until other French-language colleges are established. With no residences and none planned, La Cité expects its students will be able to find housing in Ottawa-Hull, Hawkesbury, and Cornwall. La Cité's housing service will aid in the search.

Sports and Recreation

La Cité's temporary campus has only limited athletic facilities, but the college has a couple of varsity sports teams (men's soccer, women's volleyball), intramural teams, and a program of individual recreation activities. The Ottawa campus has one large hall for nearly all of its large gatherings, but there is a lively entertainment program throughout the school year.

The City

Ottawa has always been a bilingual city, particularly around its eastern end. The communities along the road to Montreal are heavily francophone, and Hull, P.Q, is just across the river. The expansion of bilingualism in the federal government has brought more francophones to Ottawa-Hull, so the city is well equipped with entertainment, recreation, shopping, and community services *en français*.

Contact:

La Cité collégiale
2465, boul. Saint-Laurent
Ottawa, Ont. KIG 5H8
Toll-free: 1-800-267-CITE
(613) 786-CITE – Ottawa
(613) 632-CITE – Hawkesbury
(613) 938-CITE – Cornwall

CONESTOGA COLLEGE: *Updating a Technological Tradition*

Kitchener

Size: Medium

Students in the Woodworking Centre at Conestoga make quality furniture using the latest technology.

If there were a "handsome campus" award, Conestoga would be one hot contender. The college's seven buildings – including a huge sports complex – are laid out amid 144 acres of rolling ground and woodlots that form the Doon campus, close by Highway 401 south of Kitchener. This is one campus not dominated by its parking lots.

Conestoga boasts about being in Canada's technology triangle. Three universities plus Conestoga give the Guelph-Kitchener-Waterloo area the most densely concentrated educational population in Canada, and it also has a strong industrial base, plus a fast-growing high-technology sector. But Conestoga is a mid-sized college, with few glamour specialties to draw students from all over. Even its strong points, like woodworking, don't seem like areas you would find on the cutting edge of technological and commercial innovation.

Surprise! Conestoga's Woodworking Centre is extremely innovative. And behind its relaxed facade, Conestoga delivers the impression of being very strong in what it does. Placement rates are high, dropout rates lower than average.

Technology is a Conestoga strength, and that's appropriate. Though the Ontario colleges generally are not much caught up in tradition, Conestoga does manage to suggest that it is maintaining a long Kitchener-Waterloo heritage, one that goes back to the immigrant German artisans and craftspeople who made "Berlin" (the name was changed to Kitchener during the First World War) an industrial powerhouse a century ago. Among the K-W traditions continued at Conestoga are woodworking, furniture-making, and electric power technology (Kitchener people virtually invented the power grid that became Ontario Hydro). Today Conestoga students are likely to work with computers rather than chisels, but the founders might approve and be impressed.

Worth Going For

- The Woodworking Centre
- A student-centred attitude and a good job-placement record

Campuses

Conestoga has decided the best way to provide quality service to students and clients is to unite most of its facilities on a single campus at Doon: "a regional college at a single location." Though it still has facilities in Guelph, Waterloo, Cambridge, and Stratford, Conestoga plans to draw together more and more of its post-secondary activities at Doon. Part-time and preparatory studies will continue to be offered elsewhere, and a Nursing program is still offered in Stratford.

The Doon campus is centrally located in the Region of Waterloo but it is not a downtown campus. It is out on its own, with the southern suburbs of Kitchener on one side and open fields on another. Though there are bus routes to the Doon campus, Doon is mostly a campus for people who drive, and is not close to down-town services.

Programs

Compared to the average mix of program enrollments across the Ontario college system, Conestoga is relatively small in Applied Arts programming and much larger than average in Health Sciences and Technology. More than some colleges, it emphasizes three-year rather than two-year diploma programs. It has moved tentatively into co-op. It is not easy going up against the University of Waterloo, which helped invent co-op education, in the local co-op job market, but Conestoga offers a few co-op programs in Business and Technology.

Conestoga has a large General Arts and Science program (GAS), with lots of options depending on the direction a student wishes to take. GAS is mostly preparation for other studies. The University of Guelph has begun to recommend that students failing in its first year take GAS at Conestoga and then return, and a year of GAS can also be a good pathway into career-oriented college programs.

Applied Arts

Conestoga's Applied Arts division has two small clusters and no stand-out programs. The Media cluster offers a three-year Broadcasting program (for both radio and television), a combined Graphic Design and Advertising course, and a Print Journalism program.

The Community Service cluster offers the standard programs in Law and Security Administration, Social Service Work, Recreation Leadership, and Early Childhood Education. The ECE program is supported by a part-time certificate for Educational Assistants, and a part-time post-diploma program for ECE Resource Teachers working with special-needs children.

Conestoga's Radio and Television Broadcasting students gain experience in the college's closed-circuit radio and television studios.

Business

By making some clear choices, Conestoga has managed to simplify and clarify its Business programs. All Business Administration programs at Conestoga share a common first year, and students begin to specialize in the second year. Except for a General Business diploma, all the business courses are Business Admin (that is, three-year) programs. Within Business Admin, students choose among Accounting, Marketing, Management, Materials Management, and Computer Programmer/Analyst.

The Business school also offers a single hospitality program, a two-year co-op Food and Beverage Management diploma.

The only full-time Office Administration courses are certificate and diploma programs in Office Systems. Other office admin courses, including Legal Secretary, are offered on a part-time basis only.

Health Sciences

Conestoga's Health Sciences, some of which are offered at Stratford as well as at Doon, are built around Nursing and Nursing Assistant programs. They share a common first semester. The school also offers several post-diploma programs for graduate nurses in gerontology, home care, psychiatric nursing, critical care, and related areas. The only non-nursing program offered is a one-year certificate in Ambulance and Emergency Care.

Technology

Kitchener-Waterloo has a century-old tradition in skilled trades brought to the centre by German woodworkers and craftspeople, and in recent years it has also become a high-technology centre with international clout. Conestoga's Technology and trades programs are tied into both.

One Conestoga stand-out is the 50,000-square-foot Woodworking Centre of Ontario. Furniture factories with famous names have been collapsing into bankruptcy all over Ontario in recent years, so wooden furniture-making hardly sounds like a promising career. But at the Woodworking Centre, you don't see artisans tapping away with chisels or weaving cane seats.

More likely, they are working out a pattern on a CAD (computer-assisted design) terminal, then sticking the disk into huge process control machines that cut, drill, veneer, and assemble. Press a few controls, and almost instantly, it seems, a stack of wood is transformed into a complete office console. That kind of furniture-making is *not* obsolete, and the Woodworking Centre has unmatched facilities with which to teach it. The main programs are a two-year co-op Woodworking Technician diploma and a post-diploma certificate in Woodworking Manufacturing Management.

The school's electrical programs focus on the Detweiler Electrical Centre, named for a local industry pioneer and furnished with a collection of historical generating machines. Students work on a total of 400 tons of equipment, from the latest electronics to massive hydro-generating turbines. Programs are Technician and

Technologist (i.e., two years or three years) in Electrical or Electronic Engineering. The Technologist program has Computer/Communications and Telecommunications options.

All Mechanical Engineering programs have a common first year, as part of either a two-year Technician diploma, with Drafting and Numerical Control options, or a three-year Technologist diploma with options in Design and Analysis, Automated Manufacturing, or Robotics and Automation (a co-op program). Also available are Civil and Construction Engineering Technologist programs, and a two-year Welding Technician program.

Trades Training

Conestoga is one of the colleges that don't treat their trades and training projects as second-rate or bury them in old buildings and the back of the calendar. It offers a long list of trades training programs and apprenticeship programs.

Part-Time and Continuing Education

Most of the 40,000 annual users of the Conestoga Centre for Continuing Education are looking to upgrade their credentials. They are looking for credit courses, or they want a specific program to help their career. The Centre offers courses that earn credit toward a diploma, short-term certificates, and non-credit courses. In addition it offers training and consulting services to business and industry.

Getting in the Door

A lot of the colleges that talk about being student-centred should look at Conestoga. A clearly signposted Student/Client Building has everything the dazed new arrival needs on the way in. At the entrance is a large information booth – I was told there are very few questions about Conestoga that can stump the staff there.

Admission counselling, registration, scholarship and bursary info, and various other services are all close by. There's an Infoline. It's a good, friendly way into the college.

Support Services

Conestoga seems to have a serious commitment to a "student-success" learning system. Recent changes in its system actually seem to have reduced the number of dropouts.

Conestoga does a lot of pre-admission testing. Doing badly does not mean you are barred entry – but you will be pointed to services that give the kind of help you need to improve your chances of success. Students who need time or are not sure of what to choose are guided to Conestoga's strong and growing General Arts and Sciences programs and other preparatory programs. Career-oriented programs are clustered effectively and share many common first years. Counselling, peer-tutoring, faculty support – all look good.

Conestoga, in conjunction with other western Ontario colleges, does a lot of "professional development" – that is, keeping the faculty up to speed. All new teachers take training in teaching methods, and student evaluations and student focus groups are used to check up on teaching talent among both full-time and part-time faculty.

Conestoga was one of the first colleges to get into "Access" (see "The Jargon" in Part One). The people who work in the Access Departments are there to serve everyone who can't just walk in the door and enroll. If you feel you might not be a "typical" college student, head for Access. It is also a good place to start looking for aptitude and career-choice testing.

Connections

Conestoga's Technology departments have initiated a program by which high school classes do part of their science, technology, and laboratory work at the college. It is smart marketing because it eases the transition from high school to college, but it also helps popularize technology among the students. Students exposed to the program actually start increasing the number of technology courses they take in high school.

Like most colleges, Conestoga finds its local universities slow about developing cooperative agreements. For four years, the University of Waterloo has been mulling over a fairly obvious linking between its B.A. and Conestoga's Journalism diploma. But some Conestoga-Waterloo links have been established, with the college's strong preparatory English as a Second Language courses supporting many university entrants.

Scholarships

Conestoga recently started a $4.5 million fund-raising drive, mostly focused on Business programs, which will include scholarships. It has a well-developed alumni program.

Where to Live

Conestoga has not really broken through as a destination campus, and it relies heavily on its own area for recruitment. Two-thirds of its students commute from the Kitchener-Waterloo-Guelph-Cambridge area or the rural region around it. Nevertheless, a privately owned and operated student residence is under development just across from the Doon campus. Scheduled to open in 1993, it will provide residence space for 230 students. Residence space is also available at the former nurses' residence in Stratford. Conestoga also offers a housing service to help locate rental rooms and apartments.

Sports and Recreation

Since 1980, Conestoga has had the Cadillac of college sports facilities, at least among the small and mid-sized colleges. The

Kenneth E. Hunter Recreation Centre has a double-sized gym and an international-sized ice rink, each with lots of seating, plus weight rooms and squash courts. Outdoors it has a speedskating oval, lighted tennis courts, baseball diamonds, and football/soccer fields. They are used by the varsity teams (the Conestoga Condors), intramural teams, individual students, and community groups.

How does Conestoga have all this, with only one small program in Recreation Leadership? By sharing the facilities (and the cost) with the surrounding community, which also makes a pool and other services available to Conestoga students. Smart.

The City

Kitchener-Waterloo is a big double city with a strong industrial base in the midst of some of Ontario's most prosperous farm country. Kitchener has a blue-collar, industrial, ethnic German feel to it (there's a terrific Oktoberfest in the fall), while Waterloo, with two universities, seems a little more upscale, with a lot of high-technology industry settling around the University of Waterloo. With Cambridge and Guelph near, the population is large enough to support lots of culture, recreation, shopping, and sports. Highway 401 is close by, and London and Toronto are each about an hour away.

Contact:

Conestoga College
299 Doon Valley Drive
Kitchener, Ont. N2G 4M4
(519) 748-3516 – Liaison

CONFEDERATION COLLEGE: *The Distance Advantage*

Thunder Bay

Size: Small/Medium

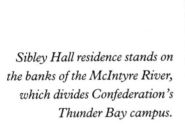

Sibley Hall residence stands on the banks of the McIntyre River, which divides Confederation's Thunder Bay campus.

Confederation College's region is that huge area at the top left of the Ontario map, from just west of the Sault to the Manitoba border. By far it is the biggest chunk of geography in the system. Confederation is a long way away from the other colleges of Ontario.

A problem? No, it is probably Confederation's greatest asset. The college has established a high profile in a proud region whose young people often don't want to leave home. Confederation also works hard to sell Thunder Bay as a place to go. I met a student from Brampton who chose Confederation over several southern Ontario schools with similar programs. He planned to make his career in the north for the quality of life it offers.

Confederation offers both diploma programs and specialized training services linked to the northern economy, particularly the pulp-and-paper and grain-handling industries and northern aviation. It is active in Distance Education for remote communities, and it has a substantial aboriginal student population. At the same time, as the only college around, it has maintained a range of general programs across the spectrum – without growing to an unmanageable size. The main campus, in a parklike setting between the Port Arthur and Fort William halves of Thunder Bay, remains small enough to be friendly and accessible.

Six months after the 1991 class graduated, Confederation reported that 84 per cent of those seeking work were employed. Sixty-five per cent had jobs related to their studies. These figures are not up to usual college standards, but troubles in the local industries have hit northwestern Ontario hard. As the recession lingers, they may get worse, but you can't blame Confederation for that.

Worth Going For

- The Aviation programs
- Northern-oriented Entrepreneurship and Business programs

Campuses

The main Confederation campus is a cluster of buildings beside the McIntyre River in an attractive wooded area between the old Fort William and Port Arthur halves of the city. There are good bus connections by city transit.

Confederation maintains outreach campuses in Dryden, Fort Frances, Geraldton, Kenora, Marathon, and Sioux Lookout, and Distance Education locations in many small communities across the northwest. Most regional campuses offer diploma courses in Business, Teacher Aide, and Social Service Work, plus skills training, pre-employment programs, and part-time courses.

Programs

The program mix at Confederation is fairly typical of the college system as a whole. Only the proportion of Confederation's students enrolled in the Business school is slightly smaller than the average for the college system.

Confederation offers several entry programs for students unready or unable to enter a career-oriented program. College Vocational (three semesters) is designed to improve the study skills and career knowledge of high school grads with Basic credentials, and it includes a field placement. General Arts and Sciences can be the prelude to either college or university, and has many options to suit individual objectives. The Pre-Technology Certificate provides the academic foundation required for Technology diploma programs.

Faced with more applicants than it can provide space for, Confederation sometimes includes high school marks among the selection criteria in some programs. You may find yourself being ranked according to marks if a program is oversubscribed.

Applied Arts

Applied Arts programs in the community and human services areas include Child and Youth Worker (three years), Development Services Worker, Social Service Worker, Recreation Leadership, and Law and Security Administration. The Early Childhood Education program supports several community outreach projects. The department believes its Law and Security program is particularly strong, though the placement record has not been impressive. Along with the usual human services programs, Confederation originated a Community Gerontology diploma, but it is currently suspended due to funding limitations.

Communication Arts programs include Broadcasting, with options in radio or television production, a Film Production program (the only two-year one in Ontario), and Arts Administration, which can be combined with a Lakehead University

Honours degree in Music through a college/university joint project.

Business

Most Business programs start with the common first-year Core Business, which leads to two-year or three-year completions. Two-year programs are Accounting, Administration, Personnel Management, and Marketing. Three-year programs flowing from Core Business are Accounting and Finance Administration, Computer Programmer Analyst, and Industrial Relations, a very demanding program that has produced some top labour negotiators. Human Resources (two years) is losing its subtitle "Employment Equity" – equity is everyone's responsibility now. Two new offerings are two-year and three-year International Business programs.

From aboriginal communities to resources towns, the north is going to have to run its own businesses, and to support them Confederation runs the Centre for Entrepreneurship and the Northwest Enterprise Centre, which offers entrepreneurial training to new and existing businesses. (The Northwest Enterprise Centre also does international consulting, including a recent project to set up entrepreneurship training in Poland.) A one-year Entrepreneurship certificate is much favoured by mature students who have capital and who plan to start businesses.

Office Administration begins with a common first year, after which students choose another year in executive, legal, or medical options.

Hospitality and Tourism programs are Culinary Management, Hotel Management, and Travel and Tourism Administration.

Health Sciences

Health Sciences programs are Nursing, Nursing Assistant, Radiography, Health Records Technician, and Dental Assistant and Dental Hygiene. Recently, Confederation's Dental Hygienists had a 100 per cent pass rate in their licensing exams, but getting in is tough: over 500 applied for the course's sixteen places. Testing is based on Confederation's own assessments, not high school marks.

Technology

Confederation's Technology stand-out (with 250 students, about a third of the Technology program) is its cluster of Aviation programs, which cover flight, management, and maintenance aspects of the aviation industry. The college's Aviation programming began partly by accident – the first president was an air vice-marshal – and they now draw half their enrollment from far beyond northwest Ontario. The Aviation programs are Flight Management, which includes commercial pilot's-licence and floatplane certification; Aircraft Maintenance; Airport and Air Carrier Management (for airport and airline ground operations); and two Aviation Manufacturing programs, a two-year Technician and a three-year Technologist diploma. There is no aviation manufacturing industry in Thunder Bay today, but these programs have been successful in placing their grads elsewhere.

Many of Confederation's other Technology programs are closely linked to the employment needs of Northern Ontario. Specific programs are Civil Engineering Technologist, which is co-op; Construction Engineering Technician (co-op); Technician and Technologist programs in Electrical Engineering; Electronics Engineering Technician; Instrumentation Engineering Technician; and Mechanical Engineering Technician. Content in all of these is conditioned by local industrial requirements. The Civil Engineering Technology program already has a strong environmental-control component and Confederation hopes to open a northern-oriented Environmental Engineering Technology program.

Aboriginal Programs

There are about 500 aboriginal students at Confederation. They actually form a higher proportion of the Confederation student body than aboriginal people do in the northwestern Ontario population. But for twenty years aboriginal students at all the Ontario colleges had a dropout rate sometimes exceeding 90 per cent.

Confederation thinks the situation there is turning around. (See "Aboriginal Students" under "Special Clients" in Part Three.) There is now strong native input both to the Board of Governors and to each program. As aboriginal organizations take greater control of education planning and tailor programs more closely to their community needs, the success rate for First Nations students at Confederation is beginning to grow.

In 1992 Confederation established an Aboriginal Studies division. Its General Vocational program is designed as preparation for employment and for entry into career-oriented programs, and it includes aboriginal culture studies. It includes a one-year Pre-Health certificate for students who need preparation for Health Sciences programs. Other programs include the three-year Native Family Worker program and the three-year Business Management-Aboriginal Organizations. Diploma programs and trades training will increasingly be offered on reserve communities, so that aboriginal people can gain skills and credentials without the dislocation of moving to the city.

Trades Training

Confederation offers one-year trades training courses in Heavy Equipment, Small Powered Equipment, Industrial Maintenance, Welding, and Stationary Engineering. Increasingly these certificates are becoming prerequisites for employment in apprenticeship programs. Confederation does the classroom side of apprenticeship training for trades such as Carpenter, Electrician, Heavy Duty Equipment Mechanic, Millwright, and Motor Vehicle Mechanic.

Part-Time and Continuing Education

Confederation's Community Education programs offer a wide range of part-time courses in Thunder Bay. Like other northern colleges, Confederation is also deeply involved in Distance Education and serves as one of the focal points for the Contact North network. In addition, the Continuous Learning Centre has been created to offer diploma program courses on a part-time basis directed by individual schedules.

Getting in the Door

There is a toll-free 800 number for the main campus and most of the satellites. The main entry is adequately marked, and there is a very helpful Information desk right inside, though the main student services are not gathered together.

Each summer, Confederation and its student government invite new students to an event called Passport. Passport participants from out of town get two days' free housing and meals at the college, including full use of the recreation facilities. During Passport visits, student hosts provide personalized tours of the college, including meetings with faculty and staff from their program area. When students are arriving to start school, Confederation offers shuttle services from the airport and bus depot.

Support Services

Confederation offers the usual range of support services, with particular attention to aboriginal student support. Its relatively small size and isolation seem to give the college an enthusiasm which suggests support should be easily available. Students I talked to thought Confederation was doing a good job in student services.

The student society recently opened its own student centre, including Sharky's Pub, paid for, owned, and operated by the students. There is also an Aboriginal Student Association.

Telecommunications equipment links Distance Education students at a northern community to instructors at the main campus. Confederation participates in the Contact North/Contact Nord educational network.

Connections

Curiously, Thunder Bay's Lakehead University is a competitor for the colleges in some technology fields. Because it began as a trade and technology institute, Lakehead (virtually alone among universities) still offers college-type diploma programs in Engineering Technology, Forest Technology, and Library Technology. Confederation does not run programs that are already being offered by Lakehead.

Perhaps because it too began as a trade school, Lakehead University has been unusually enlightened about accepting links to the college system. It is possible to combine a simultaneous B.A. in Music (from Lakehead) and a diploma in Arts Administration from Confederation, or follow up a Confederation Engineering

Technology diploma with a Lakehead Engineering degree. College diplomas in Business, Engineering Technology, Health Sciences, Natural Resources, Visual Arts, and other programs can all be used for advanced standing in degree programs at Lakehead. More joint programs are planned.

An arrangement this sensible ought to be absolutely routine, but given the prevailing attitude of Ontario universities, it is almost unheard of.

Scholarships

Money for almost 200 scholarships and bursaries, mostly quite small ($50 to $300), has been donated to Confederation, but the College has not had a special campaign to raise scholarship funds. There is no fund-raising foundation at Confederation. An alumni organization, with a part-time staffer, has recently been organized.

Where to Live

About 60 per cent of students at the main campus are from Thunder Bay, with another 25 per cent from the rest of Confederation's huge northwestern Ontario catchment area. About 15 per cent come from Manitoba, southern Ontario, and other areas outside Confederation's region.

Confederation has had one 152-bed residence for ten years, and in September 1992 it added another 132-bed residence. "We could fill a thousand if we had them," says a staffer, so places are available on a first-come, first-served basis. Get in an application early. There is an active Residence Life program. Since kitchen facilities are provided in the accommodations, there is no meal plan. The College Housing service will assist students in their searches for off-campus housing in the city.

Also in the planning stages: the Negahneewin Centre, a residence/daycare/study centre/student support centre for aboriginal students. Currently the aboriginal community of Thunder Bay can provide some housing for aboriginal students.

Sports and Recreation

The on-campus fitness centre, open to all students, includes weight training facilities and squash courts, and an air-supported bubble covers tennis, basketball, badminton, and volleyball courts. Other college sports teams use community facilities for skiing, curling, and so on.

The City

By far the largest city in its area, with about 125,000 people, Thunder Bay is the main port, industrial centre, and transportation and service centre for northwestern Ontario. If northwestern Ontario were a province, Thunder Bay would be the capital. It has excellent recreational and cultural facilities, a strong Finnish-Canadian heritage, a substantial aboriginal community, and a diverse multicultural population. There are not many other cities close by, but Thunder Bay has regular airline connections, as well as highway and railroad links, to the rest of Canada and the United States. And half the people I met at Confederation seemed to have a "camp" – what Southern Ontario would call "a cottage" – by a quiet lake deep in the woods and only half an hour from downtown.

If you are not from Thunder Bay, home is probably a long way away, and the winter is long. Better settle in and enjoy yourself.

Contact:

Confederation College
1450 Nakina Drive
P.O. Box 398
Thunder Bay, Ont. P7C 4W1
(807) 475-6110
Toll-free: 1-800-465-5005

DURHAM COLLEGE: *Hard Head, Warm Heart?*

Oshawa

Size: Small / Medium

The main campus of Oshawa's Durham College is a short walk from a new, privately developed student residence.

Interesting place, Durham College.

They talk very hard-headedly at Durham about the college's mission being economic development – building prosperity for the community, for business and industry, for the individual graduate. They have been very practical about tailoring programs strictly to the demands of the marketplace, and they have been ruthless about pruning non-performing programs. In recent years they have reported placement rates around 97 per cent. Even if you don't put much faith in placement statistics, that's high.

At the same time, they are so . . . nice. Ask Gary Polonsky, Durham's president, what characterizes the college, and he uses words like, "Integrity. Respect. Cooperation." He says them with a great deal of Sincerity (that would be another of the words). How to succeed at Durham? "Be S.W.A.N.S.," he says. "Be Smart, Work

127

hard, be Assertive, be Nice, be a Straight-shooter." That's all there is to it.

"The great majority of our clientele is just splendid," says Polonsky. "They read well. They count well. They speak well. They aren't becoming astronauts, but we don't do that program here. They treat us with respect. They make splendid students and great contributors." In exchange, Durham promises to treat everyone equally, to keep everyone informed and involved, and not to play politics with them.

Written down, it sounds like an awful pack of sanctimonious clichés. But the sincerity of that commitment to mutual respect and to giving everyone a quality college experience seems to filter down. I caught glimpses of it in the way the place is run and in the way faculty, staff, and students I met talked about it. The commitment to service and to student success does seem to run deep.

Now, when you have just lined up for an hour and they tell you the course you want is already full ("Next!"), you might find this hard to believe. Colleges tend to be bursting at the seams, money is tight, and there can be a lot of pressure around registration time. But don't be driven away. Durham says very clearly it is there to serve you, so take it at its word. If you think you are getting no respect, tell them Gary Polonsky sent you.

Or tell him.

Worth Going For

- Sports Admin and Entertainment Admin
- Strong commitment to student success
- Robotics and Automation facilities

Campuses

Durham, the first college east of Metro Toronto, serves Durham Region plus the Port Hope area. The main Durham campus is on Simcoe Street on the northern outskirts of Oshawa, with easy access by car and transit.

Durham is committed to being a multi-site campus, particularly for outreach, basic skills, and part-time programs. A former chocolate factory in Whitby is about to become the centre of Durham's trades training and apprenticeship programs. It has satellite campuses in Port Hope, Uxbridge, and Ajax, and is considering expanding its facilities in Pickering.

Programs

Perhaps surprisingly for industrial Oshawa, Durham has a smaller than average Technology school, but it is respected for its computing and robotics. Durham has a slightly larger than average proportion of students in Business and Health Sciences.

Durham administers a questionnaire to all qualified applicants to all programs and may use the questionnaire as well as high school marks in selection procedures.

If you are lacking specific credentials or need preparation for a career-track program, you can take short College Prep courses in Pre-Business, Pre-Technology, or Pre-Health. Pre-Health runs September to February, the others February to June. None gives automatic entry into career-oriented programs in the related fields.

If you have not settled on a career track, can't get into the program you want, or need general skills that can lead either to a college program or to university, Durham offers General Arts and Science. Most GAS students go to a career-oriented diploma program after a one-year GAS certificate, but a two-year diploma GAS is available.

Durham does not offer co-op programs. It is experimenting with Summer Internship programs as a way to provide job experience that requires less faculty supervision and a shorter time commitment by students.

Applied Arts

Rather than cover the spectrum, Durham's Applied Arts programs focus on a few areas, with a couple of Community Service programs and a small Hospitality cluster alongside a large and diverse Media/Communications cluster.

The Media cluster is built around two-year Journalism and three-year Public Relations programs. Both programs are project-oriented – Journalism produces a newspaper, PR takes on non-profit clients – and use a laboratory method, using facilities that look more like newsrooms and PR offices than classrooms. Other courses are three-year Graphic Design, three-year Interior Design, and two-year Advertising Administration programs. All these use Macintosh computers extensively, and Durham claims to have the best Mac labs in the college system.

Durham offers a standard two-year Early Childhood Education, plus a part-time version and a one-year certificate for ECE assistants. These are linked to a network of college-run community daycare projects and centres. The Law and Security Administration program recognizes the limited prospects for police-force employment by focusing on other aspects, particularly retail, industrial, and electronic security. The two-year Sports Administration and Entertainment Administration are unique in the province.

Two-year Hospitality programs are Catering Management, aimed mostly at catering managers in large institutions, and Food and Beverage Management, aimed more toward hotel and restaurant work.

Business

All business courses have a common first semester. Durham offers the two-year Business and three-year Business Administration options right across the spectrum of its programs: Accounting, Human Resources Management, Information Systems, Marketing, Production and Operations Management, and General Business. The only program without a two-year option is Fashion Retail Administration. It has been suspended for the 1993-94 school year and its future is uncertain.

Office Administration offers a one-year secretarial certificate, plus a full range of two-year options in Office Admin for

Engineering, Executive Secretary, Legal, Medical, and Word Processing. A three-year Legal Admin course trains law clerks and paralegals.

Durham also runs the Durham Management Centre, which does extension and outreach programs for businesses and individuals.

Health Sciences

Health Sciences at Durham are relatively large but tightly focused, with only four programs: Nursing, Nursing Assistant, Dental Assistant, and Dental Hygiene. Through Con Ed, it offers specialized post-diploma programs for working nurses, and much of the full-time Nursing program can be done on a part-time basis. Nursing and Nursing Assistant share a common first semester, but students are registered in one or the other from the start.

Technology

The Technology school is small but strong, with a commitment to computer applications and excellent computing facilities. Programs are oriented to the industrial requirements of Oshawa and its area.

There are two-year Technician and three-year Technologist options in Civil Engineering and Electronic Engineering. There is a two-year Technician program in Quality Engineering. (The Durham calendar reports this program was opened because of industry's demand for quality upgrading techniques in the wake of the Canada-U.S. Free Trade Agreement of 1989.) Mechanical Engineering is available only in the three-year Technologist program. The three-year Technologist program in Environmental Technology is closely linked to Durham Region's need for solid waste management – it's about industrial and urban environmental control, not natural resources. The three-year Food and Drug Technology program is linked to the University of Guelph's similar departments. After its first year, transfer into Med Lab Technology programs at other colleges is possible.

Electronics Engineering Technology students at Durham benefit from the college's well-equipped computer facilities.

Durham runs the Productivity Improvement Centre and Manufacturing and Automation Centre, each offering consulting and specialized courses on an outreach basis to business and industry.

Trades Training

Durham offers short (one year or less) certificate programs in a broad range of construction, industrial, electrical, and motor vehicle trades. Most of these provide entry into the trades and facilitate access into apprenticeship programs.

Part-Time and Continuing Education

Durham says it is "aggressive about partnership." It seeks to be the key training facility for industry and government in the Oshawa area, it sells its expertise overseas, and it is larger than average in the non-post-secondary areas of training.

Continuing Education sees about 42,000 clients and part-time students a year at the main campus and through large Con Ed offerings at the satellite campuses, particularly Ajax and Uxbridge. Substantial numbers complete Early Childhood Education and Office Admin programs on an entirely part-time basis, and about 60 per cent of Con Ed students have already taken at least one previous course. Mostly they are working to complete a certificate or diploma.

Getting in the Door

There is a toll-free 800 number for Durham information. Durham's publications have won international awards – they tend to be brief and clear.

If you enter from Simcoe Street, the main entrance is easy to find, and just inside the door is a Reception/Information counter surrounded by the main "front-end" services most needed and used by students and potential students.

Durham has created an Access Division. Access at Durham is the doorway to all the non-post-secondary programs for anyone who needs specialized skills training, upgrading, language skills, and life skills. It's also for anyone who needs special help getting into post-secondary college programs.

Support Services

Everyone talks "student success," but Durham seems to be one of the colleges that has been aggressive about it. (Read about study skills under "Using the Services" in Part Three.) Durham has all the usual student-support services, but it also has its own strong faculty-training programs that involve all teaching personnel in student-success work. Every program has study-skills components built into it, and there seems to be close liaison between counsellors and faculty. Durham has been working to make scheduling more flexible. In recent years dropout rates have been reduced substantially, and while a tough job market is one factor, Durham thinks its student-success programs are having an effect.

The college's serious commitment to cooperation and respect translates into strong non-academic support services – with guidance and counselling links reaching into the community. Durham Region Social Services, for instance, has been offering its services on-campus to Durham students, as a supplement to Durham's own Counselling service.

Connections

Durham is a growing region with a large population of high school age students. Compared to some colleges with large adult student enrollments, recent high school graduates still make up a relatively large part of Durham's student population. Durham does extensive work with local schools, orienting guidance counsellors (and even consulting them on the design of Durham publications), circulating information about the college and its programs and requirements, and providing its lab facilities for high school uses.

Since Oshawa has no university, Durham is quietly going about creating a kind of university inside the college. In 1989 it joined with Trent University, Wilfrid Laurier University, Ryerson Polytechnical Institute, and Atkinson College of York University to create DATE, the Durham Alliance for Training and Education. Through DATE, a growing number of university courses are offered on the Durham campus.

DATE attracts people who want a university degree but cannot leave Oshawa – a substantial number of single parents, for instance, are enrolled in DATE. Already a Trent B.A. can be completed at Durham. Meanwhile, Durham benefits from expanded library and other facilities.

Currently DATE has mostly part-time and summer programs, but Durham foresees it growing into a full-scale University Centre, where the universities will offer degree programs alongside Durham's diplomas.

Scholarships

Durham has never had a major fund-raising campaign, but it offers 98 scholarships annually (worth $30,000 in total) and 135 bursaries (also worth $30,000). The Financial Aid office reports it is able to give some assistance to most people who can demonstrate real financial need, even on an emergency short-term basis. Durham also offers athletic scholarships – twelve of them, worth $500 each to qualified varsity athletes.

Where to Live

Durham has a relatively small out-of-town student population, but a private developer, in cooperation with the college, has just opened a student residence adjacent to the main campus. It has fifty two-person suites, with bath and kitchenette, at a (1992-93) weekly rate of $85 per person. During the summer, it is intended to be a motel/seminar centre. The college runs a housing service to help students search for off-campus accommodation, but the housing situation in the area is said to be tight.

Sports and Recreation

Durham sports teams, the Lords and the Lady Lords (who sound due for a name change), compete in many varsity sports, and Durham claims no other Ontario college has done as well in intercollegiate competition. It's also one of the handful of colleges that give athletic scholarships. The athletic complex on the main campus has a 1,000-seat double gym, squash courts, a fitness gym, and outdoor playing fields. There is a sports medicine clinic in the complex. Student sports and intramurals are student-run.

The City

Oshawa (population 125,000) is a big manufacturing and industrial centre. Well known as the Canadian headquarters of General Motors, it is part of the rapidly growing eastern fringe of Metro Toronto. Oshawa itself offers lots of job placement prospects, and entertainment, recreation, shopping, and cultural facilities. Durham students are also in easy reach, by highway and GO commuter transit, of Metro Toronto.

Contact:

Durham College
2000 Simcoe St. North
P.O. Box 385
Oshawa, Ont. L1H 7K4
(416) 576-0210
(416) 571-5560 (TDD)
Toll-free: 1-800-668-5843

FANSHAWE COLLEGE: *Co-ops and Communities*

London

Size: Medium/Large

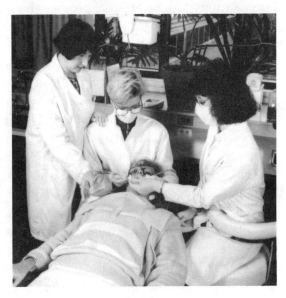

Dental Assistant and Dental Hygiene programs are part of Fanshawe's School of Health Sciences, which is closely linked to London's renowned teaching hospitals.

Fanshawe is a big college (about 7,500 students in post-secondary programs) serving a big city, so it has to offer a wide range of programs, and not surprisingly its mix of programs is pretty close to the system average. But it has a couple of distinguishing marks to set it off from the average.

Fanshawe claims to be the biggest co-op college anywhere in Canada. Along with Mohawk, it led the way into college co-op back in 1969, when the colleges were only a couple of years old. Co-op is popular with many students and a definite draw for Fanshawe. (In a survey, 90 per cent of Fanshawe Tourism and Travel students said the fact that it was a co-op course drew them to Fanshawe.) Only a third of its programs are co-op (and for many, co-op is an option), but Fanshawe offers co-op programs right across the college, not just in Business or Technology. For

137

many programs, Fanshawe is the only place a co-op option will be available.

Fanshawe's other distinguishing feature is a commitment to serving local communities. Colleges that are consolidating their services at one or two locations depend on good transit or travel ways and residences to serve people who live at a distance. But adults with jobs and families won't go "away" to college the way young students will, so colleges that are deeply involved in adult training tend to need local campuses in their students' communities. Fanshawe is big in adult training of all kinds, and its community campuses help it break down the distinction between adult and young students, and between skills training and post-secondary education. Fanshawe has always been strong in adult-literacy teaching, and it houses a Canada-wide database on adult literacy.

Fanshawe is determined to have a strong presence all through its four-county area. A new Oxford County campus has opened in Woodstock. There is already a campus in Simcoe. Fanshawe hopes soon to have a new and larger campus offering a wider range of services in St. Thomas.

The other community Fanshawe serves is London. London has some of the best teaching hospitals and medical facilities in Canada, so Fanshawe is strong in the health sciences. London has substantial automotive industries and a strong manufacturing base, so Fanshawe's technology programs are comprehensive and varied. Being in a large, attractive city with many amenities is part of what Fanshawe offers to hold local students and attract distant ones.

Worth Going For

- Strong co-op programs
- Music Industry Arts

Campuses

The main Fanshawe campus is a 100-acre plot in an industrial area on Oxford Street on the east side of London. It's really one large complex of buildings rather than a campus, though it has extensive sports fields at the rear. If you want a beautiful green campus, you have to visit the University of Western Ontario, across town, on the elegant side of London.

Fanshawe's new Woodstock campus is the key tenant in a city development there, and the City of Woodstock is going to add on a recreation complex, a public library, and other shared facilities.

Programs

Fanshawe offers General Arts and Sciences as a two-year diploma, About 400 students start GAS's first year, and all year the number grows as struggling students transfer in from other programs. But only about twenty students go on to the second year – most use GAS as a one-year stepping-stone to a career-oriented program.

Fanshawe hopes to cut down failure and dropout problems by increasing its students' opportunities to make well-informed program choices and to be well prepared for their courses. There are Foundation Year programs in Human Services, Health Sciences, and Technology. Completing a Foundation Year improves your credentials (and your preparedness) for most programs in these areas, but does not guarantee acceptance.

Applied Arts

Communications programs form the largest cluster in Applied Arts at Fanshawe. Two-year programs in Radio Broadcasting, Television Broadcasting, and Broadcast Journalism are supported by Fanshawe's own radio station, CIXX-FM, which broadcasts in a fifty-kilometre radius around the college, and by a complete closed-circuit television station. A related program unique to Fanshawe is Music Industry Arts, which has Production and Engineering options and trains graduates to work in music industry record production engineering. ("It started out years ago as a kind of airy-fairy Creative Electronics, and grew into this very focused, very practical studio production course," someone told

Fanshawe's music production studio, insulated from noise and vibration deep inside the Oxford Street campus, is home to a unique Music Industry Arts program.

me.) There is nothing like it elsewhere, and its well-equipped production studio also serves as Sony Canada's training facility. A two-year Audio-Visual Technician program is also offered.

The other stand-out Applied Arts group is Design, where all programs lead to three-year diplomas. All except Advertising Art are co-op. Other programs are Fashion Design and Fashion Merchandising, offered by few other colleges, and the unique-to-Fanshawe cluster of Industrial Design, Interior Design, Landscape Design, and Urban Design.

Fanshawe has a three-year diploma in Fine Arts, a two-year Photography diploma (with an optional third-year certificate), and a two-year Library Technician program.

Two-year Human Services programs include the standard Child and Youth Work, Early Childhood Education, Social Service Work, Developmental Service Work, Law and Security Administration, and Recreation Leadership, as well as a program in Fitness and Health Promotion. Linked to the Oxford St. ECE program is an excellent on-campus daycare centre for 150 children. (Woodstock also has daycare facilities.)

The Hospitality programs are Hotel and Restaurant Management and Tourism and Travel Counsellor. Both are co-op. Tourism is intense – with thirty-five hours of classes a week, it has one of the heaviest course loads in the system. Hospitality students gain experience in Fanshawe's Heliotrope restaurant as well as in their job placements.

Business

Fanshawe's Business programs begin with Basic Business, a first-year foundation for most business programs. Two-year diplomas emerging from Basic Business have options in Accounting (co-op), Finance (co-op), Information Systems (co-op), Insurance, Marketing (co-op), and Purchasing. There are also two-year programs in Computer Programming and Municipal Administration. Three-year Business Administration options, all co-op and all starting with Basic Business, are Accounting, Marketing, and Information Systems.

Office Administration programs start with a one-year foundation certificate, which can lead to diplomas in executive, legal, and medical Office Administration. Also available: certificates in Health Office Administration and Health Records Technician, and a two-year Legal Assistant diploma.

Health Sciences

Health Sciences programs include extensive practicum sessions in the excellent medical facilities of the London area. Nursing and Nursing Assistant are joined by Dental Assistant (one-year), Dental Hygiene (one-year, after a Dental Assistant diploma), Ambulance and Emergency Care (one-year), Radiography (two-year), Respiratory Therapy (two-year), and Med Lab Technology (three-year). There are also many specialist post-diploma courses for working nurses and nursing assistants.

Technology

Fanshawe's Technology programs are offered in several clusters: Civil/Architectural, Electrical/Electronic, Manufacturing Sciences, and Motive Power. All three-year Technologist programs and some Technician programs are co-op.

There are Technician and Technologist programs in Architectural Engineering. Civil Engineering programs are a three-year

Construction Engineering Management, a two-year Construction Engineering Supervision, a co-op Survey Technician, a certificate program in Construction Carpentry Techniques, and Civil Engineering Technology.

Technician programs in Electronic Engineering are the standard one, plus General Servicing and Robotics/Process Control. There is also a Technologist program and several post-diploma offerings, including unique biomedical options.

The Manufacturing Sciences programs are standard Technician and Technologist programs, plus specializations at the Technician level in Air Conditioning and Refrigeration, Design (co-op), and Metallurgical Engineering (co-op), and for Technologists in Mobile Equipment Technology, in Environmental Technology, and in Science Laboratory Technology. Fanshawe has a CAD-CAM training centre equipped with robotics technology.

The Motive Power division of Fanshawe is closely linked to southwestern Ontario's automobile and autoparts manufacturing industry. It includes Technician diplomas in Diesel, Automotive, and Parts Manufacturing, plus a large number of apprenticeship and modified apprenticeship programs in automobile maintenance. Only Centennial's School of Transportation has a greater range of automotive industry programs and courses.

Trades Training

Fanshawe has strong programs for apprenticeships (up to 2,000 enrollees a year) and offers skilled trades training in a large variety of fields. Training courses go on at several Fanshawe campuses.

Part-Time and Continuing Education

Fanshawe sees Outreach and local community service operations as fundamental parts of the college's mandate, and so the Continuing Education division is a large and closely integrated part of the college. Courses from many of the full-time programs can be taken on a part-time basis, and there are a great many additional courses, some mostly for interest, many more job-related and for credit.

Getting in the Door

Fanshawe has not developed a single information telephone number. Calendars are bulky, small-print, and extremely detailed.

The main building of the Oxford Street campus is huge, and because several additions and expansions have been made to it, it's not easy to find your way around it. Try entering at the southeast corner to find an Information counter, and ask lots of questions.

Support Services

Fanshawe offers most of the usual Student Support services. The Foundation Year programs were developed as part of Fanshawe's strategy to encourage student success. There are learning labs for mathematics and languages.

Connections

Fanshawe thinks student preparedness is important for college entrants – that you ought to have a clear idea what you are getting into. So, in addition to its preparatory programs for students who have already arrived at Fanshawe, it runs extensive information programs with high schools and elementary schools.

College officials throughout the system despair of the Ontario universities' lack of interest in college-university cooperation. "Ivy-league" universities tend to be particularly sceptical of any arrangements that might ease student transfer between colleges and universities. As a result, while Fanshawe has reached some agreements with the University of Western Ontario, it is also seeking "hungrier" universities to deal with. Meanwhile, Social Service Work graduates can get automatic credit toward a UWO

Bachelor of Social Science, and Fanshawe and Western agreed late in 1992 to work toward joint degree/diploma offerings in Nursing and in Engineering Technology. But these achievements took years.

Scholarships

Fanshawe has a $5-million capital campaign under way, and has raised most of it already. The money is earmarked for an athletics centre, for library and learning resources, *and* for scholarships and bursaries. So the amount of money available for students should soon be growing.

Where to Live

Drawn by its unique programs, its co-op opportunities, and London itself, almost half of Fanshawe students come from outside the college's official catchment area. Fanshawe has no residences and no plans to build any, but housing is abundantly available in the city, and the college maintains an off-campus housing registry and a housing-mediation service for landlord and tenant disputes over student housing.

Sports and Recreation

Fanshawe has the Falcons varsity sports teams and many intramural programs, plus fitness and recreation activities. Current facilities include two gyms, a fitness centre, and outdoor fields. An athletic centre is planned for the Oxford Street campus in London when fund-raising is completed, and the new Woodstock campus will be linked to civic recreation facilities.

The Fanshawe Student Union owns and operates its own Student Centre. It has student offices, a conference room, student newspaper facilities, a small variety store and snack bar, a games area, a licensed lounge, and a common room with a performance stage and a large-screen television. The campus is large enough to be well equipped with clubs, activities, and recreation, and the city of London is just down the street.

The City

With more than 300,000 people, London is one of Ontario's largest cities and the urban centre for most of southwestern Ontario. With a strong British-immigrant background (it was founded as a future capital of Ontario, which is how it got its name), London is still not as ethnically diverse as many Ontario cities.

Nicknamed the "Forest City" for its parks and tree-lined streets, London is a prosperous, comfortable, attractive city. It also has a solid industrial base. Generally, the western side of the city, which has the university and the research hospitals, is the well-to-do side. Fanshawe is on the east side, which is plainer and more industrial.

Transit connections around the city and to other parts of Ontario are good. London offers a wide range of entertainment, cultural activities, shopping, sports, and recreation. Fanshawe is unusual among the colleges in that it supports several musical groups: the London Fanshawe Symphonic Chorus, the Concert Players, the Gerald Fagan Singers, and the Woodstock Fanshawe Singers.

Contact:

Fanshawe College
1460 Oxford Street East
P.O. Box 4005
London, Ont. N5W 5H1
(519) 452-4100

Surviving – Ten Tips

I asked a lot of college students and grads – all ages, all backgrounds, all program areas – what advice they give to people coming to college. These are the kind of things they said, roughly in order of frequency.

1. "Find your support group."
   It will probably be the other people in your program who will lend you notes, trade information, keep you sane. You might find support in a college club, in the student society, in a sports team. But find it. Don't try doing college on your own.
2. "Learn some study skills."
   Most colleges have workshops and classes called Study Skills, Master Student, Success Workshops, whatever. Particularly if you have been out of school a while, do it. You learn a little about how to study, how to take notes, how to manage your time, how to handle the stress. Most students say it can make a big difference.
3. "Get involved in college life."
   Clubs, sports, student government, whatever works for you. Most student government is not very political – it's more about doing things, and it's not hard to get involved if you want to. You find out what's going on, you learn some things, you start to feel part of the place. It even looks good on the resumé.
4. "Know what you want to do."
   This one is tough – how do you know you know what you want? But researching your choice helps. And a lot of people said that feeling confident that this was really the field for them helped more than anything. (But see #5 – #4 and #5 seem to be opposites, but several people said both.)

5. "Remember: you can fail in one program and blossom in another." Some colleges estimate 30 per cent of students enroll in the wrong program. They didn't know what they were doing, they let someone else choose for them – or it just didn't turn out the way they hoped. The point is – don't graduate from the wrong program (even if you are passing).

6. "Use the services."
   Faculty advisors, counsellors, peer tutoring, health services, legal aid, special-needs consultants, the weight room, and more: they are all there, and you ought to use them. Some people said women are smarter about this, while the men go all John Wayne – trying to be strong and silent and self-reliant. Others said no, nobody asks for enough help.

7. "Get your life in order."
   Oh sure. But college can be intense. It helps if you know where the money will come from, that your family is with you on this, that you have Plan B when the stress builds up. #6 might help.

8. "Don't spend all your OSAP money before Hallowe'en."
   Student-loan money comes in a big chunk in the fall. They say waiters in the student pubs do very well on tips around then. But come February, you are going to need some of that money.

9. "Go to class."
   One prof said there's no big secret. If you go to class, take notes, do the assignments, then you will pass. (On the other hand, if you already know everything in that course, don't waste time and bore yourself silly. Talk to the prof about an exemption.)

10. "You can learn to handle the stress."
    Several people wanted to add this one, more or less in addition to any or all of the first nine.

GEORGE BROWN COLLEGE: *The City College*

Toronto

Size: Medium / Large

George Brown calls itself "The City College." Many George Brown programs link students directly to downtown industries and services.

George Brown College can make you proud of Toronto – even if you hate Hogtown. It's the "City College" and it draws on much of the best of the big city. On a good day, George Brown looks like Toronto on fast-forward.

George Brown doesn't have ivy-covered buildings on a grassy campus. Unless you are part of it, it almost vanishes into the city. It's a streetcar and subway operation, spread around in an odd collection of buildings in some lively downtown neighbourhoods. And people attending George Brown are just as diverse. They tend to have three jobs and two languages. They bring the college the ethnocultural mix of a hundred immigrant communities, and they run at the pace of the big city.

At its best, George Brown takes Toronto's achievements as a challenge. "Right here in Toronto is the biggest, most sophisticated social service network in the country," says the head of its

Community Services Division. "If we don't have the best programs in those areas, what's wrong with us?" The best departments of George Brown seem to think that way. With all the city
has to offer, they think being in the forefront is an obligation, not a
boast.

Mostly, George Brown isn't the power-broking, BMW-driving,
yuppie Toronto the rest of the country loves to hate. The college
grew out of the blue-collar Provincial Institute of Trades. It still
has the biggest apprenticeship program in Canada, and the skilled
trades and upgrading side are a big part of its operation. That may
become a problem for the college. The federal government has
been cutting back the labour-market training commitments that
cover the cost of many skills-training projects. Nobody knows if
Ontario will find the money to take over, so any college that does a
lot of trades training has to wonder where the money will come
from. But trades are still important to what George Brown does
and is, and it is the only college with a union-affiliated School of
Labour.

Still, George Brown has grown far beyond its trade-school
roots. Its Technology programs produce specialists in fields like
Electronic Instrumentation and Computer-aided Product
Design. The world-famous School of Hospitality trains whiz-kid
chefs for Toronto's elegant bistros (as well as staff for hot,
crowded institutional kitchens). George Brown has some programs tied into Toronto's leading-edge fashion and design industries, and others that lead to the Bay Street financial centre a few
blocks away. It has specialized Health Science programs no one
else in the country offers.

On the whole, though, George Brown seems more Queen
Street than Rosedale – even in the drop-dead sophistication of its
own restaurant, Plumer's. "We're a down-and-dirty, come in and
get comfortable place," brags one staffer. George Brown looks like
a place for people who want to *work*.

Worth Going For

- The city feel – but only if you like the big-city life
- The School of Hospitality
- Programs and services for the deaf

Campuses

The St. James campus is a big building, filling a city block, that fronts on King Street East. The Theatre building is a bit further east, and the School of Hospitality has its own new premises just across Adelaide Street East.

Nightingale Campus on Murray Street, close by the hospitals of University Avenue, has some Community Service and post-diploma Nursing programs. The Kensington Campus, on Nassau Street in Kensington Market, was once the School of Hospitality but now houses only Fashion programs and English as a Second Language. George Brown plans more consolidation, so Kensington may continue to shrink. Casa Loma Campus, a cluster of buildings near Davenport and Spadina, down the hill from Casa Loma, the grandiose castle home of a 1900s financial magnate, has Technology, Health Sciences, and a small Applied Arts component.

Programs

George Brown has large enrollments quite evenly divided among all areas. The only unusually large department is Health Sciences, which is one of the largest Health Science departments in the college system, with more than 1,300 students enrolled. In 1992 George Brown stopped offering co-op work terms, but it makes extensive use of field placements and other kinds of (unpaid) job experiences.

The college has preparatory courses for those lacking the requirements for college entrance. General Arts and Science can be taken on a full-time or part-time basis, and there are Pre-Health and Pre-Technology programs.

Applied Arts

Instead of the standard Social Service Work, George Brown offers an entire cluster of related programs, many of them unique to the college. Diploma programs include Activation Co-ordinator/Gerontology (roughly, someone who runs activity programs for the elderly), Community Worker, Counsellor/Advocate for Assaulted Women and Children, Intervenor for the Deaf/Blind (unique in Canada), and Human Services Counsellor (with options in Addictions, Mental Health, and Criminal Justice). More familiar programs include Child and Youth Work, Early Childhood Education, a one-year Daycare Assistant certificate program, Health Care Aide, and Support Care.

Community Service programs at George Brown include substantial fieldwork. The ECE program is linked to fifty daycare centres, eight of them college-run. It includes equal amounts of class time and field experience.

The Fashion Division offers Creative Fashion Design and Fashion Management, both of which include extensive use of computers. Other programs are Furniture Production and Design, a three-year Jewellery Arts program, and Ceramics, plus shorter courses in Apparel Pattern Drafting, Upholstery, Furniture Finishing, Gem Setting, Jewellery Repair, Gemmology, and Sewing Machine Technician. Among the colleges, only Sheridan has an equivalent range of programs and facilities.

There is a strong Graphic Arts Division, closely connected to the Toronto design and printing industry and built around a comprehensive three-year Graphic Design diploma, a two-year Graphic Sign Design program, and a two-year Technician and a three-year Technologist program in Printing. These are supported by shorter certificate programs in Desktop Publishing, Commercial Art, Offset Printing, Screen Process Printing, and Signwriting.

A three-year program in Theatre Arts trains actors for stage performance.

On-screen design work is standard practice for students in George Brown's Creative Fashion Design program.

Business

Business at George Brown includes the standard college programs as well as some special offerings. Some can be completed rapidly by a continuous schedule with no summer breaks.

The basic Business and Business Administration courses all share a common first year. Two-year diploma programs are available in General Business, Accounting, Information Systems, Marketing, and Distribution Management, and three-year options are available in Accounting, Marketing, and Information Systems.

Specialized Business programs at George Brown include Health Records Technician (one-year) and Administration (two-year), Human Resources Management, Insurance, Investment Sales Assistant (the only such college program in Canada), Property Management, and Small Business Administration. There are also three post-diploma programs: International Trade, Sports Marketing, and Workers' Compensation Claims Management.

George Brown is the only college training Official Court Reporters for courtroom work. The two-year program includes summer semesters. Graduates are eligible to write the Chartered Shorthand Reporters Association exam.

Health Sciences

The three-year Nursing program and one-year Nursing Assistant program include practical experience in Toronto's teaching hospitals, and George Brown also offers qualified nurses short specialized post-diploma programs in several fields.

The Dental Assistant and Dental Hygiene programs are supplemented by two unique three-year programs, Denture Therapy, which specializes in making and fitting dentures, and Dental Technology, which covers all kinds of orthodontic appliances.

Other health sciences programs unique to George Brown are a three-year Chiropody program, offered in cooperation with the Michener Institute for Applied Health Sciences, an Orthotic/Prosthetic Technician program, which focuses on the making of artificial limbs and braces, a post-diploma Clinical Methods in Orthotics and Prosthetics, and a certificate course in Hearing Instrument Dispensing. Fitness and Lifestyle Management is a two-year program to train staff for community and private health and fitness centres.

Technology

George Brown offers Technology programs in several clusters. Architectural Engineering includes Technician and Technologist programs in Architecture and Drafting, Civil Engineering, and Construction Engineering.

There are Technician and Technologist programs in Electrical and in Electronic Engineering, and in Instrumentation Engineering.

Mechanical Engineering programs are the heart of George Brown's Technology department. After a common first year, students can complete a Technician diploma in Drafting Design,

Product Design, Tool and Die Making, or Tool Design, after which a third year (in Design) can be completed for a Technologist diploma. There is also a Technician program in Electro-Mechanical Engineering, and Technician and Technologist programs in Air Conditioning/Refrigeration.

The Stationary Power Plant Engineering program is the only one in Ontario qualifying grads for 3rd class certification (4th class is also available).

The Technology school has certificate programs in Heating, Appliance Servicing, Gas Fitting, Machine Shop, Refrigeration/Air Conditioning, and Welding. It also offers the only Piano Technician program in Canada and a program in Residential Construction Management.

Hospitality

Hospitality is a separate school at George Brown, and the School of Hospitality has an international reputation. It has its own new Hospitality Centre, partly funded by industry donations, and it has produced many of the "star" chefs of Toronto's prestigious restaurants. The core programs are the two-year programs in Hotel Management, Food and Beverage Management, and Culinary Management, and the one-year Chef Training certificate. These are supported by many short specialized courses and post-diploma training in such fields as Italian Culinary Arts (which includes a field placement in the United States or in Italy) and Professional Wine Service. Hospitality also offers training in many food-service trades: baking, bartending, meatcutting, and so on. A shop in the School of Hospitality lobby sells baked goods produced by the classes.

Trades Training

Building on its strength in mechanical and civil engineering technology, George Brown offers training in many of the skilled trades: Gas Fitter, Carpenter, Mason, Heating Technician. In addition, George Brown runs the classroom side of the largest number of apprenticeship programs of any of the colleges, from Baking and Hairdressing to Ironwork and TV Servicing.

Part-Time and Continuing Education

George Brown has a large part-time program, which includes many of the programs offered on a full-time basis, and many advanced courses for diploma-holders, as well as starter courses and general interest offerings.

Getting in the Door

George Brown has one of the best telephone information services in the college system, with one central phone number (and 800 service for outside Toronto) providing quick access to most information that outsiders will need. The Liaison Office offers tours and orientation to the college, with special services available for deaf and hard-of-hearing clients and for students with learning disabilities. Free career-planning workshops are offered regularly.

Commercial parking lots are available around George Brown's downtown campuses, but they're expensive. On the other hand, transit connections are excellent. Special parking and transit services are available for students living with disabilities. Finding the entrance to the St. James campus is easy, and there is an Information window just to the left inside. Casa Loma, with several buildings on adjacent streets, is harder to find, so ask for directions.

Support Services

George Brown offers the full range of support and counselling services to students. It has a particular commitment to deaf and hearing-impaired students, who are guaranteed equal opportunity to participate in all programs. George Brown attracts about a quarter of all the deaf and hearing-impaired students doing post-secondary studies in Canada. It offers College Preparation and College

Orientation for the deaf and hard-of-hearing, a Deaf Futures course, and housing-search and support services. TTY phone service is available. Of course, Special Needs services are also available for people with other disabilities.

George Brown also pioneered in the creation of an Access Division, intended to open doors for all those who have difficulty moving into college programs. Access offers many upgrading and preparatory programs. It has a very well-developed centre for career counselling and career development, open (on a fee-paying basis) to all and able to do extensive testing and assessment for people at any stage of life. The Access Centre also provides support for deaf and learning-disabled students.

Connections

George Brown has formal agreements with the Toronto Board of Education, the Metro Toronto Separate School Board, and the York Board of Education. Graduates from those schools may be entitled to advanced standing in George Brown programs. George Brown graduates in various programs can receive credit toward degrees (or other certifications) from Queen's University, the University of Western Ontario, McMaster, York, Ryerson Polytechnical Institute, Lakehead, Rochester Institute of Technology, Nova Scotia College of Art and Design, and the National Technical Institute for the Deaf in Rochester, N.Y.

Scholarships

The George Brown Foundation does fund-raising for specific projects, including the new School of Hospitality building. Scholarships and awards worth more than $200,000 are offered each year to students entering second and third year. Alumni activities are run by some departments – Hospitality's is particularly active.

Where to Live

Although 73 per cent of its students come from outside the city of Toronto, George Brown has no residences. Private accommodation is abundant in Toronto, but it is expensive. The George Brown Housing Registry – office at the St. James Campus – is linked to the systems at University of Toronto and Ryerson, and it covers most of the Metropolitan area, not just the downtown core. Information on housing for the deaf and hard-of-hearing is also available.

Sports and Recreation

The St. James, Casa Loma, and Kensington campuses all have gyms with weight training and/or Nautilus facilities. The Athletics department runs recreation programs for individuals and intramural sports. The intercollegiate varsity sports teams, the Huskies, play in twelve sports, from soccer to cross-country running.

The Students Administrative Council (SAC) runs student stores at St. James and Nightingale, a campus paper and internal radio station, and games rooms at all campuses. George Brown employs a Student Life manager who can act as student advocate in dealing with the college.

SAC runs about thirty pub-night activities a year. But with Toronto just outside the door – and almost 60 per cent of George Brown students holding down jobs while they go to school – most recreation goes on outside the college.

The City

It's Toronto. Everyone already has his or her own opinion about Toronto, and no one can tell you whether to love or hate it. Some college students want the bright lights, and others want to study anywhere *but* Toronto.

There are a couple of things to consider. On the one hand, Toronto is pretty much unlimited in the range of entertainment, recreation, cultural life, housing, shopping, job placements, and career alternatives that it can offer college students – and when you are at George Brown, most of it is right in front of you. On the other hand, living in Toronto is probably going to be more expensive than other college communities.

Contact:

The Enquiry Centre
George Brown College
P.O. Box 1015, Station B
Toronto, Ont. M5T 2T9
(416) 867-2464
Toll free: 1-800-263-8995
Deaf / Hard-of-hearing: (416) 864-0535

Student Associations

College student governments tend to be service-oriented more than political. Some are pretty traditional – they run pub nights and sports events. Others work with counsellors and health staff on things like substance-abuse programs or anti-stress seminars. Or they run the Peer Tutoring and Orientation. A few have Ombudsmen to look into student complaints about the college. They all say they are the first place a student should go for help.

Some student governments get reps from all program areas. Others are dominated by Marketing (or sometimes Public Relations) students who run their campaigns like a class project. Generally you don't have to be a campus politician to get involved. There are positions you don't have to run for, and you might even get paid. It can be great administrative and people-skills experience. A couple of colleges even offer Leadership Training and a Psych credit for student government officers.

Hot trend: mature students getting involved. Northern recently had a fifty-three-year-old Student President.

GEORGIAN COLLEGE: *Finding Special Niches*

Barrie

Size: Medium

Brenda Roy, a student in Georgian's Jewellery and Metals program, won a Diamonds International Award for her diamond and acrylic bracelet, which toured world fashion centres in 1992.

Georgian College is bigger than it "ought" to be. No one thinks of Barrie as a major educational centre, and the region that Georgian serves isn't particularly heavily populated. Despite that, Georgian keeps attracting more students than some colleges in bigger centres.

Why? Location, luck, and hustle. Georgian is just outside the Golden Horseshoe – close enough for access to Metro Toronto, far enough away to offer lower living costs and a more relaxed pace. Georgian also got in on the ground floor of several programs that grew to national prominence. As the colleges started specializing, it led the way into several unique program areas.

But competitive hustle must have played a part, too. Otherwise, why would Georgian dominate all the programs related to Great Lakes shipping, when there are four other colleges (Niagara, St. Lawrence, Sault, and Confederation) within earshot of the lakers'

159

foghorns? Why is auto-dealership training in Barrie instead of at colleges in car-industry cities like Windsor, Oakville, or Oshawa? Why is it a centre for airport management? Simply by spotting opportunities, Georgian was able to create several nationally recognized training programs.

Georgian's new president, Bruce Hill, says Georgian is now big enough with about 4,700 full-time students. He says Georgian's priorities should now be quality of teaching and student success – the issues for the 1990s throughout the education system.

Worth Going For

- Canadian Automotive Institute
- Canadian Aviation Institute
- The Marine programs

Campuses

Instead of consolidating, Georgian is attempting to provide a wide range of programs on three campuses. The main campus, with about 3,000 students, is attractively laid out on a roomy site on the northern edge of Barrie, close to Highway 400. It has most of Georgian's unique programs. There is also a substantial campus in Orillia, with close to a thousand students and programs in Human Service, Business, and Marine Recreation. The slightly smaller Owen Sound campus offers a variety of programs, notably Marine Engineering and Navigation.

Programs

Georgian has slightly larger than usual enrollments in Business and Health Science, and it is smaller than the college system average in Applied Arts and Technology.

As well as the usual upgrading and preparatory programs,

Georgian offers one- or two-year General Arts and Science, for those uncertain of a program choice or seeking general academic preparation. There is also a one-semester Interim GAS starting in January, and a Pre-Health GAS for students aiming at Health Science programs.

Georgian emphasizes co-op learning. With more than 60 per cent of its full-time students participating in co-op programs, it claims to be the second-largest co-op college in Canada. It has also been developing a number of post-diploma programs in specialized fields.

Applied Arts

The School of Design and Visual Arts has a strong and well-integrated cluster of programs. All programs share a common Foundation Year. Creative Arts, training professional artists in sculpture, painting, and printmaking, has two- and three-year options. There are also three-year Graphic Design, Industrial Design, and Interior Design programs, plus a combined program offering the fundamentals of both Creative Arts and Graphic Design. Students in all these programs may also take a wide variety of art electives. There is also a three-year co-op program in Jewellery and Metals. The training includes preparation for the commercial jewellery industry, but many graduates (most are women and mature students) aim to start their own craft studios.

Georgian's small cluster of Human Service programs includes Early Childhood Education, Early Childhood Assistant (one-year), and Developmental Service Work. Law and Security Administration and two-year Advertising are offered through the School of Business.

Post-diploma courses are offered for Research Analysts in business, industry, education, and community service; in Recreation for Special Populations, which prepares social-science graduates for work with various special-needs or disabled groups; and for Communicative Disorders Assistant, which prepares social-service graduates to assist Speech-Language Pathologists or Audiologists.

Business

Georgian's stand-out business program is Business Administration – Automotive Marketing, and you can find the sleek new Canadian Automotive Institute at the Barrie campus by all the high-performance cars in the parking lot. It is the only institution in Canada with programs specifically aimed at training for the automotive marketing industry. It is linked to Automotive Dealers Associations and teaches in English and bilingually for francophone students.

Students come from all over Canada and do their co-op placements throughout the country and overseas, not only in auto dealerships, but also with manufacturers and auto service retailers. About half the students are DKs – dealers' kids – who will probably go home to run the family car-dealership. So far only 15 per cent are women, although the industry needs more women. Each September the Centre presents the largest outdoor auto show in Canada, largely student-run and attracting more than 20,000 visitors to the campus over three days.

Georgian also offers two-year Business and three-year Business Administration diplomas, with options in Accounting and Marketing. All are co-op, and Georgian has developed a common first year for them. There are co-op programs for Computer Programmer (two-year) and Computer Programmer/Analyst (three-year), and there is a single, apparently isolated program in Fashion Merchandising.

The Hospitality and Tourism School offers Culinary Management, two-year Hotel and Resort Operations and three-year Hotel and Resort Administration, plus Tourism Management, which trains planners and consultants to the travel, resort, and convention industry. All are co-op. Linked to the school is the Georgian Dining Room on the Barrie Campus, and the Kempenfelt Conference Centre, a specialized residential management-training centre and resort on Lake Simcoe, which is home to the Canadian Tourism Management Centre.

Health Sciences

Georgian offers Nursing, Nursing Assistant, Dental Assistant, and Dental Hygiene programs, and short courses in Health Care Aide and Home Support. (See also the post-diploma programs discussed under Applied Arts above.) A unique Georgian offering is a two-year co-op Ophthalmic Dispenser program, which teaches the making and dispensing of contact lenses, spectacles, and low-vision aids. This program is linked to the Canadian Optical Institute, which is located on the Barrie campus, and it prepares students to write the examinations of the Ontario Board of Ophthalmic Dispensers.

Technology

Georgian offers two unique Technology clusters: Civil Aviation and Marine.

The Civil Aviation Institute does not train pilots – for that, it's Seneca, Sault, or Confederation, and Canadore for helicopters. Georgian specializes in ground operations, with three-year co-op programs in Airport Management and Operations, Air Carrier Management and Operations, and Air Traffic Services, and it draws students from all over Canada. The first two years are common. There are no special selection criteria, and dropout rates in the first year are high. Air Traffic Services grads must still complete Transport Canada's Air Traffic Control school in Cornwall, but the diploma should improve their chances of both entering and passing.

"We offer the best Marine training in Canada," says the Georgian calendar bluntly. (St. Lawrence College's Marine Engineering programs at Cornwall are the only competition in Ontario, and they are heavily oriented toward naval engineers.) At Owen Sound, co-op programs in Marine Engineering Technology and Marine Technology-Navigation train shipboard engineering officers and navigational officers for Great Lakes and seagoing merchant vessels. Job and pay prospects are excellent. There are also certificate programs for seamen and engineering staff. At Orillia, a

Grads of the Marine Technology-Recreation program at Georgian's Orillia campus often find work with marinas, manufacturers, and boat dealers in the nearby Muskoka resort district.

third program, Marine Technology-Recreation, trains retail marina operators and staff in both boat servicing and marketing.

Georgian also offers Technician and Technologist programs in Civil, Electrical/Electronic (with an option in control systems), Environmental Engineering, and Mechanical Engineering (options in Drafting, Industrial, Tool and Die), plus a Survey Technician and a specialized Automotive Manufacturing Technology program. All are co-op.

Trades Training

Georgian offers skilled trades certification and the in-school part of apprenticeship training in a wide range of industrial, construction, and marine trades.

Part-Time and Continuing Education

At its three main campuses and several outreach campuses, Georgian offers many courses from its diploma programs on a part-time basis. There are also many courses available only through Con Ed, including a cluster of gerontology and other post-diploma human service certificates, nursing upgrades, creative art courses, and many business and computer courses.

Getting in the Door

Access to the main campus is well signposted and the main entry is easy to find. There is an information booth at the door.

During the summer, before classes begin, Georgian offers Preview Sessions, when new students are introduced to the campus, programs and services, and staff. Much of this is run by "Student Peer Ambassadors," and special activities are arranged for parents accompanying new students.

Support Services

In support of its new focus on quality rather than growth, Georgian is working intensively on improving communication between programs and faculty at its various campuses. It is exploring new techniques for self-directed learning and multi-media instruction (which usually means learning on and with computers). It has opened a Teacher Centre and given the faculty increased control over its own professional development, and it is seeking to orient all its programming to predetermined "Learning Outcomes." (About "Learning Outcomes," see "The Jargon" in Part One.)

Georgian may have a way to go in these areas. Some programs still seem isolated, without common years or supporting clusters, and others are scattered across two or more campuses. But the need to draw students from outside its own area encourages Georgian to be a student-centred college.

Connections

Georgian and nine school boards in its area have negotiated

linkages that enable high school students to enter the college with advanced standing.

The Automotive Marketing program is linked to (and modelled on) the Northwood Institute, a Michigan-based college that specializes in automotive industry programs. Successful Georgian grads can complete a Northwood degree in Business Administration in one year, and they can also enter automotive studies at the University of Windsor. The Civil Aviation programs are linked to two universities in the United States and one in Britain. Tourism grads can proceed to the Rochester Institute of Technology and Nursing grads to two New York State universities.

Scholarships

The Automotive Centre has $100,000 in scholarships and bursaries for entering students and at each year of the program. This is actually larger than the amount ($80,000) offered in the rest of the college, but the Georgian College Foundation has an active fund-raising program, and the scholarship and bursary fund is expected to grow. Georgian also has some athletic scholarships. For details on awards, contact the Resources Development Office.

Where to Live

Georgian reports that only 27 per cent of Georgian students come from outside its catchment area, so they must be heavily concentrated in its specialty programs. A few years ago, Georgian College found a surprising solution to the cost of building residences, now being adopted at several other colleges. The Georgian Green student residence, close by the Barrie campus, has been built and is managed by a private developer. It houses Georgian students, apartment-style, but it is entirely independent of the college itself. The Housing Service also has a computerized inventory of private housing and will assist housing searches in Barrie, Orillia, and Owen Sound.

Sports and Recreation

Georgian has a small gym and limited recreation facilities, but it has intercollegiate varsity sports teams (the Grizzlies), intramural sports, and recreational programs. It is also one of the colleges that offers athletic scholarships.

The Student Council organizes many activities and runs the Last Class pub on the Barrie campus.

The City

Barrie, with more than 50,000 people, is an industrial centre with several large and medium employers. It is also a service centre for the rural surroundings and the nearby recreational districts. It is close to Georgian Bay, the Muskokas, and most of southern Ontario's ski hills, and it is large enough to support a full range of entertainment, shopping, and recreation. So, like Fleming and a few others, Georgian promotes itself as a college that offers reasonably priced accommodation and great recreational potential, and is close enough to Toronto for good job and co-op placements.

Contact:

Georgian College
One Georgian Drive
Barrie, Ont. L4M 3X9
(705) 728-1951
Orillia: (705) 325-2705
Owen Sound: (519) 376-0682

How to Prepare – College Students' Advice to High School Students

I asked a lot of college students what they say about college to their younger brothers and sisters, their nieces and nephews, and the neighbours' kids. Try asking some students yourself.

1. "Keep up your English and your math."
   Amazing, how often I heard that. With solid English and math, you can get into pretty much any program and career path you want. (Though if it's Technology you are aiming at, you should do tech math and probably physics too.)
2. "Life ain't over if you made some wrong move."
   Colleges try to take people as they are, not to make everyone fit some set of rules. If you missed some prerequisite, or if your math is weak, or even if you dropped out in Grade 9, the colleges can help you make it up. It won't take forever.
3. "Do some volunteer work."
   Particularly for the human service fields, for two reasons. First, it's as good a way as any to find out what it's really like in that kind of career. Second, many of the social service programs have hundreds of applicants for every place, and you may need some volunteer credentials to get in.
4. "Check out careers."
   People often said this – but not how to do it. Bully your guidance counsellor. High school co-ops or job shadowing can be good. Canada Employment Centres have a book called *Job Futures* about every kind of career and its prospects. Volunteer or part-time work is good in some fields. Just keep asking.
5. "Keep up your English and your math."
   This is worth repeating.

6. "It's not the rest of your life."
   Your choice of some two- or three-year diploma is not going to lock you into the same job for the rest of your life. These days, people change and so do jobs. You might come back to college, or to university. You might go on to do something completely different.
7. "Do your work."
   The colleges want to get you ready to hold down a job, and they only have you for a couple of years. They pile quite a bit of work on, and they keep you busy. If you are used to doing homework, you'll get used to college.
8. "Choose college or university for what *you* want."
   If you have the choice to make, forget snobbery – there are too many unemployed B.A.s for that. Forget fear, too – university isn't that hard if you really want to be there. But college and university are two different places. If you are bright and bookish, university can be a good place to find yourself, to explore the meaning of life, to consider the secrets of the universe. But that could drive you crazy if you're goal-oriented, practical, and in a hurry to get somewhere. A career-oriented college program could be just your thing. And relax – choosing university *or* college doesn't mean you can't go to the other later.
9. "Consider GAS."
   People struggling or failing in college often get pointed toward General Arts and Science, so it has a bad rep – "for dummies." Too bad. I hear that a year in GAS is a good way to have a look around, pick up some useful credits, and have a good time before settling on a career-related program. A GAS diploma can be a stepping-stone to university, too. GAS keeps your options open, and for many people that's a good thing.
10. "Keep up your English and your math."

HUMBER COLLEGE: *Aiming for the High End*

Etobicoke

Size: Large

One of the largest colleges in North America, Humber has an international reputation for innovation. Recent expansion has given a new look to the North campus in Etobicoke.

A lot of people at Humber will let you know they think it's the best college around. They tend to assume there are two systems of Ontario colleges: Humber – and all the rest. Quite a few people at other colleges are ready to agree that Humber is often two steps ahead of the pack. It's aggressive and entrepreneurial about creating opportunities, they say. It innovates.

Robert Gordon, Humber's longtime president, says Humber is like Singapore. Singapore didn't start with rich resources. Its people had to get smart and work hard, and now it is prosperous and admired. Similarly, Humber started with little. Its Etobicoke-York catchment area on the west side of Metro Toronto is not very big. The number of high school grads in Humber's region actually shrank all through the 1980s. But instead of getting smaller, Humber did something right, because it grew and grew, to become (along with Seneca) one of the two biggest colleges in the system: close to 12,000 people in diploma-track programs.

Humber is the least community-rooted of Ontario's colleges, for it sees itself with an international rather than a local mandate. Four out of five full-time Humber students come from outside its local area. It attracts university graduates and others with advanced training whom the colleges have not traditionally considered as their market. (More than 20 per cent of Humber students have university experience.) People come to Humber because they want to, not because it is in the neighbourhood.

What draws them? Programs, lots of programs, for one thing. Humber has programs in every area and probably more unique programs than any other college. It innovated accelerated programs that allow university graduates and others with established credentials to earn a college diploma in a short, intensive program. It nailed down strong connections to business and industry, networked with top American colleges, loaned its expertise to colleges all over the world. All those things helped Humber attract good faculty, and what's been called "the best professional development in North America" keeps them motivated. It is the only college in Canada invited to join the prestigious American-based League for Innovation in the Community College.

Its programs frequently aim for the "high end" of the careers they serve, and Humber hustles for motivated students to fill them, with some of the best entrance scholarships in the Ontario college system. Altogether, good planning and good management helped Humber expand both its size and its reputation way beyond expectations.

Is there a drawback to all this? I found the staff at Humber keen to talk about their services to business, their international projects, their connections to California and Florida. It took an effort to get the subject around to the ordinary student coming in the door.

And speaking of doors, I had a hard time *finding* the front door at Humber. Humber has a Business and Industry Services Centre, doing a $30 million-a-year business selling training to top-drawer corporations all over Canada. At the Centre, they talk all the hot phrases: Total Quality Management, customer satisfaction, a client-driven operation. The Centre has its own building, free parking, an elegant lobby, all the services business needs right in one place. There's no need for the suits to walk down locker-lined corridors or rub shoulders with students.

But for students and other normal people, it's hard to be sure which is the main entrance of Humber's main campus. There's no free parking there. Humber has only just started to gather together the essential student services – admissions, counselling, housing, financial aid – and they are not in the building marked "Main Entrance." Is Humber so busy polishing its corporate connections and its international reputation that it is taking for granted its real clients?

Well, yes and no. Humber is not for everyone. It has been dropping most of its upgrading programs for students who graduated from high school with a diploma at the Basic Level and for adults who lack the credentials for college entrance. "If twelve years of remediation don't work, what can Humber do?" I was told there. It was the only time I heard an Ontario college official say anything like that. Most colleges are proud of being accessible to nearly anyone who comes looking for help – even if they won't be ready for college programs for years.

Humber seems to have decided there is a place for a college aimed more at the bright, well-educated, maybe even well-to-do students, the people with lots of options and unlimited horizons. Those students appreciate the competitive, fast-moving style of Humber. It stretches and challenges them, and they respond.

If you already feel challenged enough, and maybe want a more supportive atmosphere, there are other colleges more interested in you than Humber. But Humber has probably done more than any other college to establish college as a high-end alternative, a first choice for people who do have options.

Worth Going For

- Unique post-diploma programs for college and university graduates
- Music – the jazz program

Campuses

North Campus, the main Humber campus, is just off Highway 27 near Finch in a zone of industrial malls and corporate centres north of the Lester B. Pearson Airport. Its low-rise, blue-glass façade fits right in. North Campus has most of Humber's full- and part-time programs, the residence, the main Resource Centre, and the Technology Centre. An attractive feature beside North Campus is the Humber Arboretum, 250 acres of paths, ponds, and green space. The Arboretum is a great place to escape to when North Campus seems too big and busy.

Lakeshore Campus, on the edge of Lake Ontario near the foot of Kipling, has about 1,500 students in Community Service and Business programs. Humber also has several outreach facilities around Etobicoke and York, including The Centre for Transportation Training near the airport, Theatre Humber on the Queensway, and the Sailing Centre on the lake. It hopes to establish a major campus in the City of York eventually.

Programs

Humber is close to the system average in its mix of programs. With close to 12,000 students, it is big in all program areas.

Humber has fewer upgrading programs for individuals lacking entrance credentials than most colleges. For qualified entrants, Humber has its own Communications Placement Tests in reading, English, and math. The results of these tests determine what level of Communications and Math courses students will take, and whether "developmental" courses are required.

Humber has a diversified General Arts and Science program. Two-year Pre-University GAS is intended for students seeking transfer to university. Completion with good marks usually secures university entrance. General College is for students uncertain which career-oriented college program they wish to enter. Pre-Health and Pre-Technology provide skills and credentials needed for applications to those areas – but no guarantee of entry to them.

Humber has co-op programs, particularly in Business and Technology, but it is also one of the few places where I heard arguments against co-op. Particularly in Applied Arts, Humber has decided that intensive and closely supervised field placements can provide training as good as or better than a co-op work term. Humber integrates field placement into many of its non-co-op programs.

Humber's Institute of Language and Culture offers language and culture training, mostly to business and industry, but student exchange programs are also available between Humber and several CEGEPs, which are roughly the equivalent of Ontario's colleges in Quebec. Some of the Institute's programs also offer overseas placements.

Applied Arts

In the Arts cluster, there are two Fashion Arts programs, one focused on management in the fashion and cosmetics trades, the other including modelling as well as general fashion industry training. Theatre Arts offers a three-year Performance program for actors and a two-year program in Technical Production. Both programs are closely involved with stage performances through Theatre Humber. The renowned Music program, focused on jazz with options for performance, writing, or a combination of both, was one of the first to recognize the need for music training beyond the classically oriented conservatory system. Applicants may be guided to a Pre-Music year in General Arts and Science. There is a Creative Photography program and a post-graduate certificate in Arts Administration which is offered on a part-time basis to experienced arts personnel.

Communications programs are three-year Film and Television Production, Radio Broadcasting, Audio-Visual Technician, three-year Journalism, three-year Public Relations, and Advertising Media Sales. Some programs include a two-month internship segment. In addition, Humber sees Communications as an area where colleges can give career-oriented skills to university graduates. It offers separate, shorter diploma or certificate programs in Journalism, Radio Broadcasting, and Public Relations to students who have diplomas or university degrees. There are plans for a post-graduate Media Copywriting course as well.

Design programs are a one-year Design Foundations certificate, Advertising and Graphic Design, and three-year programs in Industrial Design, Interior Design, and Packaging and Graphic Design.

Horticulture includes a two-year Technician and a three-year Technologist program in Landscaping, with options in Horticulture or Urban Forestry. The Technologist program is flow-through, meaning that it takes one further year of study after completion of the Technician program. There is also a Retail Floristry diploma and a Tree Care certificate, plus an apprenticeship program in Horticulture. Programs use the Humber Arboretum (run jointly by Humber and civic authorities), a Construction Laboratory, and the college Greenhouse.

The School of Social and Community Services, at the Lakeshore Campus, offers three-year Child and Youth Work (which can include West Indian culture studies and travel/study to St. Vincent), Developmental Service Work, Law and Security Administration, Rehabilitation Work, and Social Service Work. Several of these include substantial field placements. Early Childhood Education programs (offered by the Health Science Division at North Campus) include the regular ECE stream and a Special Needs option, both with heavy fieldwork obligations, and an Advanced Certificate, offered on a part-time basis for holders of an ECE diploma. Humber's ECE trains in child care for all ages from newborn up to age seven and for special-needs children. The college has on-campus and off-campus daycare lab/demonstration centres.

Humber's Hospitality and Tourism programs are covered

Industrial Design students, like this group working on an automotive concept in the Humber labs, learn skills for a wide range of design responsibilities.

below under Business, though Humber happens to make them part of its Arts Division.

Business

Several Business programs have common first years. Humber calls its two-year programs (usually called "Business") Business Management. Business Management has only the general stream, but after first year students may transfer to the second year of most Business Administration programs. Three-year Business Administration has a "regular" stream plus options (chosen after first year) in Marketing, Operations Management, Human Resource Management, and Small Business Management. Also offered is Accountancy, with two-and three-year options, Retail Management, Marketing, and Legal Assistant. Post-graduate certificate courses for university and college graduates are offered in Condominium Management, Human Resources Management, and Marketing Management.

Business programs in Computing are a co-op three-year Computer Information Systems with regular and management options, Computer Programming (with optional co-op), a Systems Analyst certificate (with diploma available when demand is sufficient), and Computer Sales and Marketing.

In association with the German state of Baden-Württemberg, Humber has begun an International Business program, which includes business courses, German language instruction, and co-op placement in Germany. There is also a post-graduate International Marketing certificate with an Asia-Pacific co-op placement developed in association with the Asia-Pacific Foundation.

Humber's School of Hospitality has less diverse offerings than George Brown's but competes head-to-head for reputation in key programs like Culinary Management and Food and Beverage. The Culinary Management program is co-op. Other programs are Food and Beverage Service, Hotel and Restaurant Management (with a third year for Hotel and Restaurant Administration), and various certificate programs. Interchange between programs is easy. Hospitality students can do internships or work/study programs in Japan, Europe, and the Caribbean.

The School of Tourism and Leisure has several unusual certificate and diploma programs. Programs are Travel and Tourism (offered at North and Lakeshore campuses), Recreation Management Studies, and Horse Care and Equine Skills, plus shorter certificate courses in Arena Management, Equine Studies (with Management or Coaching options), Jockey Training, Ski Resort (or Ski Area) Operations, and Sports Equipment Specialist. Several of the short programs attract students active in the field or with prior experience. The horse and jockey programs are associated with Humber's neighbour, Woodbine Racetrack.

Humber no longer offers the one-year General Office Administration certificate that is standard at most colleges, but it has two-year programs in Executive, Legal, Medical, and Word Processor Office Administration. Its one-year certificates are a Receptionist/Word Processor course and a Legal Secretary course that has extensive law-office placement work.

Health Sciences

Humber Health Sciences offers Nursing and Nursing Assistant, plus many post-graduate and refresher courses for RNs and RNAs. Also offered are Ambulance and Emergency Care, certificate courses in Pharmacy Assistant and Health Care Aide, and the only English-language Funeral Service Education program in Ontario (which is always heavily oversubscribed). For Early Childhood Education programs, see under Applied Arts, above.

Technology

Technician/Technologist programs at Humber are flow-through; that is, a Technologist diploma in each Engineering cluster requires one extra year, which is taken after completion of the appropriate two-year Technician program. First semesters tend to be common in each cluster of programs. Technology programs are taught in the North Campus's well-equipped Technology Centre, which has a Flexible Manufacturing System based on numerical control, CAD-CAM (Computer Assisted Design, Computer Assisted Manufacturing), and robotics.

Humber offers Technician and Technologist programs in Architectural Design, with a co-op option in the third year.

There are several Mechanical Engineering programs, which make extensive use of Humber's computer-integrated manufacturing facility. There are Technician programs in Drafting Design, Tool and Die, Numerical Control, and Manufacturing, plus a Technologist program (which follows on completion of a Technician program) and Technician and Technologist programs in Electromechanical Engineering. Humber is also working with the plastics industry to create a Canadian Plastics Training Centre and expects to offer a Plastics Technician program soon.

There is a Technician program in Heating, Air Conditioning, and Refrigeration Engineering, and a Technologist program specializing in Energy Management. Humber has a Safety Engineering Technologist program, a Chemical Laboratory Technician and a Chemical Engineering Technologist program, and

Technician and co-op Technologist programs in Civil Engineering.

The Electronic Engineering programs are: Technologist in Computer Engineering, Technician and Technologist in Control Systems, and regular or co-op options in both Electrical Engineering Technician and Technologist.

Trades Training

In keeping with its "high-end" emphasis, Humber has been cutting some of its trades training programs. It currently offers a small number of skilled trades courses, mostly in industrial electronics and computer control, and the in-school part of eight apprenticeship programs.

One recent Humber innovation is the Centre for Transportation Safety, which trains commercial truck drivers and trucking managers and offers upgrading and refreshers to working truckers.

Part-Time and Continuing Education

Humber has been assertive about what it calls the "education aftermarket," particularly in business and industry. Most Canadian industries do a pitifully small amount of workplace training, and most experts agree that amount has to increase. Through its Business and Industry Service Centre, Humber sells a lot of training services to business and industrial clients, and it aims to do still more.

The School of Creative Writing, a short summer program that Humber recently developed in association with Toronto's Harbourfront Reading Series and International Festival of Authors, has already won worldwide attention for the top-flight writers who come to teach in it.

Humber also offers about a thousand part-time and evening courses to approximately 65,000 Continuing Education enrollees every year. The courses are strongly career-oriented. The typical Con Ed student is over thirty, is fully employed in a white-collar job, and probably has a post-secondary degree or diploma. Some of Humber's post-graduate certificates are only offered through the Con Ed department.

Humber offers Con Ed students telephone registration, evening counselling services, and a magazine for part-time students, produced by the Journalism department.

Getting in the Door

Humber has established an Enquiry Centre with 800-number service for all but northwestern Ontario.

The North Campus on Humber College Drive is easy to find, has good transit connections, and its own "Humbus" shuttle to other campuses and distant parking lots. Some more signs would make the main entrance easier to find. (The door labelled "Main Entrance" leads to the library and classrooms, but most student services are in an adjoining building west of there.) Humber is gathering its front-end services around the entrance to that building, close to the Information Desk.

Week-long "Discover Humber" sessions run all winter to orient potential students to the college's programs and activities. Information and contacts should be available through the Enquiry Centre. About half the people seen in Humber's Counselling Department are non-students who take career counselling and assessment on a fee-for-service basis.

Support Services

Because of its size, Humber can provide many services. It has big, well-equipped Learning Resource Centres, Language Development Centres, Math and English labs, and access to computers in all programs. It was one of the first colleges to establish an Equity Committee to deal with racial and sexual harassment issues, and the North Campus has a cross-cultural centre to make the most of its multicultural student population.

Humber offers study-skills sessions, and "Anti-Flunk" and "Anti-Stress" handbooks. For mature students, Humber offers "Balancing Home Life and School" sessions. ("Mature students tend to define themselves. An eighteen-year-old with two kids probably has a lot in common with people in our Mature Student Club.") There are large Peer Tutoring (and Tutoring in English) programs, and Humber offers a credit course in Psychology or English for students who tutor. Mostly, however, Humber points to intangibles in student service. It claims that good faculty and high morale create an attitude that students pick up.

Connections

Humber has developed a number of joint projects with high schools. One interesting one: it invites high school students to try out its English placement test. Students who may be cruising through high school get a motivational jolt if they discover they won't make the grade in college.

Humber's post-diploma courses draw many university graduates into custom-designed, accelerated certificate or diploma programs. York University accepts many graduates of Humber's Pre-University GAS program.

Scholarships

Some years ago, Humber began a capital fund-raising drive and raised $3 million, but stopped short of its goal when the recession took hold. It does not have a central alumni organization, but thirty of its program areas run alumni activities for their own graduates. Entry-level scholarships of $1,000 each have been an important part of Humber's recruitment, and the college has many other scholarships and bursaries, including the athletic scholarships discussed below.

Where to Live

With 82 per cent of its full-time students coming from outside its own area, Humber was one of the first colleges in southern Ontario to open residences. There are two residence buildings close to the North Campus and facing the Humber Arboretum. They have a total of 720 single rooms, a cafeteria with a variety of meal plans, a strong Residence Life program, and options such as "Study Floor," "Fitness Floor," and "Substance-Free Floor."

Sports and Recreation

On the North Campus, Humber has the Gordon Wragg Athletic Centre, jointly developed by Humber and the City of Etobicoke, with gyms, squash courts, weight-training, saunas, a pub, and a new swimming pool. There is also a gym at the Lakeshore campus, and Humber's Sailing Centre on the lake offers recreational sailing, competition, and lessons. Sports and recreation activities cover the spectrum. The varsity Hawks and Lady Hawks play a range of intercollegiate sports. The Student Athletic Association has raised funds for athletic scholarships. Students playing varsity sports and maintaining a passing average are eligible to have their tuition fully reimbursed. There are organized intramural teams, "fun sports" to encourage individuals to discover new activities, fitness programs, and (for a fee) instructional courses in many sports and activities.

As the average student gets older, more fitness and non-competitive programs have been added, and, as the cultural mix changes, soccer, cricket, and other sports have emerged as increasingly popular.

The City

Humber, which likes to see itself serving all of Ontario and all of Canada, points to its location close to the Pearson airport and the transportation hub of Metro Toronto. For students at Humber, there are good transit connections to all of Metro Toronto and its entertainment, shopping, housing, and recreational facilities. Adjacent to Humber's main campus is the 250-store Woodbine Mall, which not only provides many Humber students with part-time work but also houses Humber outreach classrooms and one of its several daycares. The green spaces of the Arboretum adjoin the other side of the campus.

Contact:

Humber College
205 Humber College Boulevard
Etobicoke, Ont. M9W 5L7
(416) 675-5000 – Enquiry Centre
Toll-free: 1-800-268-4867

LAMBTON COLLEGE: *Technology in a Free-trade World*

Sarnia

Size: Small

Instrumentation Engineering is part of a cluster of Lambton programs in "process control." They train technicians and technologists for Sarnia's highly automated petrochemical plants and other industries.

Lambton has always been one of the smallest colleges in Ontario, but it intends to change that. It has more than doubled its student numbers in five years, from 1,200 to nearly 2,800, and it plans to keep growing. Indeed, if Lambton's plans work out, it could be one of the most interesting colleges in the system, particularly if your interests are technological.

With only 125,000 people in its local area, the college has always had to be interested in a lot more than just the local student population. Serving local industry has been important to Lambton, and it is about to become more so.

Sarnia is the heart of "Chemical Valley," the chemical, petrochemical and oil-refining complex that lines both sides of the St. Clair River. It claims to have more Ph.D.s and use more energy per capita than any other city in Canada. The local industry struggled in the 1970s and 1980s, but it has been adjusting to global competition and the free-trade environment. Lambton aims to be a key part of that. It wants to be the training and retraining centre of Chemical Valley at every level, from entry-level plant workers to senior researchers and managers – and then to use those strengths to train Lambton's students, particularly in Technology and Business.

In the fall of 1992, Lambton broke ground for its new Centre for Advanced Process Technology. In industry, Process Technology means automation, computer-controlled machinery, and robotics. Chemical Valley's industries are moving that way, and Lambton's Centre is where they will test procedures, train workers, and learn to manage. It will be an industry-oriented centre, but by participating in it, Lambton students will be studying at the cutting edge.

Lambton hopes to open other centres in Energy Conservation, Environmental Technology, and Human Resource Management, all to be deeply integrated with local industry as well as training the college's students. Because Lambton is already heavily co-op, it expects the Centres will allow it to train its students on industries' own facilities, rather than leave it to pursue the hopeless task of purchasing up-to-date equipment for its classrooms and labs.

Chemical Valley is opening to free trade and international competition. Lambton is doing the same, in ways that break with the way Ontario colleges have traditionally operated. It has already formed an International Education Centre with St. Clair County Community College across the river. It intends to send its Technology (and Business) graduates across the border to acquire applied degrees from American universities. If a flow of Lambton-trained technologists with American degrees and certificates creates pressure for Ontario colleges to start offering their own applied degrees, well, Lambton will not be disappointed.

Worth Going For

- Technology – particularly Process Control and Environmental areas

Campuses

Lambton occupies a spacious, partly wooded campus on the eastern edge of Sarnia, a few blocks from Highway 402. There are bus connections from the campuses to downtown Sarnia, but it is a fairly long walk from restaurants, shopping, and the other services the city offers.

Programs

Compared to the mix of enrollments across the Ontario college system, Lambton has slightly more students than average in Applied Arts and Technology and fewer in Business and Health Sciences. In recent years, it added some new Applied Arts programs, but it sees its future growth coming in Technology and Business.

Along with the standard upgrading courses, Lambton offers General Arts and Science in several versions. The one-year Pre-Health Sciences, Human Services Foundation, and Pre-Technology options guarantee successful graduates entry into Lambton's programs in those fields. The College Preparation option of GAS permits students uncertain of a career choice to select courses from any program. Liberal Studies emphasizes English, Humanities, and Social Sciences. Successful graduates of the two-year GAS program may enter second year at the University of Windsor.

Lambton has co-op options available in many programs, including Applied Arts and Office Administration programs where co-op is unusual. Where there is no co-op, field placements or practicums are the rule. Not all co-op programs follow the standard schedule of four months of full-time paid work between full-time academic terms. Some have simultaneous work and study schedules, which usually means three days of paid work every two weeks during an academic term.

Applied Arts

Applied Arts programs cover a wide range without much clustering of related programs. In order to serve local students in fields
where it cannot yet sustain a complete program, Lambton offers
the first year of some programs. Students can transfer from Lambton to subsequent years of the program at other colleges.

The largest group of related programs is in Human Service,
which includes Law and Security Administration and Correctional Work (they share a common first term), Early Childhood
Education (plus post-diploma certificates in ECE Resource
Teacher and Infant-Toddler Care), and Social Service Work.

A two-year Hospitality and Tourism Management program has
second-year options in Hospitality (food, hotel, and convention),
or Travel and Tourism. A two-year Parks/Tourism Technician
program offers second-year options in either Parks/Golf Courses
or Landscape and Nursery. Lambton's only media offering is a
one-year program that combines Radio, Television, and Journalism. Students can complete a certificate in Media Fundamentals
at Lambton and transfer to the second year of the Broadcast Journalism program at Mohawk College.

Lambton also offers a one-year Art Fundamentals, after which
graduates may transfer to another college for diploma completion
in their area of specialization, and a one-year Graphic Design
Fundamentals, which gives access to the second year of Graphic
Design at George Brown (and potentially at other colleges).

Business

In two-year Business programs, Lambton offers only General
Business, which is co-op. Three-year Business Administration
options are General, Accounting, or Marketing. All but Accounting share common first years, and all are co-op. There is also a separate, three-year co-op Accounting program. There are two-year
Computer Programmer and three-year co-op Computer Pro-
grammer/Analyst programs with common semesters.

Office Administration programs are standard: one-year

General Office Administration and two-year Executive or Medical options. Unusually, the two-year program is co-op.

Health Sciences

Lambton has three small Health Science programs, all offering extensive clinical experience: three-year Nursing, Nursing Assistant (forty weeks continuous), and three-year Med Lab Technologist. It also offers shorter certificate courses to train Health Care Aides and Home Support Workers.

Technology

Lambton sees its future in Technology programs closely linked to the industrial base of Sarnia's "Chemical Valley." It is already training many of the employees of local petrochemical companies. In general, three-year Technologist programs are co-op, two-year Technician programs are not.

A unique Technology program at Lambton is Industrial Hygiene Technology-Occupational Health and Safety, a three-year program aimed at the recognition, evaluation, and control of environmental factors in the workplace. In effect, it is the indoor complement to Environmental Technology, which focuses on the assessment and control of air, water, and noise quality in the outdoor environment. The two programs have a common first year.

Process Control (what we mean when we say "automation") is becoming a Lambton specialty. There are Technician and Technologist programs in Instrumentation and Control Engineering-Industrial Automation, plus a forty-week certificate in Process Operations for the chemical and petrochemical industry.

Lambton offers two-year Technician and three-year Technologist versions of Chemical Engineering. In Electronics Engineering, the Technician program specializes in Office Information Systems, and the Technologist program is more general.

Mechanical Engineering includes three programs: a two-year Technician, and a two-year co-op Technician program specializing in Drafting, plus a three-year co-op Technologist program.

Lab work, hospital placements, and classroom learning are daily fare for college nursing students, like this group discussing spinal function in a Lambton class.

Associated with them is a Power Engineering Technician program, which is co-op and trains Third Class Stationary Engineers.

Trades Training

Lambton provides a range of employment skills programs associated with its diploma program area: Food Preparation, Home Support, Computer Operator, Office Assistant, and so on.

As well, Lambton provides certificate programs in skilled trades in Industrial, Automotive, Construction, Small Engine Servicing, and Appliance Repair. Some of these courses provide preparation for apprenticeship programs, and Lambton provides the academic part of apprenticeship training for cooks and industrial apprentices in several fields.

Part-Time and Continuing Education

Lambton has created centres that provide specialized training and consulting to business and industry: the Industrial Fire School, a group of Safety and Environmental services, and the Southwest Training Centre. It cooperates with local Native Band Councils to provide on-reserve training in many fields, including the Correctional Work and Social Service Work programs.

For individuals, Lambton offers part-time courses in many of the areas covered by its full-time programs: Business, Health Sciences, Adult Education, General Arts and Sciences, and Technology. Part-time students can take single courses or complete a group of courses to earn certificates tailored to part-time study, or work toward a complete diploma program on a part-time basis. Various general interest courses are also offered.

The Southwest Training Centre, an entrepreneurial arm of the college, offers entrepreneurial programs, microcomputer training, management and supervisory training, and quality-control programs to local business and industry.

Getting in the Door

The Liaison office within the Public Relations Department at Lambton will provide information on request, and will provide guided tours that can be tailored to the specific interests of individuals or groups.

The main entrance, by the fountain, is easy to find, but from most of the parking lots you will be entering from the back. Lambton is small enough that people and services should be easy to find.

Support Services

Lambton offers all the usual student support services discussed at the back of the book. Its Learning Centre runs a peer tutoring program, offers a variety of "coursework learning support" packages (many of them on computer), and can help students tailor individual learning packages for credit. Besides its usual functions, the Counselling office runs credit courses in life skills, study skills, and career planning.

Lambton is working toward a Prior Learning Assessment process in which all incoming students will be tested as to the knowledge and skills they already have. As a result of the assessment, students will receive immediate credit in areas where they can demonstrate competence. They will also be directed to additional instruction in areas where weaknesses are identified.

Connections

Connections to industry and to other institutions of higher learning are central to Lambton's plans for the future.

With St. Clair County Community College, across the border in Port Huron, Michigan, Lambton is creating an International Education Centre. Already Lambton's Business students go across the river to St. Clair County (not to be confused with Ontario's St. Clair College in Windsor), for some of their courses. Lambton and St. Clair County also foresee increased cooperation in Technology. In addition, Lambton has developed connections with several universities in Michigan, particularly Central Michigan, Walsh College, and Concordia. Concordia now permits diploma graduates from Lambton to complete a B.A. in sixteen months of part-time study, and Lambton intends to make it possible for all its three-year diploma graduates in Business and Technology to go on to Michigan universities to complete applied degrees.

Within Ontario, Lambton has more familiar articulation agreements. Its Business grads can receive advanced standing in Bachelor of Business Administration programs at University of Windsor, and Lakehead University accepts diploma-to-degree transfers from all the colleges. In addition, Lambton encourages college-to-college transfers in those programs where it offers only the first year.

Scholarships

Lambton expects to begin planning a capital fund-raising drive
soon, but already it has acquired funds for a substantial number of
Lambton-specific scholarships (particularly in Health Sciences)
and an established bursaries program.

Where to Live

Not quite half of Lambton's students currently come from outside
its local area, but the college expects that proportion to increase in
coming years. Lambton has 120 beds in single units in its co-ed
student residence on campus. A full meal plan is included in the
rent, which was $108/week in 1992-93. In addition, the Housing
Registry assists with searches for off-campus housing in the Sarnia
area.

Sports and Recreation

Lambton College has a gym with weight-training and aerobics
facilities, and it has outdoor sports fields and tracks. There are varsity teams in several sports, and the Athletic Department puts particular emphasis on recreation, fitness, and intramural activities.

The City

Sarnia is a small city of about 75,000, on Lake Huron at the
entrance to the St. Clair River. The world's first oil well was drilled
not far away, and Sarnia has had refineries for nearly a century. In
the Second World War, it became a petrochemicals production
centre, and the Sarnia area (along with Port Huron, Michigan,
just across the bridge) has been "Chemical Valley" ever since.
Because of its industries, the feel of the community is mostly

hard-working and industrial. The cost of living for students is relatively low, and access to shopping and entertainment in the U.S. is quick and easy. Beach and water-sport recreation facilities around Sarnia are excellent.

Contact:

Lambton College
1457 London Road
P.O. Box 969
Sarnia, Ont. N7T 7K4
(519) 542-7751 – Liaison

Crowded Doorways –
The Programs Students Demand Most

1. Dental Hygiene. (Nearly every college that offers it reported huge numbers of applicants per place.)
2. Nursing.
3. Law and Security Administration.
4. Social Service Worker.
5. Ambulance and Emergency Care.
6. Aviation – Flight.
7. Radiography.

If one college reported overcrowding in a program, the others offering it usually did too, including those offering it in French.

LOYALIST COLLEGE: *Small – And Focused*

Belleville

Size: Small

Action in the newsroom, as Loyalist's Broadcast Journalism students prepare a story for their closed-circuit television station. Outstanding Media Studies programs draw many students to Loyalist.

Loyalist, one of the smallest colleges in the system, seems to have its finger on the pulse of its communities. It draws most of its students from rural and small-town eastern Ontario, and it retains a friendly, small-town atmosphere. The main Kente Building, built twenty years ago but looking much newer, testifies to careful upkeep, due as much to college pride as to janitorial excess. But Loyalist also serves the industries of Trenton and Belleville and the hospitality businesses of the resort areas nearby, so it offers specialized technological training and extensive outreach programs for business and industry.

But not in too many areas. Loyalist focuses its efforts in a few areas, and it has always had an eye out for opportunity. There is no particular reason why Belleville should be a centre for media training, but through smart planning and the work of some talented staff, Loyalist has built up perhaps the most broadly based media school in Ontario. Now it is looking to create a similar centre of excellence in Environmental Technology. As the market for environmental testing increases, it is combining its Chemical and Civil Engineering expertise into one unified centre for testing and control of air, water, and noise pollution.

A few years ago, when the government permitted colleges to begin capital fund-raising, Loyalist was one of the first ones in. With a well-focused, well-marketed campaign, it moved quickly toward its $1.6 million objective. Now it has a growing scholarship and bursary fund, improved library resources, a new Centre for Environmental Studies and a new Training and Development Centre.

Compared to most of the Ontario colleges, Loyalist is small and expects to remain so. It will always be a small college with a small-town feel, and it's not for you if you need the bright lights. But there is an enthusiasm there that suggests good feeling, and because it lacks the profile of larger schools, waiting lists for some Loyalist programs may be shorter than elsewhere.

Worth Going For

- A small college with small-town roots
- School of Media Studies

Campuses

The Loyalist campus is a large, partly wooded property on the western edge of Belleville. Most activities are in the Kente Building, with the Daycare Centre, the new Training and Development Centre, and other facilities close by. There are few facilities within easy walking distance of the college, but there is bus service to both Belleville and Trenton.

Loyalist offers Continuing Education courses in more than a dozen communities throughout its region.

Programs

Because of its large School of Media Studies, Loyalist emphasizes Applied Arts programs more than most colleges, and all its other areas are relatively small. There are no co-op programs, but extensive field placements are used in most program areas.

Loyalist offers the usual upgrading courses for underprepared students. A one-year College Vocational Program, intended for high school grads with Basic-level high school credits, offers job preparation skills and is individually tailored.

A two-year General Arts and Science program has both September and January start dates, and there is a Pre-Technology option. If you take GAS because you could not get into an oversubscribed program at Loyalist (or got in and failed the first semester), successful completion of first year often guarantees acceptance into that program, possibly with advanced standing. Loyalist also offers a third year of GAS, permitting students to focus on a concentrated area of study after completing a diploma. There is also a one-year Pre-Technology that emphasizes Math, Science, and Communications.

Applied Arts

Loyalist's Applied Arts courses are offered in three clusters: Media Studies, Human Studies, and Administrative Studies.

Media Studies is the college's stand-out area, attracting students from far beyond its local area and even out-of-province. It began by serving small-town and community newspapers and broadcasters. But now Loyalist grads are just as frequently placed in large centres as well. The Photojournalism program is the only one in Canada, and the media-related Business Marketing, Business Sales, and Advertising programs are highly specialized. The

Print Journalism program includes a unique option in Agricultural Journalism, offered in cooperation with the Kemptville College of Agricultural Technology. Radio Broadcasting students help to operate Loyalist's own FM radio station which broadcasts in the Belleville area, and Television Broadcasting students have the use of two on-campus studios. The School boasts up-to-date equipment, satellite uplinks to all media, a closed-circuit TV station, and a college newspaper. All programs are two-year, and most include field placements.

The Human Studies cluster offers standard programs: Developmental Services, Early Childhood Education, Recreation Leadership, and Social Service Work. All include extensive fieldwork practicums after the first year or first semester. The new on-campus Loyalist Centre for Early Childhood Education is both a child-care centre and a training facility.

Administrative Studies includes Law and Security Administration. After a common first year, Loyalist LASA students choose among Police Science, Customs/Immigration, Corrections, Corporate/Commercial Security, and Paralegal/Legal Assistant, all of which include fieldwork placements of one month per semester. Information Systems is a two-year data processing program with an optional, specialized third year. There are General, Legal, and Executive options of Office Administration, plus a one-year Small Business Office Automation program focused on planning and maintaining microcomputer office systems.

Business

Loyalist offers Marketing and Office Administration programs in its Administrative Studies and Media Studies schools, as listed above.

Accounting has two- and three-year versions, with the longer one offering extensive fieldwork placements. There are two- and three-year versions of Business Administration, and a two-year Appraisal and two- and three-year Accounting programs. In addition to Travel and Tourism, there is a two-year Hotel and Restaurant Management program, which is linked to the on-campus restaurant, Club 213.

Health Sciences

Loyalist's Health Sciences offerings are the basics: Nursing and Nursing Assistant, plus a sixteen-week Health Care Aide program.

Technology

There are Technician and Technologist programs available in Architecture, Chemical Engineering, Civil Engineering, Electronics Engineering, Environmental Engineering, and Mechanical Engineering, plus Technician programs in Construction Engineering and Surveying.

In 1992 Loyalist created a Centre for Environmental Studies to link two pillars of the Technology program: the measuring, testing, quantitative side provided by Chemical Engineering, and the applications of Civil Engineering. The Centre already provides environmental testing for government and industry in the area.

Trades Training

Loyalist offers post-secondary training in several skilled trades, and a full apprenticeship program for Motor Vehicle Mechanics. Upgrading and literacy programs prepare students for further training or employment.

Part-Time and Continuing Education

Loyalist offers part-time, mostly evening, continuing education courses at the main campus and in more than a dozen communities outside Belleville. They offer mostly career-oriented skills training, but do include courses that can be used toward program diplomas. As the only post-secondary institution in its region, Loyalist also provides facilities for associations of accountants, realtors, managers, and local businesspeople to deliver their own courses, and it runs certificate courses for many of them. The college's new Training and Development Centre, opened in 1992, provides customized training for business and industry. Loyalist has a longstanding academic liaison with the First Nations Technical Institute, run by the Mohawks of the Bay of Quinte at nearby Tyendinaga.

Getting in the Door

Inside the front page of the calendar and on other publications, Loyalist promotes its information number, (613) 969-1913. The Admissions office and Counselling office provide information and assistance to prospective students. The Liaison office offers the Student for a Day program, by which potential students can sit in on any program and discuss it with students and faculty.

Loyalist almost has its own 401 exit. Wallbridge Road was going to be renamed in honour of the college, but friends of local tradition protested. So now it is Wallbridge-Loyalist Road, which does have an exit ramp (go south) just west of Belleville. The campus should be easy to find. There is an information booth at the main entrance to the Kente Building on Loyalist's main campus. The campus is small enough that a few questions should send you in the right direction.

Support Services

Loyalist staff stress that the college is small enough to provide individual attention to anyone seeking information or advice. Besides the usual Special Needs services (discussed in Part Three), Loyalist has particular services for hearing-impaired students, developed in association with the nearby Sir James Whitney School for the Deaf.

Connections

Articulation agreements with the school boards of all the four counties that Loyalist serves permit high school graduates to obtain advanced standing in programs related to their high school studies. For details, consult a school or college counsellor.

Media Studies graduates can be accepted to Carleton's School of Journalism, but Carleton is hardly being generous: they must have superior marks and "may" receive advanced standing. Law and Security Administration grads with good marks normally receive four credits toward a Carleton B.A.

Scholarships

Loyalist was one of the first colleges to begin its own fund-raising drive, and part of the aim was to raise $500,000 to create a range of scholarships, prizes and bursaries for its students. This Endowment now supports thirty-eight scholarships and bursaries worth up to $1,100. Another ninety-five academic awards, bursaries, entrance scholarships, and athletic scholarships have been funded by other donors, so Loyalist students are well placed for receiving financial support.

Where to Live

About half of Loyalist's full-time students come from outside the four-county region that is Loyalist's catchment area. Most of these are drawn from rural eastern Ontario, although Media Studies draws much more widely. Loyalist opened its first student residences in the fall of 1992: three on-campus buildings housing 281 students in six-bedroom, two-bathroom apartments. Many Loyalist students rent rooms and apartments in and around Belleville, and the Student Services office maintains a housing registry.

Half of Loyalist's students come from beyond the local area. Loyalist's new residences opened on the Belleville campus in 1992.

Sports and Recreation

Loyalist has a fully equipped gym, a fitness centre, and outdoor sports fields, and uses community facilities for many other activities. There are varsity teams in basketball, volleyball, softball, and soccer, plus intramural, fitness, and recreation programs. The athletic staff emphasizes outdoor recreation and organizes long-distance canoe and hiking trips every year.

The City

Belleville is a small city of 37,000. It is the regional centre for a large, mostly rural, area of east-central Ontario, and it also has a number of medium and small industries. There are excellent recreational facilities in the nearby Bay of Quinte and Trent River regions. As the only post-secondary institution in the area,

Loyalist has a higher community profile than colleges with universities alongside.

Contact:

Loyalist College
P.O. Box 4200
Belleville, Ont. K8N 5B9
(613) 969-1913

College to University

Unlike colleges in most provinces and the United States, Ontario colleges have never been "transfer" colleges. They don't offer the first two years of academic programs and then send students on to complete their degrees at universities. Without half the students and faculty operating a kind of junior university, Ontario colleges have been free to get on with their real work.

But many students want further learning opportunities after college. Here the problems arise. Ontario universities have been slow to accept the college graduate – so slow that many colleges prefer to send their students on to American universities instead. The Ontario universities like to "cherry-pick" – taking some students from some programs at some colleges. Often they only give one year's credit for three years of college.

College-to-university transfer is possible in Ontario. A few universities – particularly Lakehead and Windsor – encourage college students to consider them afterwards. (For more examples, see the "Connections" section in each college profile.) You can ask any college what it has arranged for further studies after graduation.

But don't count on your right to transfer into university. With all the reasons for going to college, don't look on it as a shortcut to university.

MOHAWK COLLEGE: *A Technology Powerhouse*

Hamilton

Size: Large

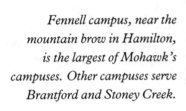

Fennell campus, near the mountain brow in Hamilton, is the largest of Mohawk's campuses. Other campuses serve Brantford and Stoney Creek.

It figures that Steeltown's college would be technological and industrial, with a workaday, down-to-earth feel to it. Like Algonquin and Centennial, it fits a big city/big college pattern: a wide range of programs and few spectacular stand-outs. Mohawk College has some real strengths but not a whole lot of glamour.

Mohawk seems to be doing the right things for students. There's strong official commitment to serving all the students' needs, a strong student organization, and "the premier student centre" of all the Ontario colleges. But perhaps the size makes Mohawk seem a bit overwhelming – it has 7,600 full-time students, and 75,000 when you include short-termers and part-timers. Or perhaps it's the building: the main Fennell campus building has some of the longest locker-lined corridors you will ever see.

Technology is Mohawk's strength, the area where everyone

concedes Mohawk is something special. Mohawk got into Technology even before it was a college called Mohawk. Before Mohawk was founded in 1967, there was a Hamilton School of Technology, and Mohawk built on what its predecessor had started. It has a very wide range of programs in all the Technology fields, with good equipment and a top-notch faculty.

Mohawk's Technology programs are also strongly co-op – Mohawk helped pioneer co-op learning in the Ontario college system. Its Technology programs are well known throughout southern Ontario's industrial heartland – and far beyond. Mohawk Technology students get good co-op experiences, and its Technology programs draw students from well beyond the Hamilton-Wentworth area.

If you find Instrumentation Engineering Technology and Mechanical Engineering Fluid Power Automation not very glamorous, you may think the same about Mohawk. But if you are interested in working hard at Technology at a school with a good reputation, the right facilities, and great placement records for Technology grads, Mohawk might top your list.

Worth Going For

- Technology programs, particularly in Industrial, Architectural, and Electrotechnology
- Innovative delivery of Health Sciences programs

Campuses

Mohawk has about twenty facilities around the Hamilton-Wentworth-Brant-Haldimand region it serves. That may be about fifteen too many. The main campus is Fennell, near the mountain brow in suburban Hamilton, but a few programs are given at a secondary campus in Stoney Creek. Also around Hamilton are the Chedoke Health Sciences Centre and the Hamilton Industrial Training Centre in Stoney Creek. The Brant-Elgin St. campus in Brantford has a broad range of programs in Applied Arts and

Business, and it has its own student services and athletics. It could be the nucleus of a Brantford college one day – though probably not in the hard-times 1990s.

Programs

Mohawk is smaller than the college average in Applied Arts and strong in everything else, with a particularly large enrollment in Health Sciences.

Mohawk offers General Arts and Science, a good way for students to hone their study skills and pick up credits before choosing a career-oriented program. Few continue into the second year of GAS.

Applied Arts

Applied Arts are a relatively small part of the program mix at Mohawk, but because it is a big school, it has a broad range of programs, and they are offered at the Fennell, Brantford, and Stoney Creek campuses. Most are "standard" programs widely available at other colleges. In the social service and human service field, Mohawk offers programs in Social Service, Early Childhood Education, Child and Youth Work, Law and Security, and Recreation Leadership. One unique program is Municipal Planning and Development, a two-year diploma preparing planning technicians for public and private agencies.

The Music and Media department offers Broadcast Journalism and both Radio and Television Broadcasting, along with Advertising and a program in Applied Music, which is rooted in jazz performance and aimed at developing professional musicians.

The Brantford campus has an unusual cluster of programs in Graphic Arts and Packaging. The three-year Graphic Arts Reproduction program aims to train Production Co-ordinators for the graphics industry, and it includes one work term. There is also a two-year Graphic Design program and a three-year, co-op Packaging Management and Technology program. The Stoney Creek campus has two Hospitality programs, Food and Beverage

Management, and Travel/Tourism, but Food and Beverage Management faces competition from strong programs at Niagara and George Brown, and Travel/Tourism from Fanshawe and Sheridan. The Brantford campus is also developing interesting post-diploma programs in service to the blind and visually impaired.

Except for Packaging, none of the Applied Arts programs at Mohawk has a co-op component. Some require questionnaires or other evaluations from applicants.

Business

Mohawk's Business programs include several with a co-op option. The three-year Business Administration program has a common first year, after which students choose a specialization in Marketing, Accounting, or Operations. There are also two-year Business programs in these areas, plus a one-year Small Business program and a two-year Insurance program. A Business Administration program in Professional Golf Management has recently been added.

The Office Administration courses cover general, legal, and medical areas and include a popular Law Clerk program and a program in Medical Transcription. Mohawk has pioneered Office Admin challenge exams. Experienced secretaries can receive full credit for fields they have mastered on the job, so they can earn a diploma much more quickly. Also offered through the Office Administration department at Fennell campus is a two-year Travel and Tourism program.

Health Sciences

Hamilton is well supplied with teaching hospitals, and Mohawk's Health Sciences programs are large and strong. The Nursing/Nursing Assistant programs claim their teaching method is unique. They start with a common program in the first two semesters. Nursing students proceed to a "self-directed, modularized" format that offers more flexibility and fewer classroom lectures than most programs. (You must complete all six modules, but you may choose what order you take them in. Within each module you set your own pace and objectives.) Because courses go year-round, you can repeat a module (instead of a whole year) if you have trouble with it, and you can take a semester off if you need to.

There are also Health Technology programs in Medical Lab Technology, Medical Diagnostic Ultrasonography (a post-diploma program), and Radiography. Offered by the Technology department, these programs are oriented to technology and not necessarily to patient care. (As they put it in Radiography, x-raying people and x-raying aircraft wings follow the same principles.)

Health Science programs require pre-admission exams and may also consider high school marks in deciding whom to accept.

Technology

Technology is Mohawk's strongest area, and Mohawk is a technology powerhouse. The Tech faculty has the greatest breadth of technology programs and disciplines in the Ontario college system and (depending on how you count it) the largest technology enrollment, too. Mohawk College's location in the heavily industrialized centre of the Golden Horseshoe has obviously influenced it to focus on technology. But Mohawk Technology places its grads all over – only 25 per cent of Mohawk Technology grads go to work in Hamilton.

To make entry to career paths simpler, Mohawk has clustered most of its Technology programs. Related programs offer common first years, so you are not forced to choose a specialty before learning what it means. Most of the two-year Technician programs and all the three-year Technologist programs are co-op.

One strong cluster of programs is Architecture, Construction, Transportation, and Civil Engineering Technology, where all the programs are co-op. There is a Technician program in Architectural Engineering, and a Technologist program with options in Design and Construction Management. Civil Engineering has Technician and Technologist programs. There is also a Construction Engineering Technician program and a Transportation Engineering Technologist program.

Computer Technology programs, both co-op, are a Technician program in data processing, and a Technologist program in the analysis and design of computer systems.

Virtually all new technology has electronics at its root, and Electrotechnology is a Mohawk specialty. In Electrical Engineering Technology, there is a Technician program in Power and a Technologist program focused on electrical control. Electronics Engineering Technology has a Technician program and two Technologist programs, one standard, one with a specialization in Computers. There is also an Industrial Instrumentation Engineering Technician program. Only the three-year Technologist programs in this cluster are co-op.

The Industrial Management and Mechanical Engineering Technology cluster has both Technician and (co-op) Technologist programs in Industrial Engineering, where the Technologist program emphasizes Management, and also in Mechanical Engineering, where the Technician program specializes in Fluid Power Automation.

In Physical Sciences, Mohawk offers a co-op Chemical Engineering Technologist program with an option in Environmental Technology, a Chemical Technician program that emphasizes laboratory work, and a co-op Technologist program in Materials Engineering, emphasizing metallurgical work.

Trades, Training, and Other Programs

Mohawk has retained a strong apprenticeship program in a broad range of careers, with eighteen apprenticeship programs, four modified apprenticeships, and six cooperative apprenticeships. Most industrial training goes on at Mohawk's Hamilton Industrial Training Centre in Stoney Creek. The newest wing of the Fennell campus is devoted to Job Readiness, Upgrading, and English Language Instruction programs.

Part-Time and Continuing Education

Mohawk has 65,000 people taking part-time courses and programs through Continuing Education every year, and it suspects that the number would double if the college had space for them.

More than a hundred certificates and 1,200 courses are offered for short-term and part-time studies. Some of these are for programs not available on a full-time basis. Con Ed develops its programs according to community need, and some programs may be aimed entirely at people holding full-time jobs. In Plastic and Fine Arts, for instance, Mohawk has part-time but no full-time courses.

The greatest demand for evening courses is in Business, Microcomputer training, and Nursing. Each semester, 1,200 people take Mohawk's Microcomputer Business Applications course, and registration line-ups sometimes form at 4:00 a.m.

David Dean, Mohawk's head of Continuing Education, says the main message about Con Ed is that it is available in almost any field to almost anyone and that it is driven more and more by the cry from employers: "We can't find trained people to do X."

Getting in the Door

When you go to Mohawk's Fennell campus for the first time, drive into the college from West Fifth Street. The main entrance by the bus loop should be easy to find, and there is a large Information counter, with a well-informed staff, just inside. Enter off Fennell Street and you can park close to the Student Centre, but you will be far from the main door.

Mohawk is one of the larger colleges in the system, and some students I met found it too large and a bit cold. To fight that perception, perhaps, Mohawk is working on a student-centred, one-stop shopping concept for information, registration, and student records. Student-oriented offices are being gathered together, and one staffer should be able to handle all the registration and information needs of any particular client. Mohawk has not promoted an information line or 800 number for telephone inquiries. Start with the general switchboard, and ask for what you need. Also, Mohawk and McMaster University run a joint Education Information Centre in the downtown Hamilton Public Library.

Support Services

Join something at Mohawk, and you may get a college credit for it. The college pioneered a college-credit Leadership Training component for everyone serving in student government and student athletic association positions. College services such as housing, peer tutoring, and legal aid are provided in the Student Centre. There is a strong Student Service department at Mohawk, and substantial cooperation between the college and the student government seems to be the rule.

Mohawk has adapted its student services to the growing number of adult and part-time students. Both mature students and part-timers are represented in student government. As the students become more diverse, Student Life programs have become more individualized. Nineteen-year-old full-timers straight from high school may want pub nights, but single parents need childcare options, and older students have led the way in supporting fitness classes, stress clinics, and life skills education.

Scholarships

Mohawk scholarships and bursaries cover 400 awards in total worth over $100,000. Many of these are listed in the calendar beside the program they relate to.

The college has not been doing extensive fund-raising. It does have a well-organized alumni association.

Where to Live

Mohawk has no residence and no plan to develop one. It does have a computerized housing registry, and housing is abundantly available around the main campus, which is located in a suburban area on Hamilton Mountain, with good transit connections throughout the city.

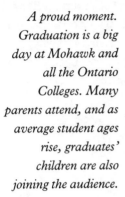

*A proud moment.
Graduation is a big
day at Mohawk and
all the Ontario
Colleges. Many
parents attend, and as
average student ages
rise, graduates'
children are also
joining the audience.*

Out-of-towners, 37 per cent of the student body, tend to come
for the co-op programs in Technology.

Sports and Recreation

Mohawk boasts that its twelve varsity teams have won more cham-
pionships than have those of any other college, and there is an
extensive recreational sports program. Mohawk currently uses
community and high school facilities to supplement its rather limited gym/fitness complex. The college hopes to add a new sports
centre at its Hamilton main campus (there is already one at Brantford).

Mohawk has one of the largest Student Centres in the system,
"the Arnie," with a full-time pub, games rooms, food services, and
shops. The student council thinks it's the best student centre at
any Ontario college, and it certainly offers an impressive range of
events and services.

The City

Mohawk's Hamilton campuses are close to the heart of Steeltown. Hamilton is a big city, with half a million people in its region, and there are lots of opportunities for off-campus entertainment, sports, shopping, and recreation. There are transit, highway, and rail connections giving easy access to Toronto, the U.S. border, and all the densely populated Golden Horseshoe.

Contact:

Mohawk College
Fennell Avenue and West Fifth Avenue
P.O. Box 2034
Hamilton, Ont. L8N 3T2
(416) 575-1212

NIAGARA COLLEGE: *Much-Needed Changes on the Way*

Welland, St. Catharines, Niagara Falls

Size: Medium

Niagara College students recently opened their own student-owned and student-run centre, "After Hours," on the Welland campus.

A couple of years ago, Niagara College started a rapid turnaround. It had been a college in trouble: big deficits, poor morale, and fewer students than colleges in less populated regions. Too many of its classes were scattered in a collection of isolated storefront locations around the region. As Niagara's financial troubles killed off costly but much-needed programs, students went elsewhere, and the college seemed to be losing the resources it needed to revitalize.

Fortunately, Niagara College seems to be breaking out of that grim spiral. It has begun funding new programs and delivering old ones better, and it has new people, a new mood, and an ambitious master plan. The Welland campus is slated to get more effective facilities, including a library and recreation facility to be shared with the community of Welland and a residence that will double as

213

a summer hostel. At St. Catharines, a new campus will eventually replace almost a dozen scattered and makeshift buildings.

Niagara's new president, John Saso, intends to see two or three new programs added every year, and about as many pruned away, until the college has the right mix of programs and a few areas of real strength. Apart from a well-regarded Centre for Hospitality and Tourism (in its own brand-new building in Niagara Falls), it has had few specialty programs to attract distant students or to fit the region's needs. It has little on marine transport, though the college is only blocks from the Welland Canal, the lifeline of Great Lakes shipping. No theatre programs have linked Niagara to the nearby Shaw Festival, and there's not even a wine-making program.

Fortunately, intriguing new programs are coming fast. The 1993 calendar lists eight of them, including a post-diploma Business program in Environmental Management and one in International Trade that is offered in cooperation with an American college just across the Niagara River. Some of its four-year Technology programs have no equivalents elsewhere. At the same time, Niagara is instituting impressive projects to test and to improve quality of instruction in all its program areas.

Rearranging all the programs at a college takes almost as long as building new campuses, and it may be a few years before Niagara fulfils its potential. But already the college is growing fast – from barely 3,000 full-time students a couple of years ago to 5,000 in September 1992, with plans for 6,000 by the end of the decade. Ideas are percolating for new programs and new ways to deliver them.

Does any of this matter to the individual student? If you have found the program you want, and the facilities and the professors impress you, a struggling college can still give you everything you need. But the drive to improve what Niagara offers and how it delivers its services has generated an enthusiasm you just might notice. "We aim to be the best mid-sized college in the system in this decade," one Niagara official told me. The college has about a dozen competitors for that title, of course, but as long as it is aiming for it, things around Niagara can only improve.

Worth Going For

- Centre for Hospitality and Tourism
- Microelectronics Technology

Campuses

Niagara College's main campus, a cluster of low-lying brick buildings, hunkers in the middle of a field in suburban Welland. Plans for renovation and expansion are in the works. In St. Catharines, Nursing programs are offered at the Mack Nursing Education Centre, but Niagara has several small and scattered other properties there. Creating a substantial and unified St. Catharines campus is a priority for the college. Niagara Falls has the college's new Hospitality and Tourism Centre.

Programs

Given its size, Niagara is less active in Technology and more active in Applied Arts than is average across the Ontario college system. Niagara has co-op placements for many of its Business and Technology programs. It is working toward clustering many of its programs into schools with common first-year courses, giving students greater opportunity to select specializations in second year.

As well as the standard upgrading and preparatory programs, Niagara offers General College, which can be a two-year diploma program or preparation for a career-oriented program. General College can be started in September or January. General College course work can be tailored toward media, human services, business, or technology objectives, and there is a one-year Health Science Preparatory option. At present, completion of General College options does not guarantee acceptance into other Niagara programs.

Applied Arts

Niagara has two Media programs, a three-year Radio, Television, and Film Broadcasting and a two-year Print Journalism. Both are lab- rather than classroom-oriented, with up-to-date production facilities, both in the studios and in a self-contained mobile production unit. Students work on the college radio station and newspaper, and do extensive work placements.

Community Service programs are Early Childhood Education (also available in French as Éducation des petits), Educational Resources and Special Needs (for classroom assistants), Law and Security Administration (with second-year specializations in Police, Security, Customs/Immigration, or Corrections), and Social Service Work. There is also a unique two-year program in Human Relations, preparing students for many kinds of community service and people-contact careers, and Niagara intends to offer Recreation Leadership in 1993.

There are programs in Fashion Merchandising/Visual Promotion (oriented more to merchandising than design), a three-year Interior Design program, and a two-year Visual and Creative Arts (Design) program that is oriented to commercial artwork or to progress into university or art college programs.

A two-year co-op Horticultural Technician program and a one-year Horticultural Management (a post-diploma certificate) are offered at the Horticulture Centre in St. Catharines. Both emphasize landscape, nursery, and ornamental horticulture for parks.

Business

Niagara offers two-year Business with Accounting (co-op option available) or Sales options, and three-year Business Administration with options in Accounting (co-op available), Human Resource Management (co-op), Information Systems, Marketing (co-op), and Operations Management. Also available is a two-year Retail Management program with a strong emphasis on entrepreneurship. The college is developing a common first year for its business programs.

In co-operation with Niagara County Community College just across the border, Niagara offers a new post-diploma certificate in International Trade taught in a module form and intended to be accessible to working professionals. It also plans to open a one-year post-diploma program in Environmental Management in 1993. Niagara's small Office Administration cluster has General, Dental, and Executive Office Admin programs (the Executive program is two years and co-op), and a two-year co-op Legal Assistant program.

Hospitality and Tourism

Niagara's programs in this area are housed in its Centre for Hospitality and Tourism in Niagara Falls. Programs are two-year co-op Culinary Skills, three-year co-op Hotel and Restaurant Administration, and a two-year co-op Tourism program, which is focused on managing Tours and Attractions. This program is also offered in French as Tourisme-Circuits et Attraits Touristiques, and part of its attraction is to Quebec francophones who come to improve their English while they study in French.

Health Sciences

Niagara offers Nursing, Nursing Assistant, and several patient care support courses. Pharmacy Assistant and Dental Assistant are each one year. Dental Hygiene was restored at Niagara in 1992. Also available are two-year Health Records Technician, a one-year Ambulance and Emergency Care certificate, and a one-year Medical Transcriptionist program focused on the management of Health Records.

Technology

Niagara's co-op Technologist programs require a total of twenty-four months of academic study and sixteen months of paid work placement, which can be completed in just under four calendar years.

Apprentice chefs practise their art at Niagara College's Hospitality and Tourism Centre in Niagara Falls.

Niagara claims particular strength in Electronic Engineering Technology, with excellent facilities closely linked to the Canadian electronics industry. It offers Technician and Technologist programs in both Electrical and Electronic Engineering, a four-year co-op Technologist program in Computer Engineering, and a four-year co-op Technologist program in Microelectronics Engineering which Niagara hopes to offer in 1993.

Other programs are four-year co-op Technologist programs in Manufacturing Engineering and Mechanical Engineering, and sixty-four-week Technician programs in Quality Control Industrial Engineering and in Stationary Engineering. There is a Technologist program in Construction Engineering.

French-Language Programs

Niagara College is also Collège Niagara, but its bilingual program offerings have shrunk to Éducation des petits and Tourisme-Circuits et Attraits Touristiques, plus some upgrading and distance education programs. It hopes to begin expanding its bilingual courses, but a new Collège du Sud may eventually be established as the French-language college for all of southern Ontario. The Collège du Sud might have a campus on the Niagara Peninsula, but its mandate would include francophone communities from Windsor to Toronto and north to Penetanguishine.

Trades Training

Niagara offers the skilled trades training and the classroom aspects of apprenticeship programs in several industrial and automotive areas.

Part-Time and Continuing Education

Niagara registers about 30,000 part-time students a year, mostly in credit courses, in a wide range of subjects. Part-time students can earn certificates and post-diploma credentials in a wide range of subjects. Continuing Education calendars appear three times a year, and courses may be added or dropped according to demand.

Getting in the Door

Telephone information is provided by the Admission office. The Counselling office also does extensive career-counselling and aptitude-testing work with non-students who are considering career changes that may include college.

As you approach the Welland campus, most of the signs say

"Permit Parking Only" as if to make you feel not very welcome, but the college promises new signage is on the way. The Hennepin Building, a low, square building to the left of the main building, currently houses most student services. It has a well-connected Information desk (with a large sign) inside the front door. However, Niagara plans to move all its front-end student services to a central location in the main building when it is renovated.

Each campus is served by local transit, but transit connections between cities on the Niagara Peninsula are limited.

Support Services

Recently Niagara started an intense program to improve the way it delivers its services to students. Related programs are being clustered into groups with common first years or semesters. The College has adopted an "Employability Skills Profile" created by the Conference Board in Canada, and is trying to work its criteria (academic skills, personnel management, teamwork) into all its programs.

Niagara has also adopted a number of anti-dropout strategies: the October Plan permits failing students to shift into a "developmental track" and return to their program when they have picked up the skills needed. Student-success and the "Master Student" study-skill workshops are offered as part of Orientation Week, and special sessions are available to older students who have been out of school for years. The faculty advisory network has been strengthened, so that academic advising and counselling are closely linked.

Connections

Agreements with local school boards have linked school programs to college programs. After Niagara established that 60 per cent of its Technology dropouts had taken Business Math instead of Math for Technology in high school, improved contacts with the schools sharply reduced the problem.

Niagara also has several agreements giving diploma grads in specific programs advanced standing in degree programs at American universities. It is also building links to Brock University in St. Catharines, permitting Niagara grads access to Brock programs, while Niagara takes over remediation (which colleges do better and far more cheaply) for students who are failing at university.

Scholarships

The college calendar lists ten prizes (for achievement) and nine bursaries, mostly for small amounts. The total amount is small – and will have to grow if Niagara intends to compete vigorously for students from all over Ontario – so apply early.

Where to Live

About 30 per cent of Niagara's students have come from outside the Niagara Peninsula. Niagara aims both to increase that number and to have residences on its campuses in Welland and St. Catharines. Meanwhile, a housing registry will help the search for accommodation in the area.

Sports and Recreation

The Niagara students' association recently opened its own freestanding Student Centre, "After Hours," on the Welland campus, with games room, snack bar, and pub. There is an active Non-traditional Students Association providing services to older students.

Niagara has a gym, tennis courts, sports fields, a fitness room, and a sauna. It has Ontario intercollegiate teams in basketball, golf, badminton, curling, volleyball, touch football, and indoor soccer, and plays hockey in a New York State league. There is also a large student-run intramural program, which involves a third of all Niagara students.

The City

Niagara has substantial operations in three cities – Welland, St. Catharines, and Niagara Falls – and it serves the whole Niagara Peninsula. All three cities have a mix of industry, services, and tourism, and they serve a heavily populated agricultural region. Commuting between the cities on public transit is not easy, but road connections are good, and each one of the cities has a wide range of entertainment, recreation, and shopping services.

Contact:

Niagara College
Woodlawn Road
Welland, Ont. L3B 5S2
(416) 735-2211

Niagara College Hospitality and Tourism Centre
5881 Dunn Avenue
Niagara Falls, Ont. L2G 1H2
(416) 374-7454

NORTHERN COLLEGE:

Not Just the Little School in the North Woods

Timmins, Haileybury, Moosonee, Kirkland Lake, Kapuskasing

Size: Small

The School of Mines in Haileybury, founded in 1912 and now part of Northern College, enjoys a worldwide reputation in Mining Technology training.

Northern College, like some other multi-campus colleges, has never been able to take unified college spirit for granted. Northern Ontario towns have always been fierce rivals, back to the days when each new mineral strike meant a new community supplanting all the older ones. When Northern College was founded in 1967, the Haileybury School of Mines was already fifty-five years old, with its own worldwide reputation, and it was not thrilled to be folded into some brand-new "college of applied arts and technology" with headquarters in faraway Timmins. Similar feelings arose when Northern absorbed Kirkland Lake's Institute of Technology. Local pride runs strong in each of the five communities where Northern has campuses.

Inter-campus rivalries have made it a special challenge to build a name and reputation for the college as a whole. Not many southerners have been inclined to go to the north for their education – to most of Ontario, Northern still looks small and a long way away – and many northerners seemed to think that real schools must be somewhere else. Since Northern was right there, it couldn't be that good.

But northerners who spend thousands to go elsewhere may be making the wrong decision. Northern has lots of strengths. With provincial funding behind it, it has the buildings, the equipment, and the faculty to deliver what all the other colleges do, and it offers great placement opportunities in all the northern industries. At the same time it is small, with good student-teacher ratios and lots of personal contact. Northern's senior faculty and staff tend to talk in examples – they give the impression of knowing all their students personally.

Northern is still the smallest college – but it seems to be doing a few thing right. Haileybury is still a world power in mining education (though Cambrian challenges it, there is room for both). Northern is strong in native programs, particularly at the James Bay Education Centre in Moosonee, and in resource-oriented Technology programs. It offers bilingual service and some bilingual programs (mostly at the Porcupine campus in Timmins). But mostly Northern's programs are standard – business, nursing, community service. Where it has been innovative is in program delivery. Program delivery is tough in a region the size of Sweden with fewer people than many southern Ontario suburbs, but Northern seems to be turning a problem into an advantage. It has moved strongly into projects to maximize student success and reduce dropouts, and it is increasing the amount of assessment it does on arriving students.

From its experience in distance learning (in which individual learners often study at their own pace), Northern is applying independent learning ideas to full-time programs, so that a skilled student and a slower one each can move through the same material at their own pace. To that end, Northern is moving into computer-managed learning. When computers do the paperwork and the testing, the September-to-May lockstep becomes less necessary.

Eventually Northern students may start when they like and take all the time they need until they master a subject. Already, Northern has rescheduled its school year from thirty-two to thirty-six weeks per year, with fewer class hours in each week. Weaker students get more time to keep up through individual learning, while strong students can use the extra time for part-time jobs and other activities during the school year.

Small northern cities have too few people to provide enough students to sustain a program year after year, and there may be too few employers to hire them anyway. So Northern rotates some programs around, offering them only once every couple of years in one city. It borrows curriculum from other colleges, and in a few programs it sends some two-year grads on to southern colleges for third year.

Northern is also a school for grown-ups. The number of high school students in the region is not growing much, and some of them either grab a job straight from school or head out for the bright lights. Adults, however, come to Northern when they come home to the north or discover there is not much future in an unskilled resource job. So Northern's average student is twenty-six, and in its new residence the average age is twenty-seven.

Recently Northern has been striving to increase cooperation and exchanges between its separate campuses, to increase its community profile, and to make student service its focus. It all looks promising.

Worth Going For

- School of Mines at Haileybury
- First Nations programs

Campuses

The main Northern campus is in Porcupine, which is part of the Timmins urban area. When I visited, the whole campus was a hard-hat area – major renovations were done during 1992 – but it

is surprisingly large and roomy. Northern has 114 acres at Porcupine, and some surprising ideas about how to develop its big,
green, lakeshore campus. (Hint: Fore!) It has just opened a student residence, and it has the most programs and the most students of any of Northern's campuses.

The Kirkland Lake campus emphasizes Technology and computer-related courses. Haileybury, with another spectacular lakeshore site and a collection of mining memorabilia that could stock
a mining museum if it chose to open one, was "pure" mining until
recently. When Business programs were added a couple of years
ago, some Haileybury veterans worried they would spoil the
school, but at last there is a substantial number of women on the
campus. Kapuskasing is small and mostly for outreach programs.
The James Bay Education Centre is devoted to serving the native
community in Moosonee and along the James Bay coast – though
it could offer southerners a great opportunity for immersion in
native culture.

Programs

Compared to the typical distribution of students among departments in the Ontario college system, Northern is larger than average in Health Sciences and Technology enrollments and has
smaller than average numbers in Business and Applied Arts. It has
co-op only for its Mining Technology program at Haileybury
School of Mines, but it uses field placements extensively.

Northern does a lot of academic upgrading to prepare students
for college. In the programs themselves, common years are rare,
but several three-year programs are "flow-through," meaning
two-year grads have the option of continuing if they wish.

Applied Arts

Northern's main Applied Arts cluster is made up of the Community Service standard programs: Early Childhood Education,
three-year Child and Youth Work, Developmental Service Work,
and Social Service Work, plus Drug and Alcohol Counsellor.

Northern is working on a Developmental Service Work diploma that will be available entirely through distance education. It will be "competency-based," meaning students will constantly be assessed on what they already know and what they still need to know, not on how many classes they have attended or how many credits they still need.

As well, Northern offers a two-year Fine Arts and Crafts, which covers many media in an open studio format.

Business

Business programs include two-year Business and three-year Business Administration programs in Accounting and Marketing, plus a two-year Information Systems program – Northern is particularly proud of the success its Marketing students have recently been enjoying in province-wide Marketing competitions. There is also a one-year Office Administration Certificate that offers extensive field placement in the second semester.

Health Sciences

Northern's Health Sciences are the basic Nursing (either two and a half or three years) and the thirty-six-week Nursing Assistant programs. It has also done some innovative distance education in Health Sciences – see below under "Part-Time and Continuing Education."

Technology

Technology programs are grouped in several clusters. Technician and Technologist programs in Architectural and Civil Engineering, in addition to a two-year Survey Technician, form the Architecture/Civil group.

A second cluster includes Technician and Technologist programs in Electrical Engineering and Electronic Engineering, Technologist programs in Computer Science and Information Systems, as well as a post-diploma certificate in Computer Process Control.

The Mechanical Engineering programs include Technician and Technologist programs in Mechanical Engineering, and Technician and Technologist programs in Welding Engineering. The Welding Engineering Technology program, which is offered at the Kirkland Lake campus, is the only one in Ontario. It is bilingual.

The Mining programs that made Haileybury famous are Technician and co-op Technologist programs in Mining Engineering, a Technician program in Instrumentation Engineering, plus a certificate program for Assistant Diamond Drill Operators.

French-Language Programs

Particularly at Porcupine-Timmins, Northern offers many of its programs in a bilingual format, and about 20 per cent of students there take bilingual programs. The aim is not so much to create an all-French environment as to train francophone students in the job terminology in both languages. But some French programs can be created on demand – Northern is the only college in the system to offer three-year Technologie du génie électrique. And all college services are available in French as well as English. When an all-French Collège du Nord is established (the government has approved in principle the establishment of a French-language college for Northern Ontario, but funding is not yet in place), French-language programming will transfer to it, but Northern will probably continue to offer student services in French.

Native Programs

Northern offers native options in Drug and Alcohol Counsellor and Social Services Work, and it has a First Nations Constable program. In addition, it offers native students a General Vocational Preparatory program as preparation for college, and a Native-core program as a prelude to Business, Community

Service, and Nursing programs. Programming at James Bay Educational Centre in Moosonee and in communities along the James Bay coast is entirely native-oriented.

Trades Training

Trades training at Northern's campuses is fairly small and closely linked to the program specialties: Millwright-mechanic, Welder-fitter, Motor Vehicle Mechanic, and so on. However, it is also extensively involved in upgrading and retraining contracts for industry. Recently it arranged to teach Sault College's pulp-and-paper program to the workers of the big, worker-owned Spruce Falls mill in Kapuskasing. Northern maintains a mobile millwright shop for on-site training.

Part-Time and Continuing Education

With about 12,000 Con Ed enrollments a year, Northern thinks it has touched nearly every family in the communities it serves. Business, Computer, and other practical, for-credit courses dominate the offerings.

Northern is also heavily involved in distance learning. Recently Northern's Health Sciences taught an upgrade-to-Nursing program by teleconferencing to RNAs in fourteen communities at once. The communications network permitted students in any one of the fourteen places to ask questions and follow the discussion. Small-town hospitals loved the opportunity it gave their staff and supported them to the hilt. "Audio-conferencing" is also used for distance-education courses in several other fields.

Experience with distance learning has led Northern into independent learning, where students learn on their own, at their own pace, supervised by the Independent Learning Centre at Northern's Kapuskasing campus. This experience, born of necessity, is already having an impact on the way full-time students are being taught.

Ontario's northernmost campus, the James Bay Education Centre in Moosonee, runs many Cree-languages services along the James Bay coast.

Getting in the Door

Staff at Northern are slightly apologetic that you can't just walk in the door and get a full-scale tour and orientation the way you used to. Now the college is big enough that they have to ask that you phone ahead first. But the same personalized service will be laid on when you come. Serving people all over the north, Northern publicizes its 800 number, and does all it can to provide information by phone and to handle registrations by mail as well as in person. All the campuses are small enough to be easy to enter and to find your way around.

Support Services

In recent years, Northern has been trying to make itself a student-centred organization. Support services are useful and easy to access. Students I talked to were impressed with the close student-faculty ties.

With a large proportion of adult students, many with family responsibilities, the student government offers a lot of mature-student programming. "But pubs are popular too," they told me.

Connections

Northern has been strengthening its relations with area high schools. It also has been promoting inter-college "brokering" – by which one college would offer another's programs. Already Northern offers students in some programs the possibility of starting at Northern and transferring to a southern college for later years. College-to-university transfer agreements are limited, but Laurentian University now offers a first-year course through Northern College, and Northern hopes to begin developing a University Centre to offer more university courses in the Timmins area.

Scholarships

Northern is currently building an alumni association (up to now, only Haileybury School of Mines had an alumni organization) and it is undertaking other ventures to increase its community profile. Northern already has a substantial fund for scholarships and bursaries.

Where to Live

Northern recently opened a 120-room residence building, with mostly private-room, private-bath accommodation, on its Porcupine campus. Cooking facilities are shared, and meal plans can be arranged. There is also a thirty-bed residence on the Kirkland Lake campus. At each campus, the housing office will assist in searches for off-campus housing.

Sport and Recreation

Until recently each Northern campus competed individually in intercollegiate sports (Haileybury's Miners won the Ontario college hockey championship in 1992), but steps are under way to unite more of the campuses' varsity sports activities. There are gyms and sports facilities on the main campuses, and each of the cities they are in has a large sports-and-recreation program.

The City

All the Northern cities are hardworking resource-based towns, and all have struggled with unemployment, plant closings, and economic crisis lately. There are strong community hockey, curling, and other recreational activities in all of them. Outdoor sports opportunities are first rate, and there are lots of bars and pubs. Northern College itself has done a lot of entertainment programming, participating actively in college booking networks and bringing in many entertainers never otherwise seen in the Northern College communities. Distances are huge in Northern's 58,000-square-mile territory, but road and airline networks link each community to each other and to the rest of Ontario.

Contact:

Northern College
South Porcupine, Ont. PON IHO
(705) 235-3211
1-800-461-2167

Northern College
Kirkland Lake, Ont. P2N 3L8
(705) 567-9291
1-800-461-4991

Northern College
Kapuskasing, Ont. P5N 1J6
(705) 335-8504

Haileybury School of Mines
Haileybury, Ont. POJ IKO
(705) 672-3376

James Bay Education Centre
Moosonee, Ont. POL IYO
(705) 336-2913

ST. CLAIR COLLEGE: *College as It Used To Be?*

Windsor

Size: Medium

Landscape students helped lay out the gardens and other amenities of St. Clair's main campus in Windsor.

St. Clair's Windsor campus, a big square building with lots of long corridors, made me wonder if this might be college as it used to be a decade or so ago. While many Ontario colleges now draw more out-of-town than local students, St. Clair's student body is still over 80 per cent from the Windsor-Essex-Kent region. It declares itself a commuter college and does not intend to build residences. While many colleges have attracted rapidly growing numbers of older students, St. Clair still relies heavily on recent high school graduates. There aren't many strikingly innovative or unusual programs in St. Clair's mix. Windsor's multicultural mix is less evident around the college than it might be. Even the decor of the college restaurant could use a makeover – though the recently renovated cafeteria is bright and modern and the main entrance lobby has been opened up and reorganized.

St. Clair has many strengths. "We do the best high school liaison in Ontario," they told me. They do a lot of high school visits, bring many classes into the college, and have firm agreements offering advanced standing for well-prepared high school grads. Even senior elementary students, brought in through the CASES (College Assists Seven and Eight Students) program initiated by St. Clair, get a valuable, hands-on introduction to career possibilities and how to prepare for them.

But success in selling college to high schools may have been balanced by less attraction to adult learners. "With 25,000 layoffs in Windsor, they should be beating down the doors," I was told. Indeed they should, but recent high school grads still dominate. In response to concerns expressed by Windsor's ethnic organizations about St. Clair's limited outreach to the multicultural population, the college recently appointed a Human Rights consultant and a native counsellor.

St. Clair is strong in Technology and trades fields and seems to be well connected to local industry. It still emphasizes traditional mechanical and industrial areas. Except for Thames's unique Energy program, St. Clair has not been one of the colleges leading the way into Robotics, Process Control, Environmental Engineering, specialized computer sciences, or other cutting edge technologies, but it does have good microcomputer labs and Computer-Assisted Design capabilities.

One undoubted St. Clair strength lies in its association with the University of Windsor. For years, the two institutions have had a joint Committee on Cooperation. St. Clair is one of the best colleges in Ontario for ease of transfer with credit from a college diploma to a university degree program. In a few programs, it also offers advanced standing to university graduates who transfer to college. Ironically, St. Clair's achievement in this area points out some of the risks of college-to-university transfer programs. I met St. Clair Business students who had no doubt they were getting better, more practical instruction than their friends at university. But they seemed to accept that they would have to transfer to a degree program before going after jobs.

Recently St. Clair has been taking steps to emphasize and improve student service, to assess the skills of incoming students, and to create flexible learning schedules to fit each student's needs. ("A three-year program just isn't automatically three years any more," I was told.) Quality of instruction has clearly become a priority. The most interesting innovation is what St. Clair calls "Paradigm Shift." This is a bold plan to reduce the amount of time students spend listening to a professor in a classroom. Instead, the college wants to encourage more independent and group work on learning projects. Much of the work will go on in labs and learning centres. Instead of acting as sole experts and absolute authorities, professors will become "learning managers."

That's certainly the direction learning is going throughout the college system, but it has its dangers. "If they leave the first-year kids to do everything on their own, there will be a lot of empty space in the parking lots after a couple of months," one student at St. Clair told me. The faculty are confident it won't be like that at all, and that support for students will be as strong as ever and better focused.

Paradigm Shift is a bold step for the college, and it has risks. If they bring it off, maybe more innovations will follow at St. Clair College.

Worth Going For

- The Architecture-Civil Engineering cluster
- Developmental Services Work at Thames Campus

Campuses

The main campus, called South Campus, is on a large grassy property off Huron Church Road south of downtown Windsor, close to the western end of Highway 401 and with good transit connections to the city. It offers a full range of college programs and services. The Industrial Resource Centre, focused on skilled trades, apprenticeship, and contract training for industry, is in the Walker Industrial Park in Windsor.

The Thames campus in Chatham has a fifty-acre site near the Thames River. With about 800 full-time diploma-bound students, it duplicates some of Windsor's programs and has a couple of its own, and it also does trades training and outreach in the region around Chatham.

Programs

Like most big-city big schools, St. Clair offers programs across the spectrum, with student enrollments in each area roughly matching the proportions common across the college system. Only the Health Sciences school has a bigger than average share of St. Clair students.

Most students starting programs at St. Clair will be tested for English and Math and may be guided to appropriate-level classes in those subjects.

St. Clair's General Arts and Science (GAS) program is primarily intended for students who have not qualified for a career-oriented program. Placement in other programs is not guaranteed to GAS graduates, but many GAS students transfer successfully after one year.

St. Clair has no co-op programs. Some programs do include workplace placements as part of the curriculum.

Applied Arts

St. Clair's main Applied Arts offerings are in the Community Service area. Programs are Child and Youth Work (three-year), Early Childhood Education, Law and Security Administration, two-year or three-year Communicator/Interpreter programs in Sign Language, and a post-diploma certificate in Gerontology, offered through Continuing Education. At the Thames campus in Chatham, St. Clair offers a two-year Developmental Services Work program, closely linked to the nearby Southwest Regional Centre (a large provincial agency serving adults with developmental disabilities), and a Gerontology program for applicants holding a certificate in a related field.

St. Clair also offers Print Journalism (with advanced standing available to university graduates), Commercial Art, Travel Counsellor, and a one-year Hairstyling certificate.

Business

St. Clair's two-year Business programs have Accounting, Information Systems, and Retail Management options. Its three-year Business Administration programs include Accounting, Marketing, and Information Systems options. There is also a three-year course in Business Advertising, which offers advanced standing to students with university or college experience, and which includes a two-week work placement, usually in Toronto.

The main Hospitality program is Food Service Management, whose students do part of their training at St. Clair's own restaurant, Chez Talbot.

Office Administration offers a one-year General certificate, as well as two-year programs with Medical, Executive, and Wordprocessing options, and a two-year Legal Assistant program.

Health Sciences

St. Clair offers Nursing and Nursing Assistant, Dental Assistant and Dental Hygiene, a three-year program in Medical Lab Technology in which most of the last year is hospital placement experience, and one-year certificates in Pharmacy Assistant and Ambulance and Emergency Care. There is also a two-year Veterinary Technician program. With the proper marks and courses, it is possible to transfer from Nursing Assistant to Nursing after the first semester, and January start dates are available in both programs.

Technology

A strong St. Clair cluster in Technology is Architecture and Civil Engineering. Programs offered are Architectural Engineering Technologist, Civil Engineering Technologist, and Construction

Clinical experience is a vital part of training for students in Nursing and all the other programs of St. Clair's School of Health Sciences.

Engineering Technician. These programs share a common first year. There are also two-year Technician programs in Furniture Production (with a one-year Techniques certificate available), Landscape (also offering a one-year Techniques certificate), and Interior Design.

There are Technologist programs in Chemical Engineering and in Electronic/Electrical Engineering, and a Technician program in Electronics. The Technician program in Mechanical Engineering specializes in Industrial Mechanics, and it can give advanced standing in registered millwright programs. St. Clair's Windsor campus has a Technologist program in Mechanical Engineering, and the Thames campus in Chatham has one which specializes in Energy Management and makes good use of the facilities and expertise of Chatham-based Union Gas as well as Ontario Hydro. Windsor campus also has a Technician program in Power Engineering, which trains operating engineers and systems maintenance personnel, and a Heating, Refrigeration, and Air Conditioning Technician program.

Other St. Clair Technology programs linked to needs of local industries are Technician programs in Motive Power (which covers automotive manufacturing and service), Mouldmaking, and Toolmaking.

Trades Training

Through its Industrial Resource Centre in Windsor, St. Clair offers trades training in a range of industrial and mechanical skills. It provides the academic portions for more than thirty apprenticeship programs, mostly in industrial and mechanical fields. St. Clair also does basic upgrading, contract training for industry and other training services for the Windsor-Essex community. The Thames campus has similar services for the Chatham-Kent County area.

Part-Time and Continuing Education

St. Clair has about 30,000 part-time registrations a year and offers courses across the spectrum. A large number of certificates in Community Service, Health Science, Business, Office Administration, and technological fields can be earned, and courses can be accumulated for diploma credit. In both Child and Youth Work and Early Childhood Education, a complete diploma can be earned on a part-time basis (both are also available full-time).

Getting in the Door

Both the South Campus in Windsor and the Thames Campus are well signposted and easy to find. At South Campus, recent renovations have provided an Information desk inside the front doors and gathered the essential student service offices nearby. Thames also has an information window and is small enough to make most things easy to find.

St. Clair offers 800 number toll-free service (for area codes 519,

416, and 705). The liaison office is ready to help with inquiries and will arrange tours on two weeks' notice. The college runs an elaborate Orientation program, with evening sessions starting well before classes begin. Information and orientation sessions are all aimed at reducing dropouts by keeping students well informed.

St. Clair recently created an Access Division to ease entry for anyone who finds roadblocks to college entry. (About Access, see "The Jargon" in Part One.) Counselling, the Learning Centre, and all the upgrading and entry-level offerings are clustered in the Access Department.

Support Services

Recently the college has been moving to implement a student-success model all through its operations. It is expanding its learning centres and working to increase students' freedom to start at their own level and progress at their own pace. Like many Ontario colleges, St. Clair is proud of the microcomputer lab facilities it makes available to all students.

The student government, dominated by Marketing students, is well run and active. It operates much of the large and successful Peer Tutoring program at the college, controls much of the Athletics program, and has put money into Special Needs programming and other valuable services.

Connections

Links to local school boards are good, and high school students can tailor their courses to fit college requirements and earn advanced standing in some areas. And, as noted above, opportunities to transfer to the University of Windsor are excellent. One recent agreement eases entry of Business Admin grads to the Bachelor of Commerce degree program at Windsor, and there are joint degree/diploma opportunities in Journalism, Early Childhood Education and other areas. St. Clair also has transfer agreements with universities in Michigan.

Scholarships

The college has a large and active alumni association, and it has been considering a fund-raising drive. (Windsor, with the most successful United Way program in Canada, has a good record in supporting local causes.) For the moment, the money available at St. Clair for scholarships and bursaries is relatively small, but St. Clair does offer twelve full-tuition entrance scholarships and a variety of other scholarships and bursaries. Emergency financial aid can be requested. Athletic scholarships are available for varsity players.

Where to Live

With 82 per cent of the students coming from the local area, St. Clair calls itself a commuter college and has no residences and no plans to build any. The Housing offices at the Windsor and Chatham campuses maintain a registry of rental accommodation in the area, but it does not provide telephones for housing-seekers.

Sports and Recreation

St. Clair is one of the few colleges with its own indoor swimming pool. Legend has it early administrators decided there would always be money for libraries and went for the pool instead. (Indeed the college today does have spacious, modern, and well-equipped library facilities as well as the pool.) There is also a gym, a weight-training room, a squash court, and outdoor sports fields.

The St. Clair Saints compete in a small number of intercollegiate varsity sports, and their Booster club provides full-tuition scholarships for varsity athletes. The student-run intramural and recreation programs are large and varied.

St. Clair also hosts the annual Challenge Cup, an annual community fund-raising event that brings dozens of teams and thousands of spectators to the campus for fun and competition in a wide range of activities.

The City

Windsor is a big city, with an industrial base built around its car plants. With the University of Windsor nearby, there is lots of student-focused activity. Recreation, entertainment, sports, and shopping are all readily available both in the city and in Detroit just across the river. "About the only course St. Clair's Con Ed doesn't offer is Shopping in Detroit," I was told. (One of the other colleges once caught hell in the Ontario Legislature for organizing cross-border shopping expeditions.) But self-directed learning is in fashion, and St. Clair students can probably teach themselves about Detroit.

Contact:

St. Clair College
2000 Talbot Road West
Windsor, Ont. N9A 6S4
(519) 966-1656 – General
(519) 972-2717 – Liaison

St. Clair College – Thames Campus
1001 Grand Avenue West
Chatham, Ont. N7M 5W4
(519) 354-9100

About Job Market Predictions and College Employment Rates

Job forecasting is like weather forecasting. You are only going to be right some of the time.

There is a whole industry to predict where all the jobs are going to be found five or ten years from now. One place you can tap into their ideas is the Job Futures book that the federal government publishes regularly. You can find it at Canada Employment Centres or at libraries.

You can ask any college for a copy of its Graduate Employment Report. Inside you will find statistics of what graduates of all the programs at the college are doing six months after graduation. If you are considering a program and a college, it is worth checking whether its grads are getting jobs in fields related to what they studied. (Remember – it's only the graduates. Nobody lists how many gave up before graduating.)

But in this book we have not used these statistics much – for several reasons. First, they are old news. They say how grads are doing now, but by the time you go through a program and graduate, the job market may have changed completely.

Second, they are not really a good way to compare two colleges. Durham College's overall placement rate may be better than Sault's, but it is a lot easier to place grads around Oshawa than in hard-hit Northern Ontario. If you are going to live and work in Sault Ste. Marie, Durham's better rates won't help you.

Third, job predictions are a lousy way to choose a career or a college program. Even if they turn out right, you don't want to choose a career you are going to hate just because it has great job prospects. College students and faculty told me over and over you should be choosing a program and a career because it seems right for you and your future.

ST. LAWRENCE COLLEGE: *Three Colleges in One*

Brockville, Cornwall, Kingston

Size: Medium

Varsity sports teams from St. Lawrence's three campuses – and all the Ontario colleges – play in provincial and national collegiate conferences. Intramurals, fun sports, and fitness programs are also important college activities.

The president and the senior staff of St. Lawrence College spend a lot of time on Highway 401.

Perhaps more than any other college, St. Lawrence is serious about being a full-service college in every community where it has a campus. So the president travels back and forth between Cornwall, Brockville, and Kingston. The administrative offices are not at Kingston, the biggest campus, but at Brockville, which is the smallest but halfway between the other two. St. Lawrence has been trying to offer a mix of programs at all its campuses.

Local pride is evident at each of the three campuses. Cornwall tried sending some of its students on to Kingston to complete their third years, but student complaints forced abandonment of that practice. For a long time, each campus tried to offer most of the programs that the others had, yet program curriculums at each

245

campus were so individualized that it was difficult to transfer to the same program at another campus of St. Lawrence.

But doing things three times is costly. Brockville has now dropped all its Technology programs, and Cornwall, strong in Technology, has dropped all Creative Arts programs. Plans are under way to ensure that when Business, Health Science, or Technology programs are offered at more than one campus, they will have common first years at all campuses.

St. Lawrence College used to be Collège St-Laurent as well, and the Cornwall campus had a large proportion of bilingual programs. With the creation of La Cité collégiale in 1989, however, French-language programming at St. Lawrence was transferred to it. La Cité shares St. Lawrence's Cornwall campus, and a substantial building program is under way to create a college and university campus that will serve both colleges and also the University of Ottawa.

In general, St. Lawrence has focused more on serving its three communities and the region around them than on creating programs that are one-of-a-kind in Ontario. More than four-fifths of St. Lawrence students come from the local area, and most stay there after graduation. However, the college says it hopes to strengthen its unique programs and begin drawing more students from beyond eastern Ontario.

Worth Going For

- Veterinary Technology at Kingston
- Combined diplomas in Developmental Service Work Child and Youth Work (at Brockville)
- Centre for Government Education, by correspondence from Kingston

Campuses

Kingston campus, with the largest number of programs and students, has a block of land in a residential neighbourhood not far from the lake in west Kingston. The western hub of Kingston

Transit is right outside the door, so bus connections in town are excellent. Brockville campus is a self-contained cluster of buildings on the outskirts of town north of Highway 401. Cornwall has a beautiful riverside site on Windmill Point close to downtown Cornwall. Its main building once housed a classical college run by an order of priests, and it still has the look of an old-fashioned boarding school. As part of the university-college Education Centre under development, substantial additions to the campus began in late 1992. The Cornwall campus also has a magnificent theatre auditorium, often used for community events.

Programs

With a nursing school at each campus, St. Lawrence is larger than average in Health Science enrollments, and slightly smaller than average in Technology. St. Lawrence has co-op programs in Hotel and Restaurant Management and the Accounting and Management options of Business Administration.

General Arts and Science at St. Lawrence has several options, and they all provide alternatives to starting in a career-oriented program. Students in the GAS Diploma Stream aim to complete a two-year GAS diploma, enjoying maximum freedom to tailor course options and schedule. It is possible to create your own major in Creative Writing, Teacher of Adults, or Women's Studies. GAS Exploratory Stream lets you look into various programs before you apply for a career-oriented program. GAS Developmental Stream lets you improve your confidence in the fundamentals and maybe collected some needed credits before applying to a career program.

GAS Integrated stream is a combination of Exploration and Development – you can improve your skills, and sample some programs too. If you are failing in some parts of a career-related program, you may be steered into GAS Integrated for a while.

Applied Arts

Kingston has St. Lawrence's main cluster of Creative Arts

programs: three-year Graphic Design, three-year Fashion Design, and two-year Fine Arts, plus a Hairstyling certificate. Brockville also offers some Fine Arts courses part-time, and Hairstyling. Cornwall has a three-year Graphic Design program.

In Social Services, Kingston offers three-year Behavioural Science Technology, a program (unique to St. Lawrence) which trains social service workers in many areas. Kingston and Cornwall also offer three-year Child and Youth Work, and Kingston has two-year programs in Correctional Work and Early Childhood Education, as well as a Social Service Work program with a specialization in Gerontology. Brockville offers both Child and Youth Work and Developmental Service Work, and has post-diploma programs that permit graduates of either program to add a diploma in the other field. Brockville and Cornwall both offer Law and Security Administration. Cornwall has a two-year Social Service Work program.

Business

Kingston has two-year Business and three-year Business Administration programs in Accounting, Marketing, Human Resources, and Information Systems. Brockville has three-year Business Administration programs in Finance, Marketing, and Accounting, and a Business Technology program in Information Communications. Cornwall has two-year General Business and Accounting, and three-year Business Administration programs in Accounting and Management (both with optional co-op), plus a two-year program in Appraisal. The main business programs at St. Lawrence are nearly identical in first year, and students confirm their choice of option toward the end of first year.

The one-year General Office Administration is offered at all three campuses. In a second year, Kingston offers Executive, Medical, and Legal options, and it also has a two-year Legal Assistant program. Brockville has Executive Office Administration, and Cornwall has Legal and Executive.

Kingston has a unique two-year program in Advertising and Public Relations, which combines aspects of what other colleges usually offer in separate Advertising and Public Relations programs. It also offers Fashion Merchandising and Recreational Marine Management. Brockville has Hotel and Restaurant Management, which has a co-op option.

Linked to the Business school is the Eastern Ontario Centre for Entrepreneurship, which offers outreach courses, seminars, and consulting to small business owners and the self-employed.

Health Sciences

Brockville, Cornwall, and Kingston all offer 2.5-year Nursing and one-year Nursing Assistant. St. Lawrence Nursing is reputed to be demanding – the pass mark is 75 per cent. Kingston has Medical Lab Technology and Medical Lab Assistant programs. It also created a unique three-year Veterinary Technology program, which trains for careers in veterinary offices and animal research labs.

Technology

Kingston has Technologist programs in Civil Engineering and Computer Engineering. It has Technician and Technologist in Electronic Engineering and in Instrumentation Engineering, which focuses on process control and automation.

Brockville does not offer Technology programs, but Cornwall is strong in that area. It has Technologist programs in Electronic Engineering and Microcomputer Engineering, a Technician program in Mechanical Engineering, and two Technologist programs in Marine Engineering: a standard one and one specializing in Control and Instrumentation. Georgian is the only other college offering similar Marine Engineering programs. For some reason, Cornwall attracts many naval technologists from the Canadian Forces, while Georgian's are mostly civilian.

Trades Training

Kingston offers the academic part of apprentice programs in the construction and mechanical areas, and skilled trades courses in

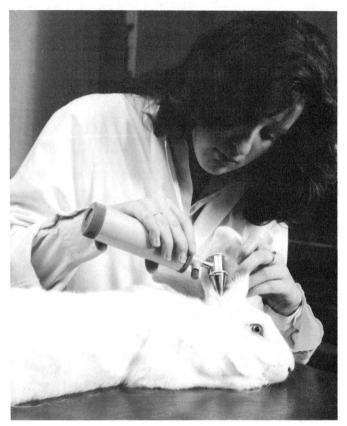

The three-year Veterinary Technology program at St. Lawrence's Kingston campus is unique in Ontario. Students frequently have a university background in zoology or another science.

the food preparation area. Cornwall has a smaller range of both. Both campuses have introduced TRAC, "TRaining ACcess," through their Training Resource Centre. TRAC allows skilled trades students to set their own pace under individual supervision. Although Brockville has no Technology programs, TRAC's individualized learning permits trades students to study there.

Part-Time and Continuing Education

Kingston has created the Community Learning Centre, which permits part-time Continuing Education students to learn skills at their own pace on their own schedule, with individual tutoring as needed. Similar centres are about to open at Brockville and Cornwall.

All three campuses have a wide range of courses which can be taken on a part-time basis as part of work toward a diploma. They also have many specialized certificate courses available only through Con Ed – these vary from nursing upgrades to management training to fine arts. All three campuses offer interest-only non-credit evening courses as well.

St. Lawrence has the unique Centre for Government Education and Training, which offers outreach courses in municipal government, including a training course for elected councillors which is now used by cities and towns in seven provinces and the Territories.

Getting in the Door

St. Lawrence has no 800 number or dedicated information line. Each campus has its own phone numbers, but you can call any campus and be connected to the right department anywhere on the three campuses.

All three campuses are easy to find and enter. All three have information services at the entrance and are clustering front-end services near the front door.

Most of St. Lawrence's orientation goes on within individual program groups, and tends to be more practical than party. For entertainment, everyone at Kingston seems to agree that it's not worth competing with the Orientation week activities at nearby Queen's. Brockville and Cornwall don't face that competition.

Support Services

St. Lawrence is beginning to institute the Prior Learning Assessment concept. Prior Learning Assessment means if you can demonstrate you have mastered a subject – by working, by teaching yourself, however – you can receive direct credit without having to take courses in that subject. At St. Lawrence they call this ALEC, the Advanced Learning Education Credit. If you have been trained in skilled technical work on the job, for instance, you should probably be entitled to ALECs toward a Technician or Technologist diploma. If you have skills in any program-related field, ask for credit toward the diploma you are seeking. The college will also grant exemptions for appropriate OAC or university coursework.

Each campus has made a substantial commitment to independent learning centres, testing centres, and computer labs. St. Lawrence has an all-IBM policy, except in Graphic Design where the Macintosh rules.

Connections

Each St. Lawrence campus has agreements with its local school boards to ease student transfer from school to college. If you do the right high school co-op, for instance, you will get advanced standing in Hotel-Restaurant Management at St. Lawrence Brockville – and you will know more of what the program does before you start it. Similar arrangements cover many other programs.

College-to-university transfers are less well developed. At Cornwall, however, St. Lawrence, La Cité collégiale, and the University of Ottawa are cooperating to create a unified Education Centre for both college and university programs, and linkages between them will develop. Veterinary Technician at Kingston draws many Science students from Queen's.

Scholarships

St. Lawrence started an alumni association a few years ago, and is gearing up for a fund-raising drive. Some of the money will go to scholarships, prizes, and bursaries. So far, the amount available for these is fairly small and mostly aimed at returning and graduating students, not new arrivals.

Where to Live

With 80 per cent of its students coming from the local region, St. Lawrence has no residences at Brockville or Kingston. At Cornwall, the student residence is about a mile from the campus. It can accommodate 210 students in single or double rooms. Cafeteria, lounge, laundry, and exercise facilities are available. Housing Registries operate at all three campuses. Kingston is a student town, and the area north of the campus there is becoming a student quarter. Permanent residents of the neighbourhood have not been entirely pleased about that, and the college runs a program to keep relations smooth. St. Lawrence Cornwall is one of the few college campuses without on-campus daycare.

Sports and Recreation

Like most colleges, St. Lawrence has varsity sports, but with three campuses, it has three varsity teams in each sport where it competes. All three campuses have gyms, weight rooms, and other sports facilities, and the Cornwall one has just been renovated and upgraded.

Midday every Tuesday is "Double X" common hour throughout the college – all classes are crossed off the schedule, creating two common hours for events, entertainment, and clubs throughout the college.

Kingston has a student centre and pub, and the TV room has an informal Soaps Hour every afternoon. The other two campuses have student lounges and pubs.

The City

Three cities. Kingston is a student city, with Queen's, Royal Military College, and St. Lawrence all close together. Queen's is very

Ivy League, and some of its preppies still think college is second-rate, but because there are so many students in the city, there is abundant youth-oriented entertainment available to all. Shopping, recreation, and outdoor sports are all available in and around the city, and travel connections to Montreal, Ottawa, and Toronto are good.

Brockville is a smaller town, with some industry and local services, and St. Lawrence is the only higher education in town. Cornwall is a blue-collar industrial town that still has some big employers – Domtar's pulp mill, in particular – but it has been struggling against industrial decline for a couple of decades. Community/college links are strong. Cornwall has a large francophone population, and although St. Lawrence turned over its French-language programs to La Cité collégiale (which shares the St. Lawrence campus), the francophone presence around the Cornwall campus remains strong. Highways and train services link all three cities to Toronto, Montreal, and Ottawa.

Contact:

St. Lawrence Brockville
2288 Parkedale Avenue
Brockville, Ont. K6V 5X3
(613) 345-0660

St. Lawrence Cornwall
Windmill Point
Cornwall, Ont. K6H 4Z1
(613) 933-6080

St. Lawrence Kingston
King and Portsmouth
Kingston, Ont. K7L 5A6
(613) 544-5400

SAULT COLLEGE: *Growing Fast in Hard Times*

Sault Ste. Marie

Size: Small

Sault College has one of the largest clusters of Natural Resources programs in Ontario. Forest Technician students do fieldwork in the northern forest.

People turn to schooling in hard times, partly to avoid the job market, partly to be better prepared when they do return to it. In recent years, few Ontario cities have seen harder times than Sault Ste. Marie. With Algoma Steel and St. Marys Paper both downsizing as they fought to avoid closing altogether, steelworkers and paperworkers flooded into Sault College for retraining or for career change. Sault, which had been getting smaller earlier in the 1980s, suddenly became one of the fastest-growing colleges in Ontario.

255

Most of Sault's new students were adults, coming to college after years in the workforce. As the average student age rose, Sault, like many other colleges, discovered that adult students make a college a different place.

Older students tend to be goal-oriented. They don't have a lot of time to float around searching for their life's direction. They identify the careers and credentials they want, and they head straight for them. They have motivation, good work habits, and clear expectations of what they want from college. They have little fear of complaining when a school does not fulfil their expectations.

On the other hand, adult students often lack academic preparation. Hundreds of the steelworkers who flooded into Sault College had quit high school to take well-paid and apparently secure jobs at Algoma or some other plant or mill, so they needed upgrading before starting post-secondary programs. Many adults are not used to school. Studying and note-taking and preparing for exams are all new to them. And adults often have families and children competing with school for their attention. Altogether, adult students behave differently from students straight from high school.

Taking in such a large group of adult learners helped Sault College focus on "developmental learning" – taking people as they are, "qualified" or not, then giving them personal and academic support to ease the transition to college and to prevent failure or dropping out. These, in fact, are precisely the same "student-centred" goals that all the colleges claim to be aiming for. At Sault, they just came home a little more forcefully.

Above all, Sault is a northern college, and as some of its people told me, "the southern colleges just don't understand." In Sudbury and the Sault and the cities served by Northern College, colleges become vital parts of the community. They are often the only source of industrial training and upgrading and they become a key part of community social-and-economic planning. With all its upgrading and industry-training activities, post-secondary education is barely half of what Sault College does.

Worth Going For

- Aviation Technology (Flight)
- Pulp-and-Paper and other Natural Resources Technology programs

Campuses

The main Sault campus is a large cluster of linked buildings on a campus in a residential/commercial area of north-central Sault Ste. Marie. Transit and driving connections around Sault Ste. Marie are good. Sault also has outreach campuses at Wawa, Chapleau, Blind River, and Elliot Lake.

Programs

Relative to the usual mix of enrollments in Ontario colleges, Sault is twice as big as average in Technology, and smaller than average in Business and Health Science programs. Some Technology programs are co-op.

In keeping with its "developmental education" philosophy, Sault has many programs designed to ease entry into its career programs. Sault's General Arts and Science program has several alternatives. GAS College Preparatory is designed for students who lack high school General credentials, or whose tests show they need additional preparation. GAS Liberal Studies may be of interest to those intending to continue on to university. GAS General Career Exploration permits students to sample programs by selecting courses from several career streams. GAS Human Sciences and GAS Health Sciences are designed as preparation for those career program areas. Completing them, however, does not guarantee entry to the target programs. The School of Sciences and Natural Resources offers GAS options that train Geological Exploration Assistants and Forestry Equipment Operators.

Applied Arts

Sault's Applied Arts programs are mostly in the Human Sciences area. Teaching-related programs include Early Childhood Education (Sault also offers a part-time, post-diploma certificate in Infant and Toddler Care and Education), Recreation Leadership, plus one few other colleges offer, Teacher Assistant program for classroom aides. Community service programs are Child and Youth Work, Developmental Service Work, Law and Security Administration, and Correctional Work. An Enforcement Services Preparation certificate is offered at Elliot Lake, and Wawa has an integrated Early Childhood Education/Teacher Aide program.

Sault also offers a three-year program in Advertising Art and Graphic Design, covering all aspects of artwork for the advertising industry. It includes extensive field placement in the final year.

Business

All Business programs at Sault have a common first semester, and Sault calls its related programs "thru-way," meaning third year is an option after completion of the two-year program, not a separate program. The basic Business program is two-year General Business. There are two-year and three-year Accounting programs, plus a two-year program in Advertising Management, and two-year or three-year programs in Computer Programmer and Computer Programmer/Analyst. Sault's Centre for Management Studies offers seminars, consulting, and training on an outreach basis.

Office Administration offers executive and legal options, plus a one-year certificate in Office Procedures and Retail Sales.

Sault recently opened its on-campus Northern Ontario Hospitality and Tourism Institute, designed to replicate a working hotel and restaurant, with its own front lobby, hotel suite, banquet rooms, and working restaurant, "The Gallery." The key programs associated with it are the two-year Hotel and Restaurant Management program and a post-diploma certificate in Tourism Marketing Management. Also offered are Chef Training (a one-year

Sault's Northern Ontario Hospitality and Tourism Institute has its own hotel lobby, suite of rooms, and working restaurant to train its students.

pre-apprenticeship certificate), and one-year programs in Food and Beverage Management and Food Service Assistant.

Health Sciences

The Sault School of Health Sciences is small and focused on Nursing and Nursing Assistant programs. It also offers a part-time program for Health Care Aides and many refresher programs for registered nurses and RNAs. It badly needs new and larger facilities.

Technology

Technology is the largest program area offered at Sault College. Some of its programs are co-op. Related programs are "thru-way," with the third year optional after completion of the first two.

Mechanical, Instrumentation, and Pulp-and-Paper programs are closely linked to the needs of local industry.

A stand-out that draws many students from outside the Sault area is a three-year Aviation Engineering Technology (Flight) program, which includes a private Pilot licence and prepares students for careers as civil aviation pilots. In Ontario, only Seneca and Confederation offer similar programs. Sault Aviation students are expected to conform to a dress code, and attrition in the first year is high.

Sault's other unique Technology area is Natural Resources. The School of Sciences and Natural Resources has a range of programs matched only by Fleming's Frost School of Natural Resources, and students come from across Canada. The Great Lakes Forestry Centre, the Ontario Forest Research Institute, and other forest-related institutions are located close by. All two- and three-year programs in this area are co-op. There are Technician and Technologist programs in Environmental Engineering, focused on water and waste-water treatment for municipal engineers. A related program is a three-year Water Resources Engineering Technology program.

The fundamental Natural Resources program is a two-year Forestry Technician program, which can lead to a third year in Technologist programs in Fish and Wildlife, Forest Management, and Parks and Forest Recreation. The Technician and Technologist programs in Meteorology, which train students for careers in the Atmospheric Environment Service and private meteorological careers, is unique in Canada. Unique to Sault is the Technologist program in Pulp and Paper Engineering, and the college also offers a one-year certificate in Pulp and Papermaking Operations. There is also a two-year program in Taxidermy. The Wawa campus of Sault College has a two-year Technician program in Log Construction.

There are co-op Technician and Technologist programs in Architectural and Civil Engineering, and a co-op Technician program in Construction Engineering. The Mechanical Engineering area offers several programs, none of them co-op: Technician and Technologist programs in Mechanical Engineering, with Technician options in Machining and Drafting. A one-year Machine

Shop certificate can lead to second-year Mechanical Engineering (Machining) or to apprenticeship. There is also an Instrumentation Technician program.

Also offered are Technician and Technologist programs in Electric and Electronic Engineering; neither is co-op.

Native Programs

With about 500 native students enrolled, Sault has a Native Education Centre with a Native Student Assembly, native counsellors, and close links to local band councils. There is a native College Entrance program, and Native Community Work programs with Child and Youth Worker and Addiction Counsellor options. Sault also runs the Four Seasons Anishinabe Art Journey, a certificate course in native art and culture.

Trades Training

Sault does extensive outreach, training the workforce of local employers. It also offers skilled trades training in a range of industrial and construction trades, many of which lead to apprenticeship. Sault provides the academic portions of apprenticeships in ten fields, from barbering to heavy-duty equipment maintenance.

Part-Time and Continuing Education

Sault's Con Ed department offers credit courses, college preparation, career-oriented refresher courses, and management seminars, and registers over 11,000 students a year.

Sault has been one of the most active colleges in the Contact North Distance Education program, particularly in teleconferencing. ("We mostly leave paper-and-pencil correspondence courses to the others," I was told.) Some of its programs are available via distance education to people working in the field.

Getting in the Door

Sault promotes its 800 number for information. The campus entrance is easy to find, and it has an information booth inside the front door. Through the summer, one-on-one informational tours are offered by appointment.

If you are unsure of your future, Sault offers a four-to-six-hour career aptitude testing process, which is followed up by counselling. This service used to be free – and heavily used by adults in career crisis. Now a fee is charged, but it is refundable to clients who enroll at Sault.

Support Services

To support its commitment to "developmental learning," Sault has built strong networks for faculty advice and counselling support to all students. Class sizes are small, so close faculty-student contact is possible.

Sault also runs an impressive placement service, available at no charge to all graduating students and graduates. Its toughest challenges: the cyclical downturns in the northern resource economy – and the reluctance of many students to leave the Sault.

Connections

Sault has built strong links to local high schools and organizes "School Days" tours of specific areas. It also has an elaborate system of links to other post-secondary institutions. The most important of these is the BRIDGE project. Bridge stands for Bi-national Regional Initiative Developing Greater Education. That may be the most carefully contrived acronym in the college system, for most of its activity depends on the bridge between Sault Ste. Marie, Ontario, and Sault Ste. Marie, Michigan. BRIDGE links Sault College and Algoma University College on the Canadian side and Lake Superior State University in Sault, Michigan.

BRIDGE runs several shared centres for regional industrial planning but, most important, it permits Sault College grads to transfer with credit to complete degrees at Lake State. Sault also has similar agreements with other Michigan universities for specific programs.

Scholarships

Sault's scholarship and bursary offerings total more than $45,000 each year, and students I spoke to felt there were lots to apply for. The college has an emergency loan fund.

Where to Live

About half of Sault's students come from outside its official catchment area. Sault has on-campus single- and double-room residence accommodation for more than 160 students in new buildings that will open in early 1993. A meal plan, included for residents, can also be purchased by off-campus students. A Residence Council and dons coordinate residence activities. The college also runs a housing service for off-campus housing searches.

Sports and Recreation

Sault has a gym, weight rooms, games rooms, and outdoor tennis and cross-country ski trails. There is an extensive intramural program and varsity teams in basketball, hockey, curling, and volleyball.

The Student Association runs movie nights, "Thirsty Thursdays," and other activities.

The City

Sault Ste. Marie is an industrial town of 80,000, with the smaller American city of Sault Ste. Marie, Michigan, just across the Sault locks at the St. Mary's rapids. The town is dominated by the Algoma Steel mill and the paper plants. Shopping, bars, entertainment, and sports are all within easy reach of the college. There are highway and airline links to other parts of Ontario and to Michigan.

Contact:

Sault College
P.O. Box 60
443 Northern Avenue
Sault Ste. Marie, Ont. P6A 5L3
(705) 759-6774
Toll free: 1-800-461-2260

SENECA COLLEGE: *All Over Town*

North York

Size: Large

Seneca is one of only three Ontario colleges that train commercial fixed-wing aircraft pilots for the aviation industry.

With 12,000 full-time students, nearly 100,000 part-timers, and 55,000 graduates, Seneca is the biggest college in Ontario. If it were three colleges, they would still be bigger than most. Before I went there, I had heard suggestions that maybe it grew too easily. With students flowing into Seneca from the fast-growing communities north of Toronto (but few coming from far away), there seemed to be hints that it never had to hustle, never had to be really good to draw students.

But if there was ever any truth to that reputation, Seneca is working hard to shake it. Seneca is using its size to lead the way in experiments with new ways to teach and learn. It is moving strongly toward a student-centred learning system. It wants to emphasize individual scheduling, hands-on lab and studio work, and computers as instructional and testing tools. "If I go into a classroom and I see someone lecturing, I have a problem," says one Seneca dean.

Seneca wants to obliterate the idea that all students must take two years, or whatever the calendar says, to complete a program. Some students need more time to master a subject. Others may have work experience or special skills that should entitle them to immediate credit. And since many students will mix full-time and part-time studies as they work toward their particular goals, Seneca wants to blur the distinction between them.

To create that kind of custom-tailored, individual learning package, Seneca has made itself the lead college in what is called "Prior Learning Assessment" – which means assessing people as they come in the door, giving them credit for what they already know, and slotting them in wherever they need to be. "If we had a perfect system," they told me, "we would test in all areas and counsel all new entrants. That's education, not mass manufacturing."

It is also expensive. In its efforts to custom-tailor education, Seneca is experimenting with computer-based instruction as one way to do more with less. That could be exciting, but it might also be dangerous. Like lectures by television, computer learning could turn out to be a wasteful, costly, techno-gimmick that simply creates a larger-than-ever gap between students and teachers. Seneca is determined to prove it will be more than that. It sees using computers that instruct, correct, and mark students in all kinds of subjects as the best way to permit students to proceed at their own pace – and to free teachers from endless lecturing, so they can concentrate on individual mentoring and supervision. If that is the future of education, Seneca will get there early.

Seneca has always been a business-focused school, with a relatively high proportion of its full-time students in Business. When the college system began, other Toronto colleges inherited a strong trades-and-apprenticeship background, and Seneca mainly stayed out of that area. (Maybe its business-school emphasis helped pin a white-collar, suburban reputation on it.) Even in

Applied Arts, it has many administrative and managerial courses with a business flavour. Many of its unique courses, in fact, are in specialized niches that aren't particularly glamorous but often attract older students with some experience in a related field.

Still, Seneca is big enough to be strong in areas well beyond the Business orbit. It is the only college in Ontario training deep-sea divers to international standards. It runs a lively School of Communication Arts, and it does leading-edge Technology training, notably in Computer Engineering and in Biotechnology. Seneca also has a wonderfully diverse student population. It has big Chinese, South Asian, Latin American, and Caribbean communities around it, some of them very affluent and strongly committed to higher education, some of them much more disadvantaged. There are more than seventy language groups represented in Seneca's student body, and large numbers of immigrants depend on Seneca to help integrate them into Canadian careers.

The Seneca students bring many cultural styles and many learning styles to the college. With 40 per cent of its students having a home language other than English (and 70 per cent of those having been born outside Canada), Seneca is actually as multicultural as downtown George Brown. It seems strongly committed to respecting all of its students' cultures. Its individualized-learning projects respond well to the very different backgrounds its students bring. The college provides counselling in as many languages as possible. It runs a special English and Orientation program for International students, and it has extensive overseas connections.

Seneca is a very big college, and some people will find that alienating. For years Seneca has had campuses all over North York and York Region, many of them offering the same programs and competing against each other for students. Like the city of North York, Seneca has been badly in need of a centre. The largest campus, Newnham, can accommodate 6,000 students in one huge, rambling building, and when you are new you are likely to get lost in it.

But find your niche and your support group at Seneca and you could be right at home. Because it is a big school, it has more services on tap – great sports facilities, top-notch computer labs, free legal clinics – than almost anyone. And with the kind of changes in personnel and policy that are going on, Seneca looks like being a school that cares about quality education.

Worth Going For

- School of International Business
- Individualized learning programs
- Outdoor-oriented programs at King Campus

Campuses

Seneca is Ontario's most glaring example of a college with too many campuses. Indeed, its campuses have often competed against each other for students, who had to choose not only their Seneca program but where they wanted to take it. Seneca needs to reduce the number of campuses it operates, but it also aims to open a major new west-of-Yonge campus to serve the western part of its territory. In the meantime, however, more departments are gathering their programs together at one or other of Seneca's campuses. Some of the campuses have remained small and developed specialized roles, so that students at them share a sense of common purpose.

The main campus, Newnham, in the Seneca Hill neighbourhood of North York, sprawls down a hillside on Finch East near Don Mills Road. It houses Applied Arts, Business, and Technology programs, the main admin offices, a theatre-auditorium, the student-run Senecentre, and an impressive athletic complex. It also has a planetarium, the Roberta Bondar Earth and Space Centre, which it uses constantly in outreach programs for local school groups. Newnham has seen several expansions and it badly needs more directional signs. If you can find your way around Newnham, you deserve an Orienteering diploma.

Sheppard Campus, at Sheppard and Yonge by the North York City Centre, houses many of the Community Service programs. Yorkdale, on Dufferin south of Lawrence, has some of the multimode learning programs where lab work and independent study replaces most classroom teaching. It also has the Office Administration programs.

The School of Communication Arts is in a business mall on Finch West near Keele. It is small and has a clear focus and an attractive in-the-workplace feel. The Computer Studies School is on Don Mills Road south of Highway 401. The Leslie campus, on Sheppard East near Leslie not far from North York General Hospital, includes a women's residence and houses most Health Sciences programs. Some courses of the Dental programs are on the Dufferin campus on Finch West near Dufferin Street.

The most attractive Seneca property is King, on North Dufferin Street in King City. King is a rolling, grassy campus of almost seven hundred acres that includes a lake and the former country estate of the Eaton family (now a conference centre), as well as the Garriock Building, which houses most classrooms, labs, offices, and student services. King campus offers several outdoor-oriented programs and other Applied Arts, Business, and Tourism and Hospitality programs.

The 20,000-square-foot Centre for Precision Skills Training, on Jane near the 400/401 interchange, houses apprenticeship and skills training services. Other Seneca properties in North York, Markham, Newmarket, Vaughan, and Richmond Hill mostly offer upgrading, evening, and outreach courses. Seneca's Aviation program has aircraft facilities at Buttonville Airport.

Programs

Seneca is very big in Business. About 45 per cent of its students are in Business programs (across the system, about a third is typical). It is relatively small in its proportion of Health Sciences students.

As part of its commitment to Prior Learning Assessment and individualized learning, Seneca tests most incoming students, particularly in English and Math. The point of testing is to determine where each student should be placed and what specialized courses might be of benefit. Expect to be tested, and ask for information about the results.

Seneca has one of the largest co-op enrollments in Ontario. It has mandatory or optional co-op in almost thirty programs, mostly in Business or Technology. Some programs require co-op applicants to have satisfactory marks in early semesters to get in.

As part of its plan to tailor all its programs to individual needs, Seneca aims to integrate most students into career-oriented programs, even if they need substantial amounts of remediation near the start. But for those in need of upgrading before entering the workforce or a college program, Seneca offers various College Preparatory courses at several campuses.

Seneca has always been more committed to "General Education" than most Ontario colleges. It offers all students a lot of options in Liberal Studies and has many Canadian Studies courses, which may be particularly useful to its large immigrant population but are available to all. Its General Arts and Science program has a common first semester for all students, but later semesters can be adapted to individual needs. There is a co-op GAS program.

Applied Arts

Seneca's Community Service programs cover not only the usual social service fields, but also a range of unusual programs in management and administrative areas. Many of these tend to attract people with some work experience in the field. They include two-year programs in Court and Tribunal Administration (co-op), Government Administration (which emphasizes property by-law supervision), Property Management, and Real Property Administration (with a strong emphasis on assessment and appraisal). There are also one-year post-diploma courses in Building Construction Regulations Administration and in Regulatory Law Administration. Also offered are a Library and Information Technician program and a Legal Assistant program.

Community Service programs include Early Childhood Education. It is ordinarily a two-year program, but Seneca also offers a four-year joint program with York University, which leads to both a diploma and a Bachelor of Arts degree. Other Community Service programs are Law Enforcement and Social Service Work (which has a Gerontology option), and the two-year Veterinary Technician program, offered at the King campus.

Seneca has an unusual cluster of Sport and Recreation programs. There are Advanced Coaching Techniques programs in Figure Skating, Gymnastics, and Tennis (all three are also available as one-year certificate courses). Other programs are Golf Course Technician (co-op), Outdoor Recreation Technician (co-op), Recreation Facilities Management, and Parks Operation (co-op). In addition, there is a post-diploma certificate in Recreational Resources Management.

Seneca has a cluster of programs in the Fashion and Retail areas. These include a three-year Fashion Arts, a two-year Fashion Merchandising, a three-year Retail Management in Fashion Merchandising, and a one-year Fashion Sales certificate. There is an Esthetician program, and also Cosmetic Techniques and Management, Visual Merchandising Arts, and one-year certificates in Cosmetic Sales and Retail Florist.

Communication Arts programs, which mostly have common first semesters and similar learning objectives in English and Liberal Studies, share facilities at the School of Communication Arts campus, which has a very "creative-studio" feel. Programs are Audio-Visual Communications, a combined program in Radio/ Television Broadcasting, Creative Advertising, three-year Design Arts, and both Computer Graphics and Technical Computer Graphics (which specializes in the hardware and software of computer graphic systems). Co-op placements are optional in both Graphics programs. Students in Audio-Visual, Broadcasting, and Advertising can earn a Seneca diploma and a York University B.A. simultaneously. There is also a post-diploma co-op program in Corporate Communications.

The Tourism and Hospitality cluster, mostly at King campus, offers one-year certificate programs in Flight Services and Tour Guiding. The Travel and Tourism studies program can be taken in two years at King (with an option in Flight Services) or on a flexible, student-driven schedule at Yorkdale. There is also a three-year Tourist Industry Administration diploma.

Business

Seneca Business programs have several clusters. Most are offered at Newnham, but a few are available at King. In the core Business subjects – Accounting, International Business, Business Management – first semester is common, and most of these programs share a common first year. Some Business programs at Newnham have a flexible completion option, meaning students work at their own pace and do a great deal of independent study. In general, however, courses with "Administration" in the title are expected to take six semesters – three years. Others are two-year unless otherwise noted. Most incoming Business students are assessed and will be placed at appropriate levels according to prior experience.

The Accounting cluster includes Accounting, three-year Accounting and Finance (with optional co-op), a one-year certificate in Microcomputer Accounting Clerk, and Business Administration in Accounting.

The Business Administration cluster includes General Business, Business Administration (with optional co-op), Business Administration specialization in Human Resources Management (with optional co-op), plus a three-year Business Computer Systems and a post-diploma program in Human Resources Management.

Marketing and Small Business includes Marketing, Business Administration in Marketing (with optional co-op), Small Business Management, Small Business Administration (with optional co-op), and post-diploma certificates in Microcomputer Systems and Sales Management.

The International Business cluster includes three-year International Business (with optional co-op) and a post-diploma certificate in International Business Management, plus two-year and three-year co-op programs in International Freight Forwarding and Customs Brokerage.

The School of Business runs an Odyssey program that sends students to work in Mexico, Singapore, and other countries to gain international business experience. Seneca also runs the

Eaton Hall Management Development Centre on the King campus. It offers live-in educational seminars on an outreach basis.

In Office Administration at Yorkdale campus, Seneca offers the general program and a two-year French-English program for bilingual secretaries, as well as Executive, Legal, and Medical options. There is also a co-op program in Records and Information Management. The certificate program in Office Systems Operations runs thirty-two weeks, but early completion is possible. This is a continuous-intake program – you can start any Monday.

Health Sciences

Seneca is almost the only college not offering Nursing Assistant, but it has Nursing and two refresher courses for RNAs, plus Dental Assistant and Dental Hygiene. Seneca's International Health certificate for RNs prepares health care workers in the multidisciplinary skills needed for work in developing countries. Entry to Nursing requires certain marks and courses from high school, and the college may test applicants.

Technology

Seneca has been introducing the "electronic workbench" concept, in which Technology students do labwork with computer simulations as well as actual machinery. The computer simulates every type of equipment, corrects errors, and permits greater student control of the pace of study. The "electronic workbench" has started in Technician programs, where it was felt students were most in need of learning support in an environment that replicates the work environment.

Seneca is one of only four colleges to offer a commercial flying program, Aviation and Flight Technology. The complete program takes almost three years of continuous enrollment, but the first two semesters are a general Pre-Technology program and only the top students will proceed to the later semesters. (In Sault Ste. Marie, I met Aviation students who chose Sault over Seneca mainly to avoid facing that cut.) Flying operations are conducted at Seneca's Buttonville airport facilities.

At the other extreme of altitude, Seneca's King campus offers a one-year certificate course in Underwater Skills for commercial divers. It is the only facility in North America that trains students to the North Sea Level One proficiency standard, and it uses the King campus lake and a Georgian Bay diving barge for training.

Seneca has an unusual cluster of programs in the Biological, Chemical, and Laboratory field. These include Technician and Technologist programs in Biology (the former being basic bio-chemistry and the latter oriented to research lab work), two co-op Technologist programs in Chemistry (one with a pharmaceuticals specialty), and Laboratory Technologist programs in Electron Microscopy and Industrial Biotechnology. A one-year certificate in Electron Microscopy is also offered.

The main Environmental Assessment programs are co-op Technician and Technologist programs in Resources Engineering. Seneca plans to expand these into a Centre for Energy Management at its King campus.

Civil Engineering programs include Technician and co-op Technologist programs and a co-op Technologist program in Building Operations Management.

Electronics Engineering programs include Technician programs in Communications, Computers, and Electrophotographic Systems, and Technologist programs in Communications and in Control Systems, plus a co-op Technologist in Computer Engineering.

Manufacturing and Mechanical offerings are a one-year certificate in Manufacturing and Machining Techniques, intended as a pre-apprenticeship course, and one Technologist and two Technician programs in Mechanical Engineering (one of which has options in either Manufacturing or Computer Numerical Control).

Two unusual Technology options at Seneca are Technician and Technologist programs in Fire Protection Engineering.

Seneca believes its School of Computer Studies, offering four Computer Programming options, is the strongest and best-equipped in the Ontario college system. Both three-year

Many Civil Engineering Technology students at Seneca earn money and gain experience doing co-op placements in the construction industry.

Computer Programming Analyst programs, one of which specializes in Electronic Data Processing, are co-op. The two-year programs in Computer Programming and Operating and the one in Computer Programming (which is sixty-four weeks of continuous study) are not co-op.

Trades Training

Seneca has mostly left trades training and apprenticeship to other Toronto colleges, particularly George Brown, but it does offer a small number of skilled trades courses, including a unique one for Farriers (blacksmiths). The Business and Industrial Training Division provides on-site contract training to corporations and other institutions.

Part-Time and Continuing Education

Seneca's part-time offerings are huge – and they attract close to 100,000 registrations a year. Seneca offers an increasing number of its full-time diploma programs on a part-time basis. Indeed, as individual scheduling begins to break down the two- or three-year lockstep of full-time programs, the distinctions between full-time and part-time should disappear. Seneca hopes to create "a seamless link" between full-time and part-time studies.

Most Seneca Continuing Education courses are taken for credit and are job- or career-focused, even if not earned toward a college diploma. Less than 10 per cent of Seneca Con Ed is in interest-level courses. Specialized certificate programs (for example, Real Property Assessment and Energy Assessment) for particular clienteles may be available only through Continuing Education.

Seneca is increasing the range of student services available to Con Ed students. Academic, personal, and career counselling is available to all part-time students at no charge, and most of it is now available during evening hours. To non-students, the vocational test fee is $300, so even if you are only taking one course, don't neglect the support services that Seneca makes available to you.

The Ontario colleges have been slow to introduce registration-by-telephone. Seneca is one of the few colleges to offer it, and so far it is only available for part-time courses, and only for students returning for a second or later course.

Getting in the Door

Seneca has no 800 number or dedicated information line. All calls go through the central switchboard. Admissions (for full-time program information and for applying) and Liaison (for general information) are the key departments to ask for.

To find your way into the Newnham campus, go around the back, by the parking lots, and look for an upper-level entranceway. In mid-1992, the college was busy moving Information and other front-end services to the area around this entrance. The other campuses are smaller, and directions should be available from the front entrance. Toronto Transit connections are good to all campuses. King is remote from the other Seneca campuses, but the college has its own shuttle from King to North York and Sutton.

Support Services

Seneca makes the most of its size by providing the largest possible range of support services to students.

As part of its move to student-directed learning processes, Seneca is making computer labs widely available. There are Learning Resource centres at all campuses – though library collections at each tend to be limited to the program areas offered at that campus.

The Counselling office offers elaborate personal and vocational counselling in several languages. There is an extensive special needs program for people with disabilities. Seneca has taken the lead in developing literacy programs designed for people with disabilities. And facilities such as the Health Service, Dental Service, Legal Aid clinic, and so on, tend to offer more services than most smaller colleges can support.

There is a strong, active, and issue-oriented student government. In fact there are eight student governments, one at each major campus, and all student government members get credit courses in leadership training through the college's Student Life program.

Connections

If you attend a high school in Seneca's area, you should be able to get advanced credit in Seneca programs for work you have done in school. Seneca now has forty of these "articulation" agreements with a dozen schools, and it has general agreements with all the school boards in its North York-York Region area.

"We have had a breakthrough with York University," I was told at Seneca. Several Applied Arts programs are now offered by Seneca and York as joint degree/diploma projects, and other departments hope to do the same soon. York now grants advanced standing to Seneca graduates in many programs who transfer to university.

But the flow of students goes both ways. Some years ago, York University replaced one of the local high schools as the largest single "feeder" of students to Seneca. Seneca offers many post-diploma/post-degree programs, and it gives university grads advanced standing in standard programs.

Scholarships

Seneca has an alumni association and strong connections to the north Toronto community, and it is beginning to plan a capital fund-raising campaign. At present, it has a scholarship/bursary fund of about $850,000 – not an outstanding amount relative to its size – and it offers 350 scholarships and bursaries. Notable among them are six $600 entrance scholarships for students coming into Seneca with outstanding high school marks. Seneca also has generous athletic scholarships, described under "Sports and Recreation."

Where to Live

More than 80 per cent of Seneca students come from the Toronto area. Except for York Hall, a former nurses' residence (400 single rooms for women) that is now part of the Health Sciences complex at the Leslie campus, Seneca has no residences and no plans to build them. There is a college-run housing registry at most campuses (with free telephones available for housing searches at Newnham and King) and it links Seneca students to a very wide range of rental housing opportunities.

Sports and Recreation

As a very large college, Seneca might seem alienating to the lone student. On the other hand, size means it offers the greatest range of services, activities, and clubs – many ways to get involved.

The Senecentre at Newnham is among the largest student-run student centres anywhere in the Ontario colleges. It has an information service and ticket outlet, a deli, a student pub, student government offices, a newspaper and radio station, and games and meeting rooms. More than two hundred students a year are employed by Campus Recreation services.

Seneca has the best sports facilities in the college system – and athletic scholarships too. The Physical Education Centre at Newnham has a triple gymnasium and an ice arena, as well as tennis courts, a 6,000-square-foot Fitness Centre, and a sports medicine clinic. The King Campus has outdoor playing fields, cross-country ski trails, an equestrian centre, and water sports facilities at its own lake. There is a swimming pool at the Leslie campus. Seneca offers all students the chance to participate in intramural sports, instructional classes, tournaments, intercollegiate fun tournaments, and full fitness and sports medicine facilities.

The Varsity Braves (for men) and Scouts (for women) play in ten intercollegiate sports: men's and women's soccer, men's golf, men's and women' volleyball, men's hockey, men's and women's basketball and badminton, and women's softball. Student Athletic Association fund-raising has provided funds for full-tuition scholarships for students on national-sport varsity teams who maintain a C average.

The City

Seneca's territory covers the whole heavily populated northern edge of Metro Toronto. It includes the polo-set country estates around King City, the highrise corridors of West Finch, the knowledge-based industrial zones around Markham, the monster-home suburbs of north Bathurst Street, and the diverse, fast-growing

City of North York. It is mostly urban and suburban but includes a rural area along the northern edge of the territory. The ethnic mix and income mix of Seneca's population is enormous.

The potential for shopping, recreation, culture, entertainment, and jobs (both part-time and after graduation) is almost unlimited in Seneca's own region and the surrounding area. The City of Toronto is right next door, and highway and transit connections are excellent.

Contact:

Seneca College
1750 Finch Avenue East
North York, Ont. M2J 2X5
(416) 491-5050

Fighting the System

Most colleges have a statement of student rights. It's usually in the calendar or the student handbook, and it sets out how to go about making an official complaint. Those statements make pretty dull reading – until you need to fight the system.

Generally, start small. Talk to faculty in your program or people in the counselling staff. Then you can start to move up. Program chairs, deans of schools or divisions, then the Vice-President Academic or the Vice-President for Student Services. Can the student government help – is there an ombudsman or a rep for your program?

And don't assume the president is out of reach. Colleges are not that big. If the college is not living up to some commitment it has made, the president ought to take responsibility. And remember: more and more, the colleges claim to be client-centred, and you are the client.

SHERIDAN COLLEGE: *The College of the Arts*

Oakville

Size: Large

In 1990, this garment won first prize for Barbara Celestine, a student in Sheridan's Fashion Technique and Design program, in the International Competition for Young Fashion Designers in Paris.

Sheridan College is named for an eighteenth-century playwright, Richard Sheridan. Well, sort of – it really takes its name from a vanished town in nearby Peel County, but *it* got its name from the writer. It's appropriate that Sheridan is the only Ontario college named for an artist, because, more than any other, it is an art school. There's artistic activity all over the Oakville campus, from life drawing and glass-blowing of the most traditional sort to cutting-edge computer work in fashion design and film animation.

Why is a college that is supposed to be training people for the job market running all these artsy programs?

Surprise! There are a lot of jobs in the arts. Compared to Ontario College of Art or most university Fine Arts programs, Sheridan's arts programs do tend to be market-oriented. Some of its graduates may be running small craftwork studios and shops out in the country somewhere, but many work in the fashion, design, and media industries, and a few have gone off to glamour positions with Industrial Light and Magic and other Hollywood institutions.

Sheridan is now the third-biggest college in the system, with 8,800 full-time, diploma-bound students, plus trades and training students and 60,000 part-time registrations. Fortunately, it does not look like a big institution with endless locker-lined corridors. The buildings, at least at Oakville's main campus, are attractively broken up. There is lots of natural light flowing in and student artwork livens up the walls. There is a substantial new student centre at the Oakville campus. In the last few years, Sheridan has been working on a much-needed reorganization to cut down on red tape and to start focusing on student service and quality of education. It still has a way to go, but already some of the other colleges have been studying its methods.

Worth Going For

- School of Crafts and Design
- Fashion and Media programs

Campuses

The Oakville campus has a block of land in a busy commercial/residential area facing Trafalgar Road north of the Queen Elizabeth Way. The Brampton campus is on McLaughlin Road just off Steeles. Oakville has most of the arts programs, and Brampton most of the Technology ones. Business and Community Services programs may be at one or the other or at both.

A Credit Valley campus close to the QEW in Mississauga houses the Health Sciences programs. And students in Heavy Equipment programs get to drive their bulldozers around a big campus on the Sixth Line in Milton.

Sheridan recently consolidated five small outpost campuses into its new Sheridan Skills Training Centre near the QEW and Trafalgar Road. It still has outreach campuses in Burlington,

Brampton, Mississauga, and Milton. All the campuses are linked into local transit, and most are close to the GO transit service.

Programs

Sheridan has many more students than the average Ontario college in Applied Arts programs, and it is unusually small in Health Sciences.

Sheridan has a relatively large number of post-diploma or post-degree certificates and programs, which offer advanced standing to applicants with college or university credits. It has co-op programs in Business and Technology, but also in Community Service and even General Arts and Science. Non-co-op programs frequently have field placements, some of them paid.

Some Sheridan programs require a questionnaire, interview, or portfolio for entrance. Many Sheridan programs can be begun in January as well as September.

Sheridan's General Arts and Science programs have several options, all sharing a common first semester. Liberal Studies permits many choices among electives and may give advanced standing in other diploma programs or university entrance. The one-year Health Sciences option may ease entry into Health Sciences programs, but does not guarantee admission. The one-year Workplace option combines academic study with a co-op placement.

Sheridan has emphasized computer applications in many of its programs, and it claims to be particularly well equipped with computer labs and support. Labs are available both on a scheduled and a drop-in basis.

Applied Arts

Sheridan's arts programs are clustered into several Faculties. Perhaps the best known is Visual Arts and Design, which is famous for its three-year program in Classical Animation and its post-diploma programs in Computer Animation and Computer Graphics. (Classical animation means hand-drawn, frame-by-frame film cartooning; computer animation is all done on the computer screen.) These Sheridan programs have been producing film cartoonists and special-effects artists for the booming film animation markets in Toronto and in Hollywood. There's even an Oscar winner (Jon Minnis, Best Animated Short for "Charade," 1985), and Sheridan's industry contacts mean its equipment is first-rate.

Another Visual Arts stand-out is the School of Crafts and Design, which has spectacular studio facilities on the Oakville campus and offers a three-year diploma in Crafts and Design. The specialty areas are ceramics, glass, furniture, and fabrics. Visual Arts also offers a two-year program in Applied Photography, a three-year Graphic Design program, and a three-year Illustration program. There is a one-year Art Fundamentals certificate (which qualified applicants can take in one intensive semester), and a unique program in Art and Art History. This can be either a three-year major or a four-year specialist co-op program, and it leads to a combined Sheridan diploma and University of Toronto Bachelor of Arts.

The other creative cluster in Applied Arts is Fashion and Media. Programs include two-year Fashion Technique and Design, which has already produced a number of fashion stars, and the post-diploma certificate in Fashion Management and Computer Design Techniques, which applies hi-tech to the needle trade. Supporting these are two-year Visual Merchandising Arts, Retail Management (not only for fashion merchandising), Esthetician, and Cosmetic Techniques and Management. There is also a two-year program in Travel and Tourism, and a two-year Interior Design program with an optional third year for advanced work.

Sheridan's unique Media Arts program (and its prerequisite year in Media Fundamentals) grew from a standard Broadcasting program into the full range of audio, video, television, film, and multi-media production and creation. Sheridan also offers a two-year Print Journalism program, which gives advanced standing to diploma holders or students with university experience. Journalism students produce the tabloid *Sheridan Sun*. There is a two-year Advertising program, emphasizing ad-writing.

Sheridan has three Theatre programs: three-year Music

Traditional handcrafts, including glassblowing, share Sheridan's art studios with commercial art processes and leading-edge computerized design.

Theatre Performance and two-year Theatre Arts Technical Production, plus a four-year co-op program Theatre and Drama Studies, offered jointly with the University of Toronto and leading to both a diploma and a degree. Theatre students perform on stage and in cabaret in Theatre Sheridan at the college's Sheridan Hall.

Community Service programs are Developmental Disabilities Work, a one-semester post-diploma program, and two-year programs in Social Service Work and Human Service Administration (which share a common first semester). Law and Security Administration and Loss Prevention Management (with co-op option available) share the first semester and there is also a two-year Correctional Work program. Sign Language Communicator is two years; the Interpreter program is a year longer, and only the first year is common to both.

Sheridan has several programs for educators. There are one-year certificates in Education Assistant and in Early Childhood Assistant, and a two-year program in Early Childhood Education (with different options available at Brampton and Oakville). There is also a four-year program entitled Early Childhood Education and Exceptionality in Human Learning, given jointly with the University of Toronto and leading to both a diploma and a degree. Also available are a two-year Library and Information Technician program and a one-year post-diploma certificate in Research Analyst.

Business

Most Sheridan Business programs are offered in Oakville and Brampton and share a common first year. Two-year Business programs and three-year Business Administration programs have options in Accounting, Finance, Human Resources, Marketing, Transportation and Distribution (co-op), or General Business. Co-op programs are available in Accounting, Marketing, and Transportation and Distribution. There is also a one-year post-diploma certificate in Human Resource Management. Sheridan offers a one-year Office Administration certificate, as well as two-year diplomas in Executive, Legal, and Medical Office Administration, and in Office Systems.

Health Sciences

Sheridan has four Health Sciences programs. Enrollments in three-year Nursing and one-year Nursing Assistant are small, with high admission standards and relatively low drop-out rates. Also offered are a one-year Pharmacy Assistant certificate program and a three-year Sports Injury Management program. Continuing Education offers many refresher and upgrade programs for RNs and RNAs.

Technology

Sheridan has Technology programs in most of the standard areas and is particularly strong in Computer Studies. All Technologist and some Technician programs are co-op.

There are Technician and Technologist programs in Civil Engineering and also in Architectural Engineering, where the

Technician program focuses on drafting and the Technologist program on design. Both Chemical Engineering programs are three-year Technologist programs, one standard, the other specializing in Environmental Engineering.

Technician programs in Mechanical Engineering have standard or Drafting options, while Technologist programs have standard or Design and Drafting options.

There are Technician and Technologist programs in Electronic Engineering, but none in Electrical Engineering. Computer Studies programs are Computer Programmer (no co-op) and Computer Programmer Analyst, three-year Technologist programs in Computer Science and Systems Analysis, plus a one-year post-diploma certificate in Telecommunications Management.

Sheridan also offers a one-year certificate in Animal Care.

Trades Training

Sheridan offers skilled trades training in Environmental Horticulture, Health Care Aide, Heavy Equipment Mechanics and Operations, and Pipeline Welding. Trades updating courses are offered in several industrial fields. There are pre-apprenticeship courses for Fitters, Mechanics, and Tool and Die Makers, and Sheridan offers the academic part of several apprenticeship programs. As well, Sheridan offers the usual pre-employment and basic upgrading programs, and a wide range of contract training to business and industry.

Part-Time and Continuing Education

Sheridan offers credit courses right across the curriculum on a part-time evening basis, and part-timers may also take courses from the daytime offerings. The Art and Craft offerings of the School of Crafts and Design, including its Summer School of the Arts, are particularly strong. Sheridan's International Summer School of Animation draws film professionals from all over the world for an intensive fourteen-week program. Some courses, such as Fund-raising and Resource Development Management and many extension courses for professionals, are only available on a Continuing Education basis. About 60,000 people register for Sheridan Continuing Education programs each year.

Getting in the Door

Signage at the main Oakville campus is limited, and the main entrance to the building is not easy to spot (look for the flagpole). The Information window is often closed, and though a sign points inquirers to another office, the people there don't think advice and directions are their job. There is no 800 number and no dedicated information line. Individual and group tours can be arranged on two weeks' notice, and there is a College Day open house every November.

Support Services

Recently Sheridan undertook a very wide-ranging review of all its programs and their delivery. As one result of that, it has been moving to make its services student-centred ("They were not at all so before," I was told) and easier to use. Sheridan intends to implement a "one-stop-shopping" process for all admissions and records matters. It has been trying to reduce bureaucracy and red tape in all service areas.

Several departments have initiated study-skills and student-success programs to ease entry and reduce drop-out rates. Mentoring and faculty advisor programs are working, and there are close contacts between faculty and the counselling staff to identify and help struggling students. The Health Services office offers innovative and popular student-run programs on sex education, substance abuse, nutrition, and other health-related topics.

Connections

Sheridan has liaison agreements with most of its local high school boards, so that students are advised of programs available and pre-requisites they need. Advanced standing is offered for OACs and other high school credits. Sheridan also offers advanced standing to applicants with university experience. Its joint diploma-degree agreements with the University of Toronto's Erindale College, noted in the "Programs" section above, are unique. Theatre graduates can also continue at the University of Windsor.

Scholarships

Sheridan has a well-developed alumni association with its own glossy magazine. However, fund-raising for student scholarships and bursaries has been limited. The largest number of them seems to be in the Business area.

Where to Live

About 45 per cent of Sheridan's students come from outside its Halton-Peel region. In general, rental accommodation is relatively easy to find in the Oakville-Brampton area, and Sheridan has no plans for new residences. Only the Health Sciences campus at Credit Valley has a residence. It has 300 beds and a Residence Life program. Most rooms are single. There is no meal plan, but there are cooking facilities.

Sports and Recreation

Sheridan's Athletics Centres in Oakville and Brampton have gymnasiums, squash courts, exercise rooms, and related facilities. Oakville also has indoor tennis courts. There are recreation, intramural, and varsity-team activities. Sheridan has been particularly strong in men's basketball.

The large and active student government recently opened the student-owned and -run 20,000-square-foot Student Centre at Oakville, which has a pub and games room and scheduled entertainment. Sheridan has a weekly common hour for college activities.

The City

These are the 'burbs. Mississauga, Brampton, Oakville, Milton, and Burlington are the generally well-off and fast-growing western fringes of Metro Toronto. Lots of kids around here grew up with spending-money. Getting the family car and tooling down the highway to the mall, the movies, the bars, tends to be the style.

If you have a different style, the area still offers lots of opportunities for sports, entertainment, recreation, shopping, and culture. GO transit and the freeways put Toronto, Hamilton, and a lot of southern Ontario in easy reach.

Contact:

Sheridan College
1430 Trafalgar Road
Oakville, Ont. L6H 2L1
(416) 845-9430

SIR SANDFORD FLEMING COLLEGE:

The Kawartha Factor

Peterborough

Size: Medium

Fleming's Centre for Manufacturing Studies trains students – and many industrial clients – in the latest industrial robotics and quality control processes.

Is it "Fleming" or "Sir Sandford" for short? I heard a lot of both, but the college uses Fleming when it doesn't use the full name. The name comes from a great nineteenth-century Canadian engineer, railway builder, and all-round innovator – not a bad role-model for any practical, hands-on college, and he did live in Peterborough for a while.

Fleming College has an attractive site on the edge of Peterborough, in the Kawartha recreation country and the valley of the Trent-Severn Canal. It is a beautiful region, the kind of place a lot of people would like to go to for college. So Fleming (like nearby Trent University) benefits from the "Kawartha factor," which steadily pulls in people from outside the area. Even though many of the programs at Fleming are not strikingly different from a lot of other colleges, the word-of-mouth from those who go is good enough to keep their younger brothers, sisters, and neighbours following them to Fleming. (One area that does not send many students to Peterborough is Toronto. At Fleming they claim that now and then someone from Toronto will call, wanting to know what subway line it is on.)

The really unusual part of Fleming, and the part that really draws students from all over Ontario and beyond, is down the road in Lindsay, at the Leslie Frost campus's School of Natural Resources.

The Frost campus is not the typical satellite campus that many colleges have. Instead of being a local imitation of the main campus, with a smaller-but-similar range of programs and services, the Frost Campus is entirely dedicated to a single cluster of related programs. It houses the School of Natural Resources, big (accounting for about a quarter of Fleming's total enrollment), world-renowned, and unique in Canada.

The School of Natural Resources began as the Ontario forest-ranger training school. It was there because of the woods, but also because Lindsay was the home of Ontario Premier Leslie Frost. That ranger-training grew into Fleming's Conservation Officer program, and the college gradually added Technician and Technologist programs – from Forestry Technician through Heavy Equipment Operator to Cartographer – all related to the use and management of land and water resources.

The Frost campus used to be very male, very outdoorsy, very hunting-shooting-fishing. That's changing now with the arrival of many more women and a strong environmental commitment (the college does vermiculture composting – yes, worms – right by the front door). But Frost still has the team spirit of a place where everyone is united by a common interest taught to an international standard. Frost students make it clear they think they are at a pretty special place. Question: Why aren't the satellite campuses of more colleges run like Frost – small and focused, instead of just small?

Worth Going For

- Natural Resource programs at the Frost Campus, Lindsay

Campuses

The main campus of Fleming is the Brealey Building, located out on its own on a large, wooded, hilly property near the eastern outskirts of Peterborough. Downtown, the Centre for Manufacturing Studies has a large building in an industrial area, where it runs Technology programs, skilled trades training, and partnership projects with industry. The Early Childhood Education lab, including the campus daycare and nursery, is on McDonnel Street in Peterborough. The three Peterborough locations are collectively called the Sutherland campus.

The Frost School of Natural Resources, fifty kilometres away, is housed on its own large woodland campus on the edge of Lindsay. Appropriately, Frost is one of the few campuses where the buildings are constructed of as much wood as brick or concrete block.

Continuing education, adult upgrading, skills courses, and industrial training are offered in Cobourg and Haliburton. Haliburton is also home to the Haliburton School of Fine Arts, which is discussed under Continuing Education below.

Programs

Because of the School of Natural Resources, Fleming is much bigger than average in Technology, with comparatively small commitments in the other areas. Particularly small is Health Sciences, where Fleming has one of the smallest departments in the system.

Fleming has a strong commitment to offering common first-year courses in related programs all through the college. It has one-year Pre-Technology and Pre-Health Science for those unprepared or unable to get into those streams, and the Frost

Campus General Arts and Science program is really Pre-Natural Resources. There is also the more usual GAS at Brealey.

The Peterborough campuses make nearly all their programs available through "February Fast-track" – programs that start in February, continue through the summer, and send students into second year in September.

Applied Arts

The sizeable Community Service cluster at Fleming includes Early Childhood Education, Educational Assistant (one of only a few preparing teacher's classroom assistants), Employment Counsellor (a three-year program offered nowhere else in Canada), Recreation Leadership, Social Service Worker, and Drug and Alcohol Addictions Counsellor. All these programs share a common first semester.

Recognizing that not all Law and Security Administration grads will join police forces, Fleming has made the standard LASA program into the basis of a cluster of law-related programs. There is a general LASA program, plus options in Customs Administration, Loss Prevention Management, and Police Education. To these Fleming has added Correctional Officer and Legal Assistant. All these programs are two-year and share a common first semester.

Another small cluster offers a unique three-year Art Conservation Techniques program and a two-year Audio-Visual Graphics Technician, which share a common first semester. A program in Arts Administration, currently suspended, may return in a different form.

Business

Fleming's School of Business offers a two-year General Business diploma (with a Customer Service option planned), but it emphasizes the three-year Business Administration programs, with options in General Business, plus Accounting, Information Systems, Marketing, Materials Management, Human Resources Management, Environmental Waste Management, and Municipal Management. There is also a three-year International Trade program. All these programs share a common first year.

Fleming Business programs also include a Merchandising program. There is a two-year program in Sporting Goods Business that is unique in Canada, and a one-year Entrepreneurship program, aimed at people intending to open their own businesses.

The Tourism and Hospitality Department offers Restaurant Management, Food Service Supervisor, and several two-year Tourism and Transportation options – Convention Management, Hotel and Resort Management, and Travel Merchandising – as well as a three-year Tourism and Transportation program. The first year is standard to all.

Fleming's Office Admin courses have standard Executive, Legal, Medical, and Word Processing options, plus a three-year Office Systems Administration, all with three semesters in common.

Health Sciences

The only full-time Health Sciences offered at Fleming are Nursing (three years) and Nursing Assistant (one year). They begin with a common first semester.

Technology

Apart from Natural Resources, covered below, Fleming's Technology programs have a strong leaning toward electrical technology. There are Technician and Technologist programs (sharing a common first year) in Electro-Mechanical and Mechanical Engineering. Technician and Technologist programs are offered in both Electrical and Electronics Engineering, with options in Consumer Electronics, Microcomputers, Telephone Systems, and Computer Systems. All share a common first year. There is also a unique one-year co-op program in Security Alarm Systems.

Fleming's Centre for Manufacturing Studies in downtown Peterborough conducts many training programs and consultant services for industry, and claims special expertise in industrial robotics (an expertise acquired when Fleming absorbed the former Ontario Robotics Centre) and quality assurance. Students in Electro-mechanical and other programs use the Centre's facilities and may be integrated into Centre projects.

Natural Resources

Many of the programs at the School of Natural Resources are unique, and no other school offers such a cluster of expertise (supported by impressive labs and equipment) in Forestry, Earth Sciences, Parks Management, Off-Road Equipment Operation, and Cartography. Ninety-four per cent of its students come from outside the local area. All Natural Resources programs share a common first semester. Several are co-op.

Resource Management programs include Technician and Technologist programs in Forestry. There are a group of programs in Parks and Forest Recreation and in Natural Resources Law Enforcement. Animal-oriented programs include Fish and Wildlife, Aquaculture, and Environmental Pest Control.

Resource Technology programs cover the use of equipment (Heavy Equipment Operations and Well Drilling), earth sciences (Technician and Technologist programs in Terrain and Water Resources, Geology, Geoscience, and Geotechnology). There are Technician and Technologist programs in Cartography, which can lead to a specialty called Geographic Information Systems – essentially the use of computers to assemble and map data. GIS has options in Applications Specialist or Mapping Specialist, and it attracts many university graduates. The Cartography section's maps are frequent prize-winners in international competitions.

Trades and Training

Fleming offers the in-school part of more than a dozen apprenticeship programs, plus skilled trades training in construction, small powered equipment and marina techniques. The Natural Resources school trains greenhouse workers and urban tree and urban parks specialists.

The award-winning cartographers who study at Fleming's comprehensive School of Natural Sources in Lindsay include many university-trained geographers.

Part-Time and Continuing Education

Fleming has been working to break down distinctions between part-time and full-time programs, since students in both areas often have common objectives and may move back and forth between the two modes. Many programs or parts of programs are equally available on a part-time basis.

Fleming is proud that its Haliburton Summer School of Fine Arts is becoming "the Banff of the east," which means something if you know the high reputation of the Banff School of the Arts. It draws thousands of students every summer, and top-rank artists and artisans come each year to teach and study. More than 180 arts courses are offered at Fleming's Sisco Centre and at other facilities in Haliburton during the summer, and some courses continue in fall and winter at the other campuses. A diploma in Visual and Creative Arts can be earned.

Getting in the Door

The Brealey and Lindsay buildings have clearly marked access roads and entrances, and the entrance lobbies have information booths and student services clustered nearby.

Fleming does not advertise an 800-number information service, but the Liaison office and the Information desk welcome questions. Calendars and brochures are clear and useful. There are Visitor Information Programs and Student Ambassador Programs to orient newcomers to the college, and Community Information Nights aimed at adult clients. Fleming faculty claim to be readily available for information sessions and questions.

Fleming recently created an Access Centre, intended to be the "open door" for all potential clients who either are not ready for diploma programs or are seeking some other kind of training. Access at Fleming includes Independent Learning, upgrading, part-time courses, and general interest courses.

Support Services

Fleming's commitment to clustering programs, using common semesters, adding February intakes, and linking part-time to full-time courses all suggest clear planning of the delivery of academic services.

On entry, all first-year students are given a questionnaire to determine their confidence about academic success and career choices. Faculty advisers are assigned to all students and encouraged to intervene early when problems loom.

Connections

Fleming has good relations with local school boards and has

developed programs to inform high school students about college, and about high school courses that could let them enter college with advanced standing or enhanced qualifications.

Like many colleges, Fleming has at least as many links to American universities as to Canadian ones. "American universities recognize what applied courses are," I was told. "Canadian universities don't value them." American "applied" universities offer degrees in college-type programs such as Early Childhood Education, Marketing, International Trade, Recreation Leadership, Convention Management, and other subjects. Several U.S. universities will allow Fleming diploma-holders to complete a degree in one year.

Fleming's neighbour, Trent University, is trying to improve its links to the college system and is slowly working out joint programs and transfer agreements with Fleming. Trent's Geography degree can be linked to the Geographic Information Systems programs at Frost.

Scholarships

Fleming runs Alumni activities through its departments. It has not moved actively into fund-raising, but the departmental alumni offices plan to begin doing so. Already, individual and corporate donations have created about 150 scholarships and bursaries, so the potential for financial support is good. Contact the Financial Aid office for details.

Where to Live

There are privately owned residence facilities at both Brealey and Frost, and housing services help with searches for accommodation. Since students and staff at the Frost campus comprise nearly 15 per cent of the population of Lindsay, accommodation tends to be scarce, and the campus broke ground for its own residence in the fall of 1992.

Sports and Recreation

Fleming is one of only a couple of Ontario colleges with an indoor swimming pool, so its aquatics recreation activities are substantial. There are also weight-training rooms, racquet courts, and outdoor playing fields. The Recreation, Fitness, and Lifestyle Department runs large intramural and individual fitness programs, as well as a dozen varsity sports programs. The Lindsay campus uses community recreational facilities, and its students excel in men's and women's Timbersports.

The City

Peterborough is a small comfortable city, with an industrial base, many services and shopping outlets for its region, and great opportunities for outdoor recreation. With Trent University nearby, it is a "student town," and transportation connections to the rest of the province are good.

Contact:

Sir Sandford Fleming College
Brealey Drive
Peterborough, Ont. K9J 9Z9
(705) 749-5546

Leslie Frost School of Natural Resources
P.O. Box 8000
Lindsay, Ont. K9V 5E6
(705) 324-9144

Post-Graduate – University to College

"Of course you have to be a lot more mature to go to college." That's not the way people usually compare university and college. But the speaker was a young woman who had finished a degree and then entered a college diploma program.

She had done a lot of learning and growing at university, and she loved her philosophy studies, but she never imagined working as a philosopher. When she got serious about a career, she went to college. When I met her, she was thriving in a Public Relations program.

She's not alone. Universities don't talk about it much, but a growing number of their grads head for college to get real-world skills and career prospects. Arts grads often head for Media or Community Service areas. Science grads turn up in Lab Science, Technical Writing, and Veterinary Technician programs. Specialized Administration and Management programs in Business also attract university grads.

Some colleges, particularly Humber (where one student in five has university experience), run accelerated programs, open only to degree- or diploma-holders. Other programs give advanced standing to students from university or the workforce.

College students who have university experience report that at college the workload is heavier, the material is not so intellectually demanding, and the teaching is far better.

OTHER COLLEGES AND INSTITUTES IN ONTARIO

The twenty-three colleges of applied arts and technology are the backbone of the non-university post-secondary education system in Ontario. However, there are some other institutions you may want to consider as alternatives to the CAATs.

The Universities of Ontario

There are seventeen universities in Ontario. Generally they teach liberal arts and sciences, do abstract and theoretical research, and train for professional careers. Their programs take longer and their minimum requirements are generally higher than those of the colleges.

Several guidebooks to universities are now available. *Linda Frum's Guide to Canadian Universities* is brash and opinionated and irreverent, and the universities mostly hate it – read this one for sure. *The Student Guide to Ontario Universities* by Dyanne Gibson and *The Complete Guide to Canadian Universities* by Kevin Paul are more informational than critical.

Lakehead University
Thunder Bay, Ont. P7V 5E1

Lakehead is the only Ontario university that also offers some two- and three-year diploma programs of the type the colleges normally offer. It requires some OACs for entry to them. (About OACs, see "The Jargon" in Part One.) The School of Engineering offers diploma programs in Chemical Engineering Technology, Civil Engineering Technology, Electrical Engineering Technology, and Mechanical Engineering Technology. These programs – or similar ones from the colleges – are the prerequisite for entry into Lakehead's Bachelor of Engineering degree program. There are also two-year diploma programs in Forest Technology and in Library Technology. Lakehead also has Bachelor of Outdoor Recreation programs with subject matter that overlaps with some colleges' Resource Management or Recreation programs.

Ryerson Polytechnical Institute
350 Victoria Street, Toronto, Ont. M5B 2K3

Ryerson, in downtown Toronto, looks more and more like a university. It grants degrees, its programs usually take four school years to complete, and it requires some OACs for admission to most programs. Its departments get involved in things like aerospace research, and it is campaigning to be allowed to grant Bachelor's degrees in Arts and in Science, just like the universities.

On the other hand, Ryerson has the same "applied" orientation as the colleges, granting Bachelor of Applied Arts or Bachelor of Technology degrees or, in some cases, diplomas. It teaches in many of the fields the colleges cover: Early Childhood Education, Business, Journalism, Engineering Technology. Its tuition fees per semester are about double what the colleges charge.

In Applied Arts, Ryerson has Bachelor of Applied Arts degree programs in Applied Geography, Fashion Design, Fashion Merchandising, Graphic Communications Management, Interior Design, Journalism, Photographic Arts (with options in Film Studies, Media Arts, and Still Photography), and Radio and Television Arts. It has three-year diploma programs in Theatre Acting, Theatre Dance, and Theatre Technical Production, and a Diploma in Arts.

In Community Service, there are Bachelor of Applied Arts degree programs in Early Childhood Education; Environmental Health; Food, Nutrition, Consumer and Family Studies; Nursing; Social Work; and Urban and Regional Planning.

In Business, there are Bachelor of Applied Arts degree programs in Administration and Information Management, Business Management, and Hospitality and Tourism Management.

Ryerson's Engineering and Applied Science department offers Bachelor of Technology degree programs in Aerospace Engineering, Applied Chemistry or Biology, Applied Computer Science, Architectural Science, Chemical Engineering, Civil Engineering, Electrical Engineering, Industrial Engineering, Mechanical Engineering, and Survey Engineering, and a three-year Diploma in Landscape Architectural Technology.

Ryerson has residences, counselling and liaison services, and a full range of other student services and activities. The Ryerson Information Centre can be reached at (416) 979-5036.

Specialized Colleges

There are four publicly run Colleges of Agricultural Technology, one Institute for Applied Health Sciences, and one School of Horticulture in Ontario. Like the Colleges of Applied Arts and Technology, they offer two-year diploma programs, usually require a general-level high school diploma or equivalent, and have a practical, career-oriented outlook. Tuition fees at the agricultural colleges are less than $500 per school year, about half what the CAATs charge. Fees at the others vary.

Centralia College of Agricultural Technology
Huron Park, Ont. N0M 1Y0

Centralia College of Agricultural Technology, fifty kilometres north of London, has about 200 full-time students and a large part-time enrollment. It offers diplomas in Agricultural Business Management, Veterinary Technology, and Food Service Management. Residence is available for all students. For information call (519) 228-6691 or toll-free 1-800-668-1454.

Kemptville College of Agricultural Technology
Kemptville, Ont. K0G 1J0

Kemptville, in the Rideau Valley south of Ottawa, has just over

200 students, and extensive community outreach programs. It offers Diplomas in Agricultural Journalism (in association with Loyalist College), Dairy Cattle Production and Management, Ornamental Horticultural Production and Management, and Food Service Management, and ten certificate courses or apprenticeships in agricultural trades. Residence accommodation is available. For information call (613) 258-8335.

New Liskeard College of Agricultural Technology
New Liskeard, Ont. P0J 1P0

New Liskeard College, in the Clay Belt north of North Bay, has 100 students in full-time programs. It has diploma programs in Dairy Technology, Livestock Technology, and Equine Technology, and a certificate in agricultural production techniques. For information call (705) 647-6738.

Ridgetown College of Agricultural Technology
Ridgetown, Ont. N0P 2C0

Ridgetown College, near Chatham, has about 200 students and a 450-acre research and demonstration farm. It offers two-year diploma programs in Agricultural Business and Production (with options in Agribusiness Management, Crop Production, Fruit and Vegetable Production, or Livestock Production), Ornamental Horticulture, Quality Control Laboratory Technology, and Ag-Industry Technology. Three-year co-op programs are also available. Students live in residence. For information call (519) 674-5456.

Michener Institute for Applied Health Sciences
222 St. Patrick Street, Toronto, Ont. M5T 1V4

The Michener Institute in Toronto is affiliated with more than sixty hospitals and has a full-time enrollment of about 500. It offers diplomas in Cytotechnology, Radiography, Medical Lab Technology, Nuclear Medicine Technology, Respiratory Therapy, and a three-year Chiropody diploma offered in association with George Brown College, plus a one-year Medical Laboratory Technician certificate. The Institute requires a high school diploma with at least six OACs. It has no residence. Tuition fees are less than $1,000 per school year, similar to those at the CAATs. For information call (416) 596-3177.

Niagara Parks Commission School of Horticulture
P.O. Box 150, Niagara Falls, Ont. L2E 6T2

The School of Horticulture in Niagara Falls accepts twelve students a year into a three-year Niagara Parks Diploma in General Horticulture program that begins in April and continues for thirty-six consecutive months of forty-hours-a-week classroom or work experience. Tuition fees are $850 per year, but room and board are included for the first two years, and students receive a small stipend for their work. For information call (416) 356-8554.

Private Colleges

Many registered private vocational schools in Ontario offer diploma programs, mostly in business, office administration, and technology. They are private commercial enterprises, but they are inspected by the Ministry of Colleges and Universities, which sets standards regarding curriculum, teacher qualifications, and advertising. Some of them are more open to having their programs certified by outside certifying associations than the Colleges of Applied Arts and Technology have been. They will generally require a high school diploma or equivalent.

How do they compare to the public colleges? None has anything like the range of any of the Colleges of Applied Arts and Technology. Most specialize in a single specific field – welding, modelling, truckdriving, secretarial skills. Others cover a range of business or technology fields. Private vocational schools tend to be fast, expensive, very open in access (often with continuous entry all year round), very responsive to the job market, and very attentive to client (that is, student) service. Questions: do they offer the programs and services you expect, can they provide a certificate that employers will recognize wherever you go, will they stay in business?

Well-known private colleges include the DeVry Institute of Technology, the Radio College of Canada, the nine Ontario

Business Colleges, and the Toronto School of Business (which, despite its name, has sixteen campuses around southern Ontario). There are more than 300 registered private vocational schools in Ontario, and they enroll about 40,000 students a year.

The most complete source of general information on all post-secondary education in Ontario – private vocational schools, agricultural colleges, and specialized colleges plus the CAATs and universities – is the book *Horizons: Guide to Postsecondary Education in Ontario,* which is published annually by the Communications Branch, Ministry of Colleges and Universities. (In French it is *Tour d'Horizon.*) Every secondary school in the province gets copies of *Horizons,* and you can also consult it at public libraries, Canada Employment Centres, or college information offices.

Not Enough Qualifications?

It is pretty standard. To get into college, you need a high school diploma at the General level, or something equivalent.

No high school diploma? Don't decide that is a wall keeping you out of college. Colleges have a tradition of being open to as many people as possible (and the government holds them to it).

You can't start in a program aimed at a college diploma and a career until you are ready to handle it, but the colleges have many courses and classes intended to get adults ready. You can complete several years of high school as fast as you are able. You can improve your English. You can pick up Math credits. You can work on "life skills" and job skills if you need to.

Some of these courses are taught at the colleges, but paid for by Canada Employment Centres or by the Ontario Government – if you fit their rules. The courses offered at the colleges include Ontario Basic Skills, English as a Second Language, Futures, and Basic Training for Skills Development. Apprenticeship and trades training courses may not require a high school diploma for entry.

If you are an underqualified adult, the colleges can probably give you what you need to get into a career-track program. To find out, ask to make an appointment with a college counsellor. If the college has an Access department (see "The Jargon," in Part One), start there. That kind of counselling is usually free. If there is going to be a fee (for a whole series of career-planning tests, say), they might refund your money if you enroll in college.

PART THREE

Colleges: Who Pays?

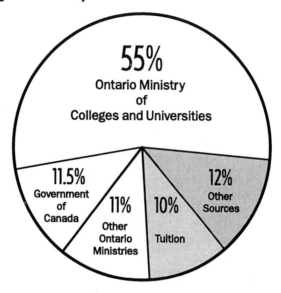

Running the Ontario college system costs more than $1.5 billion dollars a year. Who puts up the money?

Mostly, the people of Ontario pay for their college system. Two-thirds of all the money the colleges get comes from the Government of Ontario. Your $1,000 a year in tuition feels like a lot, but tuition fees only provide about 10 per cent of the money that keeps the colleges going.

Government's direct share of the bill looks certain to shrink during the 1990s. Money from government – from taxpayers, in other words – just won't be so available. The slices of the pie that are going to be bigger in future are the ones labelled Tuition and Other Sources.

The colleges are trying to get more income from selling their training services to private business and industry, and from fund-raising. But they are sure to look at tuition too. A few years from now, tuition fees could cover 20 per cent or even a quarter of the cost of college education.

One idea floating around is to balance tuition increases by a new kind of linked-to-income student loan. More student-loan money would be available, and how much you paid back (over fifteen years, say) would depend on how high your income turned out to be.

PLANNING AND APPLYING

College Liaison Offices should be able to lay on customized college tours to focus on the programs and services particular students need.

Let's assume you have some idea what colleges do, and the feeling that college might be for you. Perhaps you even have some programs and some colleges in mind.

Getting Started

This book won't be enough to get you enrolled in college, and you will probably want more than you can find in the library or your high school guidance office. Plan to get in touch with some colleges directly.

Ask for their publications. Take in the information sessions they run. Talk to the admissions staff, liaison officers, and faculty in the program that interests you, about what they can offer you. Visit the campus if you have a chance. Then you might be ready to start filling in some applications.

1. Publications.

All colleges publish a lot about themselves. Their publications are their main marketing vehicle, and they should be ready to get them to you as soon as you ask.

The main college publication is the CALENDAR. This is the official statement about what courses and programs are available, what the requirements are, the rules and regulations, and how to go about applying. Each college goes to a lot of trouble deciding what to put in. Some aim to include everything (Algonquin's runs to nearly 500 pages), others aim to be slim and easy to use (Durham's is 80 pages).

Each college publishes a new calendar every year (or every second year), usually in the fall, listing precise details about everything that will be offered the following fall. You have to have one for any college you are serious about. Some colleges offer a pocket-sized mini-calendar as well. At most colleges, the CONTINUING EDUCATION CALENDAR of part-time courses is a separate publication, which appears several times a year.

Most colleges also publish PAMPHLETS or booklets about each program (or cluster of programs) they offer. If you are starting to focus on particular programs or program areas, request more information from any college that interests you. Often you can get pamphlets on sports and various other services as well. If the college has a residence, it probably has a RESIDENCE BOOKLET, with information about residence and how to apply.

Many colleges produce a VIEWBOOK or COLLEGE GUIDE. It is shorter and glossier and has more pictures than the calendar. Usually it will list the programs, but it's mostly to tell you what a great place the college is. It covers student activities, lifestyle, residences, maybe a little about the city around the college. And it will tell you who to call and how to apply. Some viewbooks have a postage-paid postcard you tear off and mail for information.

2. Information Sessions, Workshops, College Introductions.

Colleges run informational sessions on weekends and evenings or by arrangement, whenever and wherever they can get groups of potential students together. Every college has its own name for these and its own way of organizing them. Some colleges routinely publicize them in the local newspapers. Some are drop-in, some need an appointment, some are tailored to particular groups. If you are a high school student, your school may have direct contact with its local college. Many colleges also participate in the College Information Program, which tours high schools around the province on behalf of all the colleges. If you are interested, ask any college about information sessions you might attend.

Some of the colleges are not very active in the College Information Program and prefer to do their own marketing. Colleges that depend heavily on out-of-town recruiting will often set up information sessions wherever they find sufficient interest. Many will put you on their mailing list if you ask. Notes on individual colleges' outreach programs can also be found in the section "Getting in the Door" of each college profile. In general, the Liaison office of the college handles information programs about the college for non-students.

3. Personalized Information.

I met a woman at Fanshawe College who did her diploma there because of a phone call. She had approached several post-secondary institutions, but she went to Fanshawe (and has since worked there for many years) mainly because the head of the program she was interested in telephoned her at her home in New Brunswick to discuss it.

That was years ago. Does much of that personal service really go on? Nearly every college assured me that faculty and chairs of programs will give personal attention to particular needs, questions, or requests for information about their programs. Obviously, requests for personal attention will be more successful if you are not asking at the last minute and if you have done enough preparation to be able to ask informed questions.

With a little advance notice, every college should be able to lay on personal or group visits to the campus that will include visits to the programs that interest you and perhaps even a meeting with faculty and students. Often these tours are led by students. Confederation will provide free residence accommodation for new students from out of town who are visiting during the summer. Many colleges will let you sit in on classes.

4. Admissions Counselling.

College counselling offices do a lot of their work with non-students. People who are thinking about careers and considering college as one option are frequent Counselling customers. The Counselling Office is not the place for general information about college programs; for that, contact Admissions or Liaison, or use the college publications. Counsellors specialize in the personal, academic, and social issues that may complicate your life as a student.

Some of the colleges still provide basic career counselling and advice to non-students at no charge. However, if you want a complete assessment, aptitude-testing, and career-planning package, there will be fees to pay. Some colleges will rebate counselling fees to non-students who enroll in the college after counselling.

Eight colleges have established Access Departments to assist entry to college for anyone facing particular obstacles to their further education (see "The Jargon" in Part One for details). Access Departments may have their own counselling programs or workshops to help handle these problems. If you feel you have more problems with college entry than the "typical" student, look for an Access Department. If there isn't one, go to the Counselling Office. Counselling is always confidential.

Applications

Read the calendar and contact the college itself about specific requirements for any programs that interest you. Selecting a college and a program is too important a decision to leave to any other source of information, including this guide book.

Through the fall of 1992, the way it worked was that you sent your applications to all the colleges that interested you, and each college decided whether or not to offer you a place. If you were accepted into any programs, you paid a $50 deposit to confirm your place. It was all done between you and the individual colleges.

For the fall of 1993 and all future years, there has been a change. Now applications for all post-secondary programs (see "The Jargon," Part One, for an explanation of what that means) have been centralized. The colleges have established the Ontario College Applications Service, or OCAS, with offices in Guelph. It will keep track of all the applications and acceptances for all the colleges' programs.

OCAS only handles the paperwork. You still seek out calendars and information from each college yourself. (The colleges will also supply application forms.) And each college still sets its requirements, assesses its own applicants, and decides which to accept. But applications to all of the twenty-three colleges must now go through OCAS. OCAS takes in the applications and passes them on to the colleges. And it is to OCAS that you send confirmation of acceptance if a college offers you a place in a program.

The new central applications system is certainly simpler. (Some of the paperwork will actually be paperless. Many high schools are equipped to send applications and transcripts to OCAS electronically, and links between OCAS and the colleges are all computerized.) You only have to send one OCAS form for all your applications, and the college system will finally know how many individual people are actually behind all the applications they receive. But it does create some limits on how you apply.

There are only five lines for program choices on the new Central Application form. You can only apply to five programs, and only three at any one college. And no matter how many offers of admission you get, you can only accept one. Right at the start, you have to send $25 to OCAS with your application form, and even if no college accepts your application, you don't get it back.

So: starting with post-secondary programs beginning in the fall of 1993, you get an application from any high school, any college, or OCAS itself, and you fill it out and send it to OCAS in Guelph.

Ontario College Application Service
P.O. Box 810
Guelph, Ont. NIH 6M4

The OCAS Information Line is (519) 763-4725. Amazingly enough, they do not have a toll-free 800 number.

For part-time studies or any course that is not a post-secondary program, you still apply to the college itself.

Deadlines

The most important application dates for college applications are January 1 and March 1.

January 1. On the first working day in January, the Central Applications Service begins to accept applications for fall programs. Colleges do a lot of their marketing and recruiting in the fall for students who will start in the fall of the following year. If you want to get into a college program in the fall, you should have a lot of your research complete before Christmas of the previous year. Come January, the applications start to flow in.

March 1. The first deadline is March 1. Before March 1, there is no first come, first served. All applications received in January and February are considered to have equal priority. (If you are expecting to complete high school in June, you can apply before March 1. You can receive conditional acceptance – conditional on your successful completion of high school.)

Applications postmarked after March 1 are not rejected, but they are wait-listed. Everyone who applies to OCAS before March 1 has priority over everyone who applies after. Applications to OCAS postmarked after March 1 will only be considered, in order of receipt, as space becomes available.

If there are too many qualified applicants for a program before March 1, the program is "oversubscribed." Ontario residents get priority in oversubscribed programs. The college may also consider prior academic success and work or volunteer history, or it may use tests or questionnaires to identify the applicants with the most potential for success. Marks alone do not establish a pecking order, but marks may be considered along with other factors. Each college publishes its procedures for making selections for oversubscribed programs.

May 15. The colleges make their decisions by May 15. On that day, they begin sending out their offers to successful applicants. If you receive an offer from a college, you have to confirm your acceptance – to one program only – to OCAS in Guelph. If you received more than one offer, OCAS will automatically notify all the colleges whose offers you are not accepting, so they can offer those spots to someone else.

July 15. They want the money. If you are a new student, the college that has accepted you will want payment of the full tuition fee for the upcoming year. If you are a returning student, they will wait until July 31.

About Waiting Lists

You can apply after March 1 and still get into college. In fact, you can apply right up to the beginning of September and still hope to get in. Don't count on it, but it happens every year.

Remember, not every offer of acceptance is going to be confirmed by the students who get them. When the colleges find out which of their offers have been declined (or who doesn't pay up when fees are due), they turn to their waiting lists. Of course, many of the people on the waiting lists will also have made other plans. Many programs get through a long waiting list before having a final and complete list of students. For Dental Hygiene, some Community Service programs, and others, however, there are so many on-time applicants that if you are on the waiting list your chances of getting in are very small.

Some programs are undersubscribed. With more places than qualified applicants, they never build up a waiting list. In undersubscribed programs, an application sent in right at the start of classes, or even shortly after, might be accepted. Remember, however, that residence, daycare, parking, even locker spaces, may have been scooped up by earlier applicants.

Applications for Trades, Upgrading, and Continuing Education Courses

These fill up too. Apply on time.

Applications for everything that is not a post-secondary program are handled by the college itself. Each college will have its own application dates. Part-time course applications are usually accepted each semester, and other course application dates depend on the start date. Some courses have continuous (or frequent) entry, and you can apply at almost any time during the year.

Contact the local college for information about its start dates and application dates for all these courses. Canada Employment Centres and some Ontario training programs may also have information about college courses for which they sponsor students.

Applying for Residences, Daycares, Scholarships

Residence and daycare applications are handled by the colleges themselves. Scholarships and bursaries are a little more complicated.

Generally, colleges that have student residences will send residence information and a residence application form to all out-of-town students along with the offer of acceptance into a program. After that, places are given out on a first-come, first-serve basis. Residence places at most colleges fill up quickly. Apply as soon as possible. If you need more information, contact the Residence Manager.

All the colleges have daycare services – see more information under "Using the Services" – but that doesn't mean you can get your children into them automatically. Like colleges themselves, college daycares get oversubscribed. I met a woman who postponed going to college for a year because she couldn't get daycare space. You should look into daycare availability and cost while you are researching your application. If you are confirming an offer of acceptance, apply to the college daycare as soon as possible.

The Ontario Student Assistance Program, OSAP, is covered in the next chapter, "Getting the Money Together." However, all the colleges have their own scholarships and bursaries. Some colleges list the funds available to new students in the calendar; others have a Financial Assistance booklet. While you are investigating colleges, look into entry scholarships at each particular college. And apply as early as possible. The Financial Aid office at the college has the information about all the scholarships and bursaries and how to apply for them.

GETTING THE MONEY TOGETHER

Finding daycare can be a critical part of preparation for college. Most colleges have daycare on campus or nearby, but waiting lists are common.

Tuition

Call it a thousand dollars. College tuition fees are set by the Ministry of Colleges and Universities in Toronto; the amount is the same for all programs at all the colleges. In 1992-93, the tuition for a September-May school year in a full-time post-secondary program cost $856. (In 1991-92 it was $800.) Tuition will go up again, to $916, for 1993-94. Colleges don't collect GST on top of that, but there are other fees that will put the cost over $1,000 a year.

Your tuition covers barely 10 per cent of the cost of a year at college. But it is still $1,000.

Tuition rates are calculated differently for upgrading and skills courses at the colleges, since they vary greatly in length and have many starting dates. The standard rate for most of them in 1992-93 was $23.90 per week. That does not sound like much, but it adds up to $382 for a sixteen-week course and $860 for thirty-six weeks – the same as a diploma program, in other words.

A few special tuition rates apply. Persons over sixty get substantial discounts on tuition fees. And international students pay close to the full cost of their schooling – $7,115 a school year in 1992-93 (see also the chapter "International and Out-of-Province Students").

Other Fees

All colleges charge students various fees in addition to tuition. They cover the cost of student activities, recreation and intramurals, insurance, and other miscellaneous expenses. If the college student association has built (or is planning) a student centre, there may be a building fund charge.

These fees vary from college to college. For 1992-93, for instance, Confederation was charging $106 in addition to the basic tuition fee, Fleming $112, George Brown $124, Northern $146, and Niagara $273.

Co-op Fees

Students in co-op programs pay a co-op fee to cover some of the additional costs of administering co-op. In recent years, for example, Fanshawe has charged co-op fees of $115 a school year, Humber $175, Sheridan $250, and Mohawk $369.

Materials Fees

Depending on your program, you may be charged a materials fee for supplies and equipment you use. These fees are particularly evident in creative arts, design, and media programs. Durham, for instance, recently charged a $60 materials fee in most of these areas.

Books and Supplies

Book and supply costs are not a fee charged by the college, but you have to buy your own texts and school supplies for all programs.

The colleges say you should expect to pay a minimum of $500 for books and supplies for one school year. For some programs, particularly design and art courses, the cost may be far higher. Fanshawe, for instance, recently estimated first-year book and supply costs for Business Administration (Marketing) at $390, and compared to most programs, that was a bargain. For Electronics Engineering Technology the cost estimate was $693, for Audio-Visual Technician $920. In Industrial Design, it was $1,674. In Photography, it was $2,497, and Photography students were also expected to have their own single-lens reflex camera.

Residence Costs

Residence costs vary widely, depending on the location of the college and the type of accommodation provided: single room, double room, townhouse, etc. Some college residences include a mandatory full-meal plan. Others have kitchen facilities and no meal plan. Whether meals are included or you are buying your own food, expect to spend perhaps $4,200 ($80/week for accommodation and $35/week for food) for a school year in residence.

For up-to-date information about residence costs, contact the Information Service or the Residence Manager's office at the colleges that interest you.

Parking Fees

The free-parking days are gone. Pretty well every college now charges for parking – though at George Brown, the student handbook says, "Because of George Brown's downtown campus locations, good luck in your search for parking." Sheridan, in Oakville, charged $4.50 a day recently, or $120 for a school year. At Sault College, you put a quarter in the slot every time you use the parking lot.

The Cost of Going to College for a Year

The total cost of a year at college really depends on how you calculate it – and how you live. If you include the "opportunity cost" – all the wages you might be giving up for the year – you can concoct a huge figure. But then you should allow for the extra income a college diploma might eventually earn you. Let's leave those calculations for people in Accountancy programs.

For 1992, Fleming College in Peterborough calculated the minimum cost of a thirty-six-week school year at Fleming if you lived "at home" (i.e., rent-free) or away from home:

	At Home	Away from Home
Tuition and fees:	$ 968	$ 968
Books and supplies	500	500
Housing		
room and board		3,600
[or residence		4,140]
Transportation		
local transit	320	320
visits home		240
Personal expenses		
[just $20/week!]	720	720
Miscellaneous		
[another $14/week]	504	504
TOTAL	$3,012	$6,852
		[or with residence $7,392]

You *might* be able to live close to Fleming's minimum, though probably not in Metro Toronto, where housing costs more. On the other hand, some financial officers I talked to used the rule of thumb that a year of college will cost $6,000 if you live at home,

$12,000 if you go away. Where you fit between these figures and the Fleming minimums depends on where you live and your own spending habits.

Most college Counselling and Financial Aid offices provide cost-of-living estimates along with worksheets and advice (and sometimes workshops) on budgeting.

Financial Aid

Every college has a Financial Aid office. It can provide forms, information, and advice about OSAP and every other kind of financial aid. Talk to them.

Ontario Student Assistance Program (OSAP)

Apart from what you may be able to get privately from family (or your employer), financial aid comes under two headings: OSAP and everything else. OSAP is the main government program for helping Ontario students with the cost of post-secondary studies.

In November 1992, Ontario announced that it intends (with the cooperation of the Income Tax people at Revenue Canada) to move toward an "income-contingent loan repayment" system. If and when it is fully established, that system would mean you would borrow roughly what you needed while you studied. Once you graduated, however, you would repay according to your income over the next fifteen years or so. High income earners would pay a lot, low income earners not very much. But that is for the future. Right now, there is only a tiny element of "income contingency" in the student loan system.

1. Grants.

Grant money is money you do not have to repay. Until 1992-93, about 45 per cent of college students got Ontario Study Grants through OSAP each year. Then, late in 1992, the Ontario government cancelled that program. The only people who will be eligible for OSAP bursaries that do not have to be repaid will be students with child-care expenses and students with special needs because of disabilities.

That does not mean that every other student will now have to repay all the OSAP money he or she gets. But it does mean that each student will start with a loan, rather than a grant, even though a portion of the loan (or the interest on it) may later be forgiven.

2. Loans.

If you go to OSAP for money, you start with the Canada Student Loan (CSL) and the Ontario Student Loan (OSL). Most college students getting OSAP support will have a combination of Canada and Ontario Student Loans. (With both the CSL and the OSL, you are really borrowing from a bank. In effect, OSAP "co-signs" with you and helps with the interest while you are in school, but eventually you will have to repay the loan and the interest to your bank.)

OSAP will want details on your studies and on your financial situation and, where applicable, that of your parents or spouse. It uses this information to calculate your "Allowable Education Cost" and how much you should be able to pay for yourself. For each thirty-six-week college year, you may be entitled to borrow as much as $3,780 ($105 a week) from the Canada Student Loan plan. If you can show you need more, you get it from the Ontario Student Loan plan.

CSL and OSL are interest-free while you are a student. Six months after you stop being a full-time student – and the two plans define full-time differently – you start repaying the amount you borrowed plus interest. (Interest rates are calculated by a complicated formula, and they change, but it is a real interest rate, not some token amount.) You can take up to nine and a half years to repay the total.

The main difference between CSL and OSL: CSL considers you a full-time student only if you are taking at least 60 per cent of a full course load. Drop below that and you have to start repaying the CSL. But the OSL level is 20 per cent, so you can become, in effect, a part-time student without having to repay your OSL money.

Although there are no more grants available for the average

student, it is possible that you may not be required to pay back a portion of your student loans. Here is how it works after the changes of late 1992.

You still borrow what you need according to your "allowable education cost." If that amounts to more than $5,570 (CSL and OSL combined) for a school year, you will not have to repay the amount over that. The Ontario government has shifted money from the Grant program to the Loan program, so you borrow as much as you can justify each year, and you will only repay a maximum of $5,570 for each year.

There is also a complicated system to give you some help if your income after graduation is lower than a certain amount. For 1993-94, grads with incomes under about $20,000 will get all the interest on their student loans paid by OSAP for up to eighteen months, and grads with incomes up to $35,000 will get some of their interest paid.

3. Other OSAP plans.

The Ontario Work Study Plan has a nice idea. You need money, and your college needs work done, so the Work Study Plan helps the college pay you up to $1,000 a term for part-time work you do for the college. You still have to show serious financial need beyond what is covered by other OSAP plans, and you have to be recommended by the college's Financial Aid Office. Late in 1992, Ontario doubled the funding for this plan to $5.4 million, with the extra money earmarked for disadvantaged groups.

The Ontario Special Bursary was designed to help both part-time students and students doing academic upgrading or other studies classed as "non-post-secondary." Now that the OSL covers part-timers, OSB is mostly used by students in upgrading courses. You can apply for the bursary if, for instance, you are at college working on the equivalent of a high school diploma so that you can enter a career-oriented program. The bursary does not have to be repaid, and the maximum amount given is $2,500 per school year. Late in 1992, Ontario doubled the funding for this plan to $5.4 million, and aimed the new money at disadvantaged groups. You cannot have a Special Bursary and OSAP loans at the same time.

Part-time Canada Student Loans are available to part-time students, but you start repaying the loan right away – one month after it is negotiated. In Ontario most part-time students can borrow from the OSL instead, so most do.

Applying for OSAP

You can apply for OSAP money (through any college's Financial Aid Office) when you apply for a college program, but applying to OSAP more than once complicates the process. Usually your application will be handled in about eight weeks, so OSAP suggests that in most cases you should not apply for money until you are sure which college and program have accepted you. If you are applying to several colleges and the deadlines are looming, ask a Financial Aid Office for advice – during the spring some of them run workshops on OSAP applications. If you have both CSL and OSL money, the CSL money for your entire year will come at the start of the year, and the OSL halfway through. Most colleges will provide Book and Tuition Credits, or some similar help, if you cannot meet your expenses while you wait for OSAP money.

Other Scholarships and Bursaries

Don't stop with OSAP if you need money. All the colleges have their own scholarship and bursary programs (scholarships are for academic or athletic achievement, bursaries are for need). Some have much more money available than others, and some use entry scholarships as a way to attract students. A handful of colleges offer athletic scholarships to varsity athletes. Many of the colleges require that you apply specially for a particular scholarship or bursary.

Students with disabilities and others with special needs may be eligible for specific financial aid programs. See the following section on "Special Clients."

I spoke to college Financial Aid officers who said that each year some scholarships and bursaries go unclaimed because many students think they could never get one and do not bother to apply. If you need money, ask the Financial Aid office what might be available. See the notes on "Scholarships and Bursaries" in each college chapter in this book.

Emergency Aid

What if your financial plan collapses in March? Most college Financial Aid offices do have emergency loan funds available. At one large college, they told me they can help pretty well everyone who comes to them – if they have enough notice, and if the crisis is short-term. (If you have no money and no prospect of money, and it is only November, talk to them – but don't count on being carried through to graduation.)

As the cost of living increases, as OSAP funding gets tighter, and as financial stresses increase, the colleges are having to become more versatile in the kinds of financial aid they provide. Some colleges already operate food banks and clothing banks for their students, and no doubt most will soon.

Financial Aid offices can do more than point out sources of money. They also offer budgeting courses and other kinds of financial advice – and it is free. "Don't just tighten your belt and hide from your landlord" is the advice I heard. Talk seriously to the Financial Aid office about your situation, and do it early.

USING THE SERVICES

Training in study skills can be a crucial confidence-builder for all students, particularly adults returning to school after a long absence.

These days, a well-organized college probably has a Vice-President for Student Services (you can check in the calendars). If all student services have been organized into one department and assigned to a Vice-President, the college has probably decided that service to students is important.

But however the college is organized, there are a variety of student services that all colleges offer – and that too few students use. Whether you consider that student services are "free," or that you have already paid for them through your college fees, you ought to make use of them.

329

Academic Services

Business and Industry Organizations

At some colleges, students become associate members of local business or industrial associations related to the program they are studying, so they can begin gaining "real-world" experience and building career contacts while still in school.

More rarely, there are links between programs and labour unions. George Brown's School of Labour is working to improve college-union contacts, and in strong labour towns such as Sault Ste. Marie and Sudbury, unions are usually well represented on college advisory committees and boards of governors.

Computer Labs

Access to computers is vital to an increasing number of college programs. Most colleges have computer labs available to students (sometimes around the clock). Sometimes you may be assigned in groups to do coursework in the computer lab. Other times you can use the lab facilities to work on your own assignments. All labs have staff to assist you.

Faculty Advisors

Most programs will assign one faculty member to keep an eye on the progress of each student coming into the program. Faculty advisors are supposed to notice if students are getting into difficulty – and to intervene before the crisis stage is reached. Identify your faculty advisor – he or she is the natural person to turn to regarding any problem you encounter with your program.

More and more, faculty advisors cooperate with Counselling staff (see "Counselling," below), since academic difficulties can often be mixed with family or personal issues. All counselling is confidential, but faculty members may introduce you to the counselling services if they see non-academic problems are preventing you from doing well in your program.

Learning Centres

Most colleges call their libraries "Resource Centres," to suggest they have a lot more than books in them. Many of them also have Learning Centres attached (they might be called English Labs, Math Labs, or some other name). Learning Centres provide support to individuals needing help with fundamental academic skills. If your Math skills or English skills are not as good as they ought to be, the learning centre can tailor a course of study to your individual needs, or group you with others with similar problems for self-help.

Many Learning Centres are equipped with computer-based Instructional Programs, so you can practise skills at your own pace. Learning Centres are also becoming headquarters for unscheduled Individual Learning Programs, where students do mostly independent study at their own pace. Frequently a Test Centre is located nearby, where students from several different programs may be seated alongside each other, taking entirely different exams.

Mentoring

Some colleges and programs use a mentor system, by which a senior-year student is linked to an incoming student. (In Health Sciences the mentor may be a working nurse who mentors a student during hospital placements.) Ask the faculty advisor about mentoring.

Peer Tutoring

Peer tutoring is an extremely popular program in which senior students help new ones with academic problems. If you are having difficulty with one or two courses in your program, you can apply for tutoring from someone who has already taken and passed the same courses. The tutor is paid (peer tutoring is a good part-time job for some students), but the service is free to the person receiving help. Peer tutoring may be run by the Counselling Office, or by the Student Association. Ask your faculty advisor or professor about it.

Study Skills, Student Success, and Master Student Programs

Many colleges have started programs to teach study skills. These short workshops provide pointers and practice in such topics as note-taking, research skills, essay preparation, studying for exams, and time management. I found that adults who return to school after being away from schoolwork for years were particularly enthusiastic about these programs, but they can benefit anyone.

Some colleges integrate study-skills material into scheduled course hours near the start of a program. Others offer workshops on a volunteer basis for anyone who chooses to enroll. I heard these programs strongly praised as a good, painless way to get off to a strong start in college.

Non-Academic Services

Alumni

The colleges as a whole have not made up their mind about alumni. Some colleges have elaborate alumni associations, with homecomings, glossy magazines, and a range of alumni services. Some are just starting to assemble a list of alumni addresses and have only a rough idea of how many alumni they actually have.

Apart from their social and sentimental side, alumni associations can be a useful source of mentoring for students, for job and placement contacts – and for college fund-raising. In return, alumni associations can often offer group discounts to members on life insurance, recreational activities, and many other services. Northern has launched an "affinity" credit card – each time you use it, some money goes to the college.

Counselling

Counsellors are available to assist students with everything from career planning to stress management, and they can be key people in pointing you toward other services. Most college counselling tries to stick to issues directly related to your college experience – though the line between student issues and personal issues often becomes blurred. Faculty advisors often work closely with counselling staff, but all counselling is confidential – you can consult a counsellor without word getting back to the people running your program. Most counselling is free to students, and counselling may also be available to non-students considering college.

If you need long-term personal counselling, the college counselling office may recommend you to a community-based counselling agency. Durham College, for instance, has counsellors from Durham Regional Social Services on campus regularly. Durham, like Seneca and some other colleges, also provides Legal Aid clinics on campus.

Many colleges have opened their counselling services to part-time and evening students, and many have counsellors who come from minority cultural groups and speak languages other than English and French. Particularly in the north, but also at St. Clair and other southern colleges, there are native counsellors to work with aboriginal students.

Daycare

Every college runs a daycare. Many of them are showcases, operating as Early Childhood Education research centres as well as caring for the children of students, staff, and neighbours of the college. College daycares have many different forms. At Algonquin, Centennial, Loyalist, and Fanshawe, the college-run daycare is right on campus. Other colleges run their daycares on sites provided by the local community or a local business. St. Clair's Thames campus in Chatham runs a daycare in cooperation with the nearby headquarters of Union Gas. One of George Brown's daycare centres is in the Scotia Tower highrise office building and serves office workers as well as college students. Cambrian runs separate French and English daycare centres, and its native ECE students often do placements in reserve community daycares.

Check with the daycare manager as soon as you begin investigating a college. It may have special facilities or services worth knowing about. Also, keep in mind that daycare places do fill up fast – don't take it for granted that space will be available.

Financial Aid

Financial Aid has the forms to fill out when you want to apply for OSAP money or a college scholarship. But it may also provide advice on these and many other sources of money and how to go about finding them. Financial Aid offices run budgeting workshops and may even be able to provide emergency help. See the previous chapter, "Getting the Money Together," for more information.

Health Services

Particularly if you are away from home, the College Health Services office can substitute for a family doctor. Most colleges have nursing staff full-time and scheduled doctors' hours. At many colleges, Health Services are also involved in health- and wellness-oriented educational programs: AIDS awareness, sex education and substance-abuse workshops, nutritional advice. Sheridan College has a student-run Peer Health Counselling project, and its "Sexual Pursuit" educational board game proved wildly popular around the campus recently.

Housing

Every college has a Housing office to help you find places to live in the community around the college. Some go out of their way to provide maps and free telephones. Others remind you to bring a supply of quarters. They take no responsibility for student-landlord relations in off-campus housing, but some offer mediation services in case of disputes.

Placement and Career Counselling

Colleges take job placement seriously. Some programs have placement counselling integrated into their coursework. Placement offices also become involved with co-op and internship placements, and most will continue to support the job-search and career-change needs of alumni long after they graduate.

Placement offices can also offer – or guide you to – training in job-search techniques, resumé writing, and other career-finding skills. How else can placement office staff help? "Don't wait until the week before graduation to find out," was the response of one of them.

Program-related Services

If your college has a Hospitality or Food Service program, chances are there is a restaurant on the campus providing fine dining at terrific prices. Most colleges have services like these: teeth-cleaning from the Dental Hygiene labs, haircare and beauty treatments from the Hairstyling, Cosmetics, and Esthetics programs. Every morning at George Brown's School of Hospitality, you can buy up goodies from the Bakery program. Look into what is available – prices are usually well below commercial rates.

Recreation

Every college has extensive recreation and sports organizations, and most have impressive facilities for them. See the details in each college chapter.

Special Needs Office

Every college has a Special Needs office, with consultants to ensure that students with disabilities – physical disabilities or "invisible" learning disabilities – have full access to college life. For more details, see "Special Clients" below.

Student Associations

Student societies vary widely across the college system. Some are focused on "clubs and pubs" and social activities. Others are deeply involved in running Peer Tutoring, Orientation, Athletics, Health programming, Equity and Intercultural Awareness, and Ombudsman programs. Student governments also provide financial support to all the college clubs and societies. Student representatives sit on all colleges' boards of governors.

Most colleges have student councils at all their major campuses. Some have separate francophone or native student societies, and there are strong ethno-cultural clubs at the Metro Toronto colleges and some others. A native student recently held the student presidency at Sault College. At several colleges, strong Mature Student Associations and Part-time Student Associations have led to adult participation in student government. Northern recently had a student president in his fifties.

Mohawk and some other colleges support student government members with college-credit leadership training courses. Student government officers can also get involved in OCCSPA, the Ontario Community College Student Parliamentary Association. (Two that I met at Centennial had just come back from a student-leadership conference in San Diego.)

Student society officers I met were keen to "sell" student government, but they seemed genuinely convinced that participation could enhance the college experience of anyone who got involved. Several student society officers mentioned they never got active in "that kind of thing" in high school, but student government seemed more practical and more important at college.

SPECIAL CLIENTS

The college system's commitment to Special Needs services has made a college education possible for many people living with disabilities of all kinds.

Both by their nature and by law, the colleges are committed to open access and equity. Colleges operate a wide variety of special services tailored to the needs of students and other clients with special requirements.

Students Living with Disabilities

The Manager of the Office of Special Needs at Mohawk College told me there are three important things people with disabilities should know about the colleges. One, access to college exists for people living with disabilities. Two, you should be prepared to identify yourself to the college as a person with special needs. Three, a Special Needs consultant will help develop an individual profile of what you need from the college.

Today there are some remarkable pieces of adaptive technology to enhance access to education: not just ramps and elevators, but large-print computer screens, FM transmitter-receiver systems, TDD telephones, Kurzweil machines that read out loud any written text placed on them, and so on. Particularly for the visually impaired, the deaf, and the hard-of-hearing student, technology has gone a long way to open up the colleges and their services.

But people and services are as important as machinery. Every college has an Office of Special Needs, whose consultants will help people with disabilities acquire equal access to college services. Special Needs services can include personal support from notetakers, interpreters, and readers. A student can arrange reduced course loads, revised schedules, alternative exams, adaptive computer systems, and academic support. Specially adapted co-op programs and internships can be developed. Most physical barriers in college buildings have been removed or compensated for.

Almost half of the clients of Special Needs offices in the colleges have "invisible" disabilities – that is, they are living with learning disabilities or psychological disabilities. The rest are visually impaired, hearing-impaired, mobility-impaired, or have other visible disabilities. As recently as the mid-1980s, the colleges had few Special Needs services, and only small numbers of students with disabilities went to college.

In the last five years, however, the expansion of Special Needs services have encouraged larger numbers to attend college or to identify themselves as students with special needs. Cambrian, Algonquin, Centennial, and Mohawk are acknowledged to have been leaders and innovators in Special Needs services, but all colleges have Special Needs offices and are committed by law to provide equal access for students with disabilities.

Students with disabilities can apply for OSAP financial support in the usual way, but they may also be eligible for support from Ontario's Vocational Rehabilitation Services (VRS). Some colleges have specific scholarships and bursaries for special-needs students, and college residences reserve specially equipped rooms for them. All students with physical disabilities who are starting college can apply for Aird Scholarships, which provide $2,500 to successful applicants. For more information, discuss financial support with a Special Needs consultant.

Harassment, Discrimination, and Safety Issues

The 1992 *Report on Harassment and Discrimination in Ontario Colleges of Applied Arts and Technology* from the Ontario Council of Regents suggests students, faculty, and staff at many colleges still have a long way to go on issues of safety, anti-racism, and anti-sexism. Most colleges had Equity Committees and Committees on Personal Safety. About half had safety procedures or safe-walk escort programs in place, and almost all had improved lighting in dangerous areas. Only half employ full-time security staff. The report suggested that the colleges, in general, needed better procedures and increased education about all these issues.

The Report recommended much stronger procedures for circulating information about dangerous situations, for anti-harassment education, and for dealing with incidents of harassment or discrimination when they occur. It also recommended that all full-time and part-time students and employees be required to attend orientations where anti-discrimination and anti-harassment information is presented and discussed.

Students of Colour and Ethno-cultural Minorities

Many of the colleges have substantial minority populations, which may include recent immigrants, international students, and long-established Canadian minority groups. Many minority groups have their own clubs and organizations within the colleges. Colleges and student governments may cooperate to offer multicultural experiences and anti-racism and anti-discrimination workshops. Colleges with large minority populations often have counsellors or support staff who can provide support in the groups' own languages and cultural contexts. On the other hand, visible minorities do seem much more evident in most colleges' student bodies than among faculty and staff.

What is the situation for minority students at Ontario colleges? I met aboriginal students and students of colour who were enthusiastic about minority-group access to college and about the acceptance they found there. But note the findings of the report on discrimination and harassment, covered above.

Aboriginal Students

At several of the northern colleges, I heard two stories. First, of two decades of failure in trying to serve aboriginal students, with dropout rates of 90 per cent or more having been common. Second, of the beginning of a change in the last few years, almost always associated with greater native control over native training in the colleges.

Confederation, Cambrian, Sault, and Canadore have all begun to attract and retain significant minorities of native students. All have native-oriented curriculum, native staff and counsellors, and strong input from native educational organizations. Most of these colleges also provide services directly to reserve communities. See details of these programs in the chapters on these colleges.

Some southern colleges have smaller, but similar, initiatives linked to nearby reserve communities. St. Clair now employs a native counsellor to support its programs for local native communities.

Francophone Students

All colleges in areas with significant francophone populations are obliged to provide service in French. There is already one and there will soon be three colleges operating entirely in French, and several others offer a few or many programs in French or in a bilingual form. For details, see the chapters on Algonquin, Cambrian, Canadore, La Cité, and Northern, and the box entitled "Pour les francophones."

Mature Students and Seniors

Who is a mature student? See "The Jargon" in Part One. But more and more adults are going to college. Only half of new college students come directly from high school. At many colleges, a quarter of the student body is twenty-five or older, and students in their thirties, forties, or fifties no longer seem unusual.

The presence of so many more adult students is changing the look of college classrooms, and also changing the services and activities that colleges provide. Adults with families and community commitments may have less time or interest in many traditional recreation and entertainment activities. On the other hand, mature students have become an important constituency for better daycare services, more fitness and anti-stress activities, and many other practical innovations in student service. I also heard suggestions that adult students, because they are unwilling to be patronized or to accept poor service, have done a lot to push the colleges toward a truly client-centred attitude regarding service to students.

Many colleges now have Mature Students Associations, but their boundaries are hardly fixed by age (as someone said, teenagers with kids may have more in common with mature students than with students their own age), and adult students are increasingly integrating themselves into all student organizations.

People over sixty should know that special, reduced tuition rates apply to them.

Single Parents

If you are a single parent, it is likely you will not be the only one in your program. You should be able to build up a support network – in fact, some colleges help to organize Single Parent Support Groups. Single parents should consider identifying themselves to Counselling offices for consultation on particular services that might be useful to them. Health Services, Financial Aid, and other offices may also prove useful and supportive. Students with childcare expenses can apply for OSAP bursaries to help with those costs.

Are Women Special Clients?

Across Ontario, women are a majority among college students, although male-female ratios vary greatly in different programs. See the box entitled "Changing Male-Female Ratios" for details.

Women's Studies courses are in the curriculum at Conestoga and St. Lawrence (which offers a Women's Studies Certificate in its GAS program), but these are more the exception than the rule. In general, the not-very-political style of student associations at the colleges extends to women's issues. I saw little evidence of strong women's organizations or feminist caucuses in the colleges, although women did seem to be well represented on student (and college) councils.

On the other hand, there is a strong policy commitment to equity issues, partly from the colleges themselves, partly from Ontario government directives and human rights legislation. Women are gaining an equal share of faculty positions. Women are barely 20 per cent of long-service faculty, but recent hirings have created a more equitable situation. The proportion of women among full-time faculty members ranges from 30 per cent (at Fleming) to almost 54 per cent (at Sheridan). A 1991 study by Seneca College reported that if current trends continue, women will be equally represented in Seneca faculty by 1996, and similar trends seem to prevail elsewhere. Only a handful of college presidents are women, but women are becoming strongly represented in senior administrative positions. Most colleges have progressive policies on daycare, support for single parents, women's sports, and other issues of concern to women, and they are moving on safety and anti-sexism programs.

A particular focus of attention has been the small number of women taking Technology programs at the colleges. Many colleges now undertake outreach programs aimed at promoting math and technology to female students at Grade 7 and

8 or earlier, and female enrollment in Technology programs is officially encouraged and supported. Resistance to hiring women in non-traditional jobs remains a problem for grads, but where equity programs have taken hold, particularly in public agencies, women college grads have been strikingly successful.

Most colleges have participated in programs such as WITT (Women into Trades and Technology) and INTO (Introduction to Non-Traditional Occupations), in cooperation with provincial and federal agencies. College experiments with how best to integrate women into technology and non-traditional careers have had varied results. At Conestoga, I heard of the striking success of an all-women trades course, where the women quickly formed a close-knit, supportive group, but at Durham I heard suggestions that women had been moving ahead faster in mixed courses because they could benefit from the practical experience that male students had had opportunities to accumulate.

Colleges, particularly those with Access divisions, may run special programs to assist single parents, victims of violence, minority women, and others in attaining college education.

INTERNATIONAL AND OUT-OF-PROVINCE STUDENTS

I met exchange students from Jamaica at George Brown College and from Zimbabwe at Northern. A group from Spain was just leaving Mohawk when I arrived. At Sheridan's Animation Summer School, I met filmmakers from Sydney and Bombay. I met Humber Technology faculty just back from Indonesia, and Confederation Business faculty who had been teaching entrepreneurship in Poland. Georgian's new president had just come back from running a college in Abu Dhabi.

The colleges run two kinds of international activities. One is outreach, where Ontario college staff "train the trainers," either by travelling overseas or by bringing teachers to Ontario for intensive training. The other is accepting international students who come to Ontario to enroll in college programs, either on their own or as students sponsored by governments and institutions at home.

Outreach and "train the trainer" programs are becoming a more important part of the Ontario colleges' international programs. They help to develop the educational institutions of the foreign country, they provide excellent "professional development" for Ontario faculty and staff (in a few cases, students too), and they can be more cost-effective than projects which bring individual students to Ontario.

International students remain welcome in Ontario colleges,

with two important limitations. First, international students pay close to the full cost of their education. For 1992-93, international students pay $7,115 per year – more than eight times what Canadian students pay – and they cannot receive federal or provincial financial aid through OSAP unless they have permanent residence visas. Second, Ontario students have priority in oversubscribed programs. As the colleges become more crowded and as more applicants seek entry to every program, fewer places become available for foreign students.

Nevertheless, the Ontario college system has admirers throughout Canada and around the world, and students continue to come to Ontario to enroll in programs or to take short-term training in teaching or in special fields. In some countries, local agents of the Ontario colleges are authorized to provide information and accept applications. International students interested in the Ontario colleges should contact the International office of any individual college, or Ontario Colleges International, P.O. Box 6800, Agincourt, Ontario M1S 3C6, Canada. A detailed booklet, "International Education for Career Success," is available.

With the largest and most diverse college system in Canada, Ontario also draws students from other provinces. Eastern Ontario colleges, particularly Algonquin, La Cité, Canadore, and Northern, have always drawn students from Quebec. Traditionally, Maritimers have also been drawn to Ontario colleges, though the recent expansion of colleges in Atlantic Canada may reduce the need to leave home. And Confederation has always drawn some students from Manitoba and Saskatchewan.

The strongest out-of-province draws, however, are the unique programs offered nowhere else (or not in the same form): Georgian's Automotive Marketing, the Aviation programs, Fleming's Natural Resources, and other one-of-a-kind programs and schools that see themselves as having a national mandate, frequently have a high proportion of out-of-province students. Many colleges also do co-op placement and permanent job placement right across the country. Ontario students still have priority in oversubscribed programs, but students from elsewhere in Canada pay the Ontario tuition fee rates.

Students from other provinces can apply to their provinces'
student assistance programs to support their studies at Ontario
colleges. Contact the provincial agency for details, restrictions,
and application forms.

If You Don't Live Near a College

If you don't live near a college and can't move to one, the college might
come to you.

1. Outreach campuses.
   Many of the colleges have outreach offices or training services
   offering courses in communities, institutions, and industrial sites all
   around their area. Check with the college nearest you.
2. Distance Education.
   Particularly but not only in the north, the colleges use Distance
   Education to teach people they cannot reach directly. Distance
   Education can mean several widely scattered classrooms with
   complete audio-visual hookups to each other. Sometimes it means
   educational television supplemented by print materials. Sometimes it is a more traditional correspondence program with print
   and cassette materials. Several colleges participate in Contact
   North/Contact Nord, an educational delivery service for northern
   Ontario. Again, check with the nearest college.
3. Independent Learning.
   Southern colleges are also looking to Independent Learning as a
   way to market their unique programs, to reach shut-ins, or simply to
   reduce crowding by offering courses that students take at home (or
   in college Learning Centres) at their own pace. The Con Ed or
   Independent Learning offices of each college can give information
   on these.

ACKNOWLEDGEMENTS

It was people in the Ontario college system who first saw the need for this book. They also saw from the start that the guidebook had to be independent. McClelland & Stewart and I took on this project with complete editorial freedom. The Association of Colleges of Applied Arts and Technology of Ontario (ACAATO) provided funds that enabled me to visit all the colleges in Ontario, and I was made welcome at every college, but no one made any attempt to control what went into the guidebook.

I am particularly grateful to Christopher Trump, Executive Director of ACAATO, for his enthusiastic support of the guidebook and his insistence on its independence, and to the College Advisory Committee on Public Affairs, which provided contacts at every college. Many "stakeholders" inside and outside the college system granted me interviews, and I am indebted to them all. Chris Trump, Terry MacGorman, and Dan Cushing were an informal support committee whenever I needed advice.

I met friendly interest and assistance from faculty, staff, and students at each college. (The number of times someone in a lab or classroom gave this bewildered visitor a spontaneous tour or explanation was in itself evidence of the commitment of many people in the college system.) I am specifically grateful to the following people, more or less in the order in which I met them. None of these people and none of their colleges can be held responsible

347

for the contents of this book, but I could not have done my work without them:

Dianne Spencer at Loyalist College, Dan Cushing and Jill Holroyd at George Brown, Lyn Russo and Patti Faragelli at Niagara, Terry MacGorman and Mark Toljagic at Centennial, John Sawicki at Conestoga, Joe Kertes at Humber, Janet Taylor and Mark Hall at Georgian, Don Curry at Canadore, Linda Renaud and Linda Wilson at Cambrian, Robin Dorrell at Algonquin, Guy-Marc Dumais and James Bardach at La Cité collégiale, Andrew Cane and Jean Bujold at Confederation, Rick McGee at Sault, Christine Day at Mohawk, Emily Marcoccia at Fanshawe, Cheryl Bird at Durham, Rodney Gilchrist at Sheridan, Nicole Basciano and Paul Halliday at Fleming, Carole Rondeau at Northern, Newman Wallis and Tony Tilly and Marilyn-Anne Welsh at Seneca, Nancy Acheson at Lambton, Shannon Van Norman at St. Clair, and Robin Pepper at St. Lawrence.

PHOTO CREDITS

INDEX OF PROGRAMS

Below is a listing of the full-time diploma programs mentioned in Part Two and the individual colleges that offer them. The precise titles of the programs may vary from college to college. The names of the colleges are abbreviated as follows:

Alg Algonquin
Cam Cambrian
Can Canadore
Cen Centennial
Cit La Cité collégiale
Cga Conestoga
Cfn Confederation
Dur Durham
Fan Fanshawe
Geo George Brown
Ggn Georgian
Hum Humber

Lam Lambton
Loy Loyalist
Mow Mohawk
Nia Niagara
Nor Northern
StC St. Clair
StL St. Lawrence
Soo Sault
Sen Seneca
She Sheridan
SSF Sir Sandford Fleming

COMMENTS

Look for a new edition of *The M&S Guide to Ontario Colleges of Applied Arts and Technology* in the fall of 1994. To help us make it more useful, let us know what you think about the colleges and about this edition of the guide.

How can we make this guidebook more useful?

_____
_____
_____
_____

What kind of information would you like more of? or less of?

_____
_____
_____
_____

What's your opinion – of Ontario's college system, or of any particular college in Ontario?

_____
_____
_____
_____

What has college done for you? (Or, how did it let you down?)

_____
_____
_____
_____

Write to Christopher Moore, *The M&S Guide to Ontario Colleges of Applied Arts and Technology*, c/o McClelland & Stewart Inc., 481 University Avenue, Toronto, Ontario M5G 2E9. Or fax your comments to (416) 760-9165.